Yes, Taoiseach

Irish politics from behind closed doors

FRANK DUNLOP

PENGUIN
IRELAND

PENGUIN IRELAND

Published by the Penguin Group
Penguin Ireland Ltd, 25 St Stephen's Green, Dublin 2, Ireland
Penguin Books Ltd, 80 Strand, London WC2R 0RL, England
Penguin Group (USA) Inc., 375 Hudson Street, New York, New York 10014, USA
Penguin Books Australia Ltd, 250 Camberwell Road,
Camberwell, Victoria 3124, Australia
Penguin Books Canada Ltd, 10 Alcorn Avenue, Toronto, Ontario, Canada M4V 3B2
Penguin Books India (P) Ltd, 11 Community Centre,
Panchsheel Park, New Delhi – 110 017, India
Penguin Group (NZ), cnr Airborne and Rosedale Roads,
Albany, Auckland 1310, New Zealand
Penguin Books (South Africa) (Pty) Ltd, 24 Sturdee Avenue,
Rosebank 2196, South Africa

Penguin Books Ltd, Registered Offices: 80 Strand, London WC2R 0RL, England

www.penguin.com

First published 2004
1

Set in 12/14.75 pt PostScript Monotype Bembo
Typeset by Rowland Phototypesetting Ltd, Bury St Edmunds, Suffolk
Printed in Great Britain by Clays Ltd, St Ives plc

A CIP catalogue record for this book is available from the British Library

ISBN 1–844–88035–4

In memory of Cathal

Contents

Prologue

When I went to UCD in 1969, at the age of twenty-two, I knew practically nothing about politics. Since I had seen that my family had an affiliation with Fianna Fáil – at election times its candidates got a somewhat warmer reception in our house than those of other parties, and I recalled a party car coming to collect my grandmother on polling day – without much thought I gravitated towards the Kevin Barry Cumann. It was a desert of political thought and activity compared to the maelstrom raging through the left-wing organizations. Its members' easy-going dispositions were in stark contrast to those of the Fine Gaelers, who were serious, staid even – except for those ambitious young politicos who participated in the Literary and Historical Society, where occasionally events took a nasty turn when a Saturday-night debate was invaded by the gurrier element of the student population. Their outraged reaction was redolent of an earlier era, and it didn't take much to recall the party's Blueshirt history. Matters got so out of hand on one occasion that the gardaí were called.

In contrast the activities of the Kevin Barry Cumann were sparse, to say the least. It seems astounding now, in these days of communications skills and transparency, that senior Fianna Fáil politicians – ministers – were reluctant, even afraid, to set foot on campus for fear of action by uppity students, regardless of political hue. I remember a particularly raucous meeting shortly after the arms trial of 1970 at which the Minister for Lands, Seán Flanagan, made an appearance. The cumann had never seen so many people at one of its meetings, and the reason became obvious within a short time of the minister's arrival. It was known that Flanagan had no great *grá* for Jack Lynch and leant more towards Charlie Haughey in his sympathies. Trying to defend the actions of the government in those circumstances was difficult enough without also having to contend with students intent on protesting about the use of the Offences Against the State Acts. Brian Lenihan was one of the few others to brave the student scene. I cannot recall who organized it, but certainly every member of the cumann went on the march to Merrion Square after the events of Bloody Sunday in Derry in January 1972. I was amongst those who watched the burning of the British Embassy with unconcealed glee. The only other political experience I had was getting a clip in the ear from the late Kevin Boland when I was watching proceedings during the arms trial with some fellow students, and he overheard me expressing what he appeared to take as an irreverent comment.

Apart from taking part in those few, rather conservative activities, I got on with my studies, progressed to my degree in history and politics and almost immediately joined RTÉ, courtesy of Brian Farrell. He had been my tutor on a Master's degree programme that I had started but abandoned for financial reasons, and he introduced me to Séamus Smith, the editor of the current affairs programme *7 Days*.

Initially I gloried in the title of Researcher, and my sole ambition was to be a reporter in the current affairs or news area. The 1973 general election was a watershed in many ways, not least in RTÉ's television coverage. It was the first occasion that continuous commentary was provided by Brian Farrell and Ted Nealon, together with a panel of experts. It was a phenomenal success. My role was minor – minuscule minor – and was totally in the background, but I did get to meet with various political figures who would, barely a year later, loom much larger in my life: Jack Lynch, Brian Lenihan, Liam Cosgrave, Brendan Corish, George Colley, Garret FitzGerald and others. Afterwards, Ted Nealon and I cooperated in producing the first *Nealon's Guide*, which covered the general election in the Republic and the first Assembly elections in the North.

As a result of the efforts of newsroom editor Mike Burns I was recruited as a reporter. Shortly afterwards Jim McGuinness, the head of news, asked if I would be prepared to go to the Belfast Office with Liam Hourican. I jumped at the chance. While Liam was the frontman, and an authority on what was happening in the

North, there was plenty of meaty reporting for the other members of the Belfast team: John O'Callaghan, Brian Black, Owen Hand and now myself. This was the time of Sunningdale and the establishment of the first Northern Assembly, with the SDLP and the Alliance Party sharing power with Unionists under Brian Faulkner. I recall interviewing both John Hume and Austin Currie in their new ministerial offices on the first day of the administration. Despite the trauma, the death, the destruction and the intimidation, it was a fascinating and exciting period. I travelled right across Northern Ireland, visiting places I had never even heard of before, and began to get some insight into the thinking of both Catholics and Protestants. Although hard-line public stances were adopted by many – in particular Ian Paisley – I still found Northerners to be kind, hospitable and open to discussion. On one occasion Paisley asked about my name and when I told him that my grandfather was a Scots Presbyterian, there were no further barriers to the inquiries of a 'Republican' journalist. My interest in events down South diminished, and, apart from the odd foray for the weekend, I spent virtually all of my time in the North for a year or more.

Fianna Fáil was in chaos at this time. The amazing reality was that, despite the trauma of the arms crisis, when two ministers were sacked and two more resigned, despite internal wranglings, despite untold incompetence, they were nearly re-elected at the 1973 general election. The voting pact between Fine Gael and Labour – agreed a short time before the actual election – guaranteed seats for the coalition that would not have been remotely possible without it. Fianna Fáil not only resented this, but also the role of the press in the promotion of the coalition's prospects.

After losing the election, the party was useless at communicating with the media. This is not to suggest that it was good at it prior to that defeat; but much of the media's attention between 1970 and 1973 related either to the North or to the fallout from the arms crisis, and it could handle both these issues reasonably well in the *Irish Press* (the newspaper founded by Eamon de Valera with money supplied by ordinary Fianna Fáil supporters and run by the de Valera family) if not elsewhere. But whatever control it had was lost altogether after the 1973 election, and Fianna Fáil fell into a torpor from which it either did not wish to be aroused or could not awaken. It is true that an opposition has to work hard to gain attention: journalistic interest is in the decision-makers. In the penetrating light of opposition Fianna Fáil's true abilities – or more accurately, the lack of them – became obvious, and the only outlet for grass-roots disenchantment, as well as back bench disillusion-ment, was to turn on the media. This issue of publicity, or rather the failure to get any, boiled over from time to time and then deputies turned on their colleague Vivion de Valera, TD, the paper's managing editor. Matters would be resolved temporarily by organizing a profile of, or an in-depth interview with, Jack Lynch by somebody of the stature of Seán Cryan of the *Sunday Press.* Things would rest a little easier until another outbreak of hostility resulting from some ill-defined lack of coverage of some obscure speech by a member of the front bench, and the saga would start all over again.

Before the change of government, media coverage of Fianna Fáil, including the more penetrating TV programmes presented by Brian Farrell, David Thornley and Ted Nealon, was relatively tame. After the coalition was elected, and especially after the appointment of Muiris MacConghail, former editor of *7 Days* and other RTÉ current affairs programmes, as head of the Government Information Service, there was a subtle change in approach by the media, including the *Irish Press.* Whereas Fianna Fáil had had a hostile and uncooperative attitude to the media, the new government instituted a more open procedure in which a government spokesperson – MacConghail – would brief the political correspondents twice weekly after cabinet meetings. Some newspaper editors were sus-picious of this development and thought that their correspondents might become enmeshed in a propaganda machine. But they over-came their concerns when they saw the flow of copy from Leinster House. Fianna Fáil found it difficult to come to terms with this organized, professional communications strategy. The party began to believe that it was being confronted by what it perceived –

wrongly – to be a new and sinister enemy: 'a bought press'. Given that the *Irish Press* was founded to counteract what Fianna Fáil regarded as the propaganda of the Free State *Irish Independent*, and that the party had had to suffer jocose references to its motto, 'The Truth in The News', it was a bit ironic that Fianna Fáil politicians were complaining about 'a bought press'. But even smart Fianna Fáilers believed that their own beloved organ had been seduced by the government's spoon-feeding of journalists, while the less cerebral elements in the party thought that there was a plot to promote the new government and to keep Fianna Fáil out of power for as long as possible. This paranoia deepened as a consensus developed amongst political commentators that for the first time in the history of the state a coalition government would be returned to office for a second consecutive term.

Even those who did not buy into this blinkered view of political life thought that there was an unhealthy relationship between the new government – particularly ministers like Justin Keating, Garret FitzGerald and Conor Cruise O'Brien – and journalists, all orchestrated by spin-meister Muiris MacConghail. It was no coincidence, they believed, because as a broadcaster MacConghail had clashed with the Fianna Fáil government over the broadcasting of an investigation into money-lending. Whichever way you looked at it, either from the backwoodsmen's point of view or from the standpoint of those who feigned a more sophisticated outlook while secretly plotting revenge on certain papers and programmes, the relationship between Fianna Fáil and the media was fraught and fragile.

These run-ins with the media were symptomatic of underlying anxieties within the party about its spokesmen's underperformance, about a lack of substance with regard to policies and a general disbelief that the coalition was really running the country. Within six months Fianna Fáil settled into a resigned acceptance that the government would not let go of the reins of power too easily. Jack Lynch later told me that he had met Peter Barry and his wife at some official dinner, and Peter's wife had told him how

much Peter loved being in office. Talk about rubbing salt into
the wound. Fianna Fáil found the freedom that Liam Cosgrave
apparently gave his ministers difficult to comprehend. Any minister
could talk on any subject, and frequently did, particularly Conor
Cruise O'Brien. This, naturally, generated considerable coverage
and reinforced the view that the media was in the government's
pocket. Meanwhile the newspapers, together with radio and television, were giving Fianna Fáil a hard time about its dismal performance from the opposition benches. The party could easily come to
terms with its great *bête noire* – Conor Cruise O'Brien, Minister for
Posts and Telegraphs – to whom the head of the Government
Information Service reported. After all, TDs argued, O'Brien had
been in charge of, or at least played a significant role in, the Irish
News Agency in the 1950s. And they vaguely accepted that when
they were back in government they would have to at least attempt
to operate a similar system. But what they could not accept was
that some other party was using a sophisticated communications
technique that made the approach of the largest political party in
the state look naive, and that this was detrimental to their electoral
support. The matter became personal at times, and individual
journalists – Michael Mills of the *Irish Press*, Chris Glennon of the
Irish Independent, Arthur Noonan of RTÉ, Liam O'Neill of the
Cork Examiner and Dick Walsh of the *Irish Times* – felt the wrath of
senior members of the front bench when they met in the corridors
of power.

These spats merely postponed the moment that neither Jack
Lynch nor the party as a whole wanted to arrive, the moment when
– if they were to beat the new system, if they were to buy into
the new communications strategy – they would have to employ
professionals and pay them accordingly. Politicians, until confronted and told otherwise, like to believe that they are either
omniscient or infallible. By and large politicians do not like professionals, except in circumstances where they can dictate to them
or control them. But gradually the penny dropped.

In early 1974 an advertisement appeared in the national
newspaper seeking applications for the new post of Press Officer

for the party. I don't believe I even saw the ad. It was brought to my attention by a friend, and some time later, just short of the deadline, I received a phone call asking me to apply. While both the caller and I would prefer to keep his identity confidential, none the less I was somewhat surprised, but also flattered, to have him call me, given his prominent position in Irish life. He had heard of me through another UCD graduate, a contemporary of mine. On foot of that call, I applied for a job about which I knew little and probably would never even have considered as a career move. Suffice to say that person was responsible for a sea-change in my life, a roller coaster of great experience, sadness, recriminations and enjoyment that lasts up to the present day.

It is an indication of my casual attitude at the time that when one of my colleagues in the RTÉ newsroom in Belfast handed me the phone early in April 1974 with the words 'a Jack Lynch for you', I did not immediately think of the leader of Fianna Fáil; I thought it was one of my Republican Club contacts on the Falls Road and, much to his amusement, I reacted with less urgency, or respect, than I would have, had I known who was on the line. I explained the circumstances. He invited me to Dublin. I met him together with Hugh O'Flaherty, later a member of the Supreme Court, Ruairí Brugha, then a front bench spokesman, and Esmonde Smyth, the party's newly appointed head of research. I was offered the job and accepted it.

Virtually all my colleagues – at least those of any repute or substance – advised me against the move. In doing so, they made clear their feelings and views regarding Fianna Fáil in a way that not only surprised me but showed a significant anti-Fianna Fáil attitude in RTÉ. This was based, in the main, on the sacking of the RTÉ Authority over the Kevin O'Kelly interview with the IRA's Seán MacStiofáin in November 1972, but also on resentment towards the party for its attempts at controlling events at the station since the opening night of RTÉ TV on New Year's Eve 1961. Liam Hourican – whose political sympathies were with Fine Gael (and who subsequently became Government Press Secretary under Garret FitzGerald) just laughed and said that I was ruining my career. Jim McGuinness, the head of news, bluntly told me that I was mad, that those Fianna Fáilers were piranha fish and would devour me.

With some trepidation, therefore, I presented myself at the Fianna Fáil offices in Leinster House in late April 1974. The first item on the agenda was a press conference with the political correspondents – Michael Mills, the doyen of the group, Chris Glennon, Liam O'Neill, Dick Walsh and Michael McInerney of the *Irish Times*, and Arthur Noonan and Donal Kelly of RTÉ – to announce my appointment. I had never met the political correspondents before. This tightly knit group formed the core of political commentary throughout the seventies, and it wasn't until the early eighties that it widened to include Sunday and evening papers, local radio stations and a host of commentators who demanded access to the 'lobby'. Much of my daily life, as well as parts of my nightly life, would be conducted in close association with this group. There were many rows. There was much fun. There were frightening insights into the fragile relationship between politicians and the media. And there were long frustrating days when the interests of both were at odds, and there I was, the meat in the sandwich.

Jack Lynch, in his innocence – and he was innocent, perhaps naive, in many ways – decided that if I was to work with his TDs and senators, I should meet them formally. When he introduced me at a parliamentary party meeting, there was total silence. Everybody stared at me as if I had just landed from an alien galaxy. Having thanked Jack for the welcome, I spoke briefly to what could only be described as a suspicious, even hostile audience. More silence. Then Jack asked if anybody had anything to say. The great vista of what was ahead of me opened up when Paddy Smith – a veteran of many governments under de Valera, Lemass and Lynch – asked, 'What is it exactly you will be doing for us, young fella?'

1. A party in chaos

My immediate reaction to what I found in Fianna Fáil was shock: shock at the disarray, shock at the ignorance of prominent members as to the workings of the media, shock at the blatant and naked antipathy that existed amongst former senior ministers towards named journalists. This antipathy, of course, worked two ways, and there was no concealing the satisfaction felt by some senior journalists at the spectacle of Fianna Fáil – and in particular some individual senior members – out of power after an unbroken run of sixteen years.

The truth is that the party was suffering from what would now be seen as post-traumatic stress and it was in a time warp. It had come through the arms crisis, the subsequent trial, the acquittals and the inevitable recriminations. Senior members had started laying the foundations on which they would construct their versions of what had happened. In doing so, they were also creating the fissures that would eventually widen and split the party and lead to the formation of a new entity in the shape of the PDs. On top of that, the only evidence of fresh blood on the front bench was John Wilson, a new TD, who became spokesman on education. Most of the others had been around, in one capacity or another, for the best part of a decade, and some of them owed their positions to the events of 1970 when, following the disclosure that there had been an attempt to import arms into the country illegally, four senior ministers left the cabinet. Whatever the country was expecting, to say nothing of the hopes of Fianna Fáil supporters around the country, the front bench line-up didn't augur well for revolutionary new ideas or policies.

From the moment of their defeat at the polls the majority of these men, and they were all men, believed that they were not required to do very much in opposition and that when the general election was called they would be returned to power automatically. Holding to the Fianna Fáil mantra that coalitions did not work, they were convinced that the new government would disintegrate or implode within less than two years. This attitude accounted largely for the lethargic way in which they approached the role of opposition. Likewise it went a long way towards explaining why they failed to understand the huge volume of criticism of their performance in opposition, not only by the media, but also by their own supporters.

It was a source of constant amazement to me – but I was a newcomer, and maybe a little idealistic about the workings of politics – that these men who were dependent on the grass roots for their positions took such a nonchalant attitude to the party supporters' views. It was as if they took the support for granted and that no matter what the TDs said or did in Leinster House the grass roots would vote for them unquestioningly. It was an arrogance that, as I was to learn later, when working with politicians from other parties, permeated the thinking of all TDs after they were elected. They believed that they were untouchable. They had 'a mandate from the people' that allowed them to adopt an air of invincibility. But deep down they all knew that they had to face the electorate, so there was always a fear of losing the seat. This was particularly the case where there was more than one Fianna Fáil TD in a particular constituency. The rivalry was intense, and the famous Churchillian adage about the House of Commons applied, viz., that the opposition is in front of you but the real enemy is behind you.

In my early days working with the party, eager to show that changes were afoot, I made a speech at a Fianna Fáil youth conference in which I attempted to excuse the alleged shortcomings of some of the senior members of the front bench by alluding to the difficulty of turning sows' ears into silk purses. It was something of a populist thing to say and I knew immediately that I would upset some deputies. Some days later the Donegal TD, Joe Brennan, came to see me. His appointment in the previous Fianna Fáil government in May 1970 had been for tactical and geographical rather than meritocratic reasons (he had the sacked Neil Blaney in his neighbouring constituency), and he was prone to getting himself into hot water. On one occasion, without any forewarning, he announced the cancellation of the dole. This caused consternation, and eventually it was put down to a misunderstanding on the part of the minister caused by a misreading of a briefing prepared for him by his civil servants. In any event Joe was sensitive to anything that he regarded as implied or direct criticism. He believed that my sows' ears reference had been directed at him and told me that he had complained to the leader. It was a revealing incident, showing me the depth of insecurity and sensitivity front bench members were feeling. It was also an early example of how quickly politicians react when their *amour propre* is offended. Unlike some other politicians from Donegal, Joe's bark was worse than his bite. He was not one to hold a grudge and was subsequently helpful, as an auctioneer, in advising me about the purchase of my first house.

Fianna Fáil as a parliamentary party was totally lost. At sea. Rudderless. There was little, if any, coordination in its stances to government policy or action. Everything was ad hoc. People who had been ministers, and who had become accustomed to the trappings of office such as chauffeur-driven cars, instant advice from civil servants, prepared scripts and the like, found it difficult to operate politically on a TD's salary and therefore they reverted to their previous professions. Politics – at constituency level and at national level, for those who were members of the front bench – took second place. George Colley and Des O'Malley resumed their solicitors' practices. Michael O'Kennedy and David Andrews returned to the Law Library. Jim Gibbons and Brian Lenihan were appointed to the European Parliament. And Charlie Haughey continued on in isolated splendour in his mansion in Kinsaley. (Though the place-name Kinsaley has been modernized to Kinsealy, Charlie Haughey uses the older spelling and it is the one used in this book.) It is difficult to realize it now but senior members of the party had become used to having everything done for them – in some instances even their thinking – and it was cataclysmic for them not only to lose office and to have to organize themselves on their own initiative, but also to have to begin to think about how they should react to the policies of the new government.

It was in these circumstances that Tony Hederman, SC, suggested to Jack Lynch that he appoint Esmonde Smyth as head of research and that various backroom groups of volunteer experts should be established to help the party, and the front bench in particular, with policy formulation. At the same time, over at Fianna Fáil HQ, Séamus Brennan, who had been appointed General Secretary of the party a few months prior to my arrival, was desperately trying to drag the organization into the twentieth century. He and I had only one safeguard: Jack Lynch. Lynch invested a significant amount of trust in both of us and ignored the stated, and unstated, criticisms of old stagers to the effect that the party was being handed over to people who had little experience of its workings or, worse still, little knowledge of the somewhat convoluted ethos of the party as evinced over the previous forty-odd years by those who had established it and ran it ruthlessly.

Séamus and I worked reasonably well together, but he always resented the fact that I would not work from Fianna Fáil headquarters in Upper Mount Street. I recognized from the beginning that to do so would oblige me to work through a filtration system – in other words, my contact with the leader of the party, with the front bench and with the media would, in effect, be through him. I knew that this would frustrate me, so I took up residence on the third floor of Leinster House, a few doors down from Jack's office, and I resolutely refused to move from there. I knew that Séamus complained to Jack Lynch that I was running what in effect was an independent republic and that I was responsible only to the leader, who could not possibly know at all times what I was or was not doing. Mind you, I learnt never to underestimate the capacity of a party leader to find out about the strangest activities. Séamus Brennan and I discovered that while we were running matters reasonably well, and were not causing any difficulties for Jack, we had no interference. As soon as trouble brewed, Jack, reluctantly, became involved. He smoothed ruffled feathers and in the main Séamus and I worked very amicably together. I cannot say the same for my relationship with Esmonde Smyth. Our personalities just didn't gel.

As head of research Smyth appeared to have assumed significant powers that were deeply resented by some of the front bench and most of the back benchers. I recall George Colley seeking my advice as to how to calm the anger of some members of the parliamentary party at Esmonde's role. They felt that he didn't want to know anything about back benchers' problems. As far as they were concerned, he only looked after the interests of the party leader and was solely responsible for the coordination of the backroom research committees. Most of the back benchers regarded these committees as talking shops made up of various self-interests; they hadn't quite come to terms with the new-fangled strategic approach to politics their party was now taking, nor with this retinue of experts who seemed to be running the show. The ordinary back bencher spends most of his or her time responding to queries raised at constituency clinics or through letters for information or assistance. What the back bencher doesn't have time for is research – be it into relatively simple matters regarding legislation or statutes, or more difficult issues relating to policy. That is what the back benchers wanted Esmonde Smyth to provide on demand. Smyth resolutely refused, and a deep sense of antagonism developed that began to affect the leader's office.

Eventually, George Colley reconciled matters, probably through Martin O'Donoghue. O'Donoghue had been appointed Economics Adviser to Lynch in the latter months of the previous Fianna Fáil government and after the 1973 general election he assumed the role of *éminence grise* to Lynch; he had great influence on the attitude adopted by both Lynch and the parliamentary party to a wide range of issues, economic and otherwise. With Smyth he coordinated the backroom committees and was in charge of the opposition leader's state allowance from which Smyth's and my salary, and those of our respective staffs, were paid. However effective Esmonde was – and there is no doubt that the publication of the 1977 Fianna Fáil election manifesto, which emanated in the main from his research committees, was spectacularly impressive – he did not appear to be a party-political man, and when Fianna Fáil won the 1977 general election he returned to the bar whence, on the nomination of the Progressive Democrats, he was subsequently appointed to the bench (he is now President of the Circuit Court).

Having other people do the day-to-day running of the party and formulate policy suited Jack's purposes down to the ground. The truth of the matter was that Lynch had an unchallengeable popularity. It was even said that when the electorate woke up the morning after the 1973 general election and realized that the coalition had been elected, most people said, 'What have we done to poor Jack?' He was the best, if not the only asset that Fianna Fáil had at the time. He was extremely televisual and went down a treat with key portions of the electorate – sports people, women (particularly nuns), etc. But this patina of popularity and acceptability, valuable and all that it was (and it was shown to be invaluable in the 1977 general election), concealed a startling truth: Jack was basically hands-off in his approach and this intellectual laziness got him into trouble. It took some time for me to realize that there were quite a few people around him – in the parliamentary party, in the wider organization and, after Fianna Fáil returned to power in 1977, in the civil service and the wider public service, particularly the semi-state bodies – who knew how to play Jack in situations where it suited his purposes.

I believe that this characteristic – one of allowing matters to progress a certain distance without troubling himself to look into them – was a key factor in the events leading to the arms crisis of 1970. It was just four years since the arms crisis had torn the party, and the country, apart, and it was fresh in the minds of those with whom I worked closely. After all, two colleagues, Charles Haughey and Neil Blaney, had been fired from the cabinet following allegations that they had illegally conspired to import arms for Northern nationalists; a third, Kevin Boland, had resigned in sympathy; and a fourth, Micheál Ó Móráin, resigned for health reasons. In time Charles Haughey was tried for, and acquitted of, involvement in the scheme – but not before his evidence was contradicted in court by another cabinet member, Jim Gibbons, the state's chief prosecution witness, and a judge declared that one of them was not telling the truth. The judge's words haunted members of the front bench, and Lynch, convinced, of necessity, by the Attorney General's prosecution case, was on the side of Gibbons. The generally accepted political view was that there was an attempt to import arms illegally, that Charlie was involved, and that in court he preferred to deny it. (The notion that he had somehow instigated the founding of the Provisional IRA – as some of his detractors had it and would still have it – flies in the face of his history as Minister for Justice. The former Secretary of the Department of Justice, Peter Berry, later wrote that when Haughey came to the department in 1961, at a time when such a move would have been unpopular in Fianna Fáil, he identified the crushing of the IRA as his primary objective and initiated a highly successful strategy against the organization.)

While most were reluctant to talk about these events, none the less those who had played leading roles in the drama occasionally gave glimpses of their mindsets. Gradually, as I became somewhat more intimate with them, they became increasingly talkative, and while none – with the exception of Gibbons – would go into explicit detail about the events, there was sufficient public and media interest in the affair even then to allow me to broach the matter with the main participants. When I raised the topic a few years later, nobody of seniority or standing in the party at the time was in any doubt that the government as a whole knew that 'certain actions' were being taken to try to alleviate the situation for the Nationalist community in the North. The details of such actions probably were never alluded to, and this suited Jack Lynch and others, both in the cabinet and in the parliamentary party. Something was being done but the details were an unnecessary encumbrance.

When the details – correct or otherwise – were provided to Jack Lynch by Liam Cosgrave, who was informed by a Fine Gael supporter either in the Garda or the Customs and Excise Service, Lynch acted. Had Cosgrave not contacted Lynch, would he have

ever acted? This, and other details like it, suffused debate internally
in Fianna Fáil for years and, amongst a diminishing group of party
stalwarts, probably still does. But the essential point in the affair is
Jack Lynch's psychological make-up. He was unwilling to confront
unless forced to do so. The general view of Jack's personality around
Leinster House at the time of the arms trial was that when he was
playing both hurling and football at national level, he would make
sure the referee was looking the other way before he hit you. In
other words, he didn't mind going against the rules, as long as there
was no danger of getting caught.

Jack Lynch rarely initiated anything and he was great at delegat-
ing. Most new ideas for regenerating the party, for new policies
and for attracting new blood came from other people. In truth he
had switched off, but this was masked by a positive presentation.
The events of 1969/70 had exhausted him. The constant pressure
to keep up the nice-guy image sapped his energy. After the defeat
in 1973, the Littlejohn affair a few months later (in which he had
to admit that he had forgotten seeing a report on two English
brothers who sought immunity from prosecution for bank rob-
bery in the Irish courts by claiming to be British agents acting to
provoke the Irish government into introducing internment) and
then breaking a bone in his foot in a boating accident at his west
Cork holiday home, he began to relax and allow others to run the
show. Hence the power of Martin O'Donoghue, Esmonde Smyth,
Séamus Brennan and, to a lesser extent, myself. Much of the
reorganization of the party, the vast proportion of the preparation
of new policies and the general day-to-day business of Fianna Fáil
was left to others, mainly non-elected personnel – a fact that was
the cause of considerable angst among back benchers, most of
whom, however, were concerned only about keeping their seats at
the next election.

Complicating everything was the role played by Máirín, Jack's
wife. It was commonly believed in political circles that because
they had no children she had a greater influence on him than would
normally be expected of a political wife, and Jack contributed to

the perception by saying, at the time of the 1966 succession of Seán Lemass, that he would have to ask Máirín before committing himself to accepting the job of Taoiseach. Pádraig Ó hAnnracháin, who was head of the Government Information Service under de Valera, Lemass and Lynch, once described Máirín's role as 'government by hatpin'. It was always my impression when I worked with him that while he had a number of brothers and sisters they were not particularly close. He and Máirín formed a tight unit, and she viewed his role as leader of the party in a protective way. But it never struck me that her interest was other than on behalf of Jack; it didn't extend to the party as a whole.

Numerous stories about Jack and Máirín entertained the cynics in Leinster House but endeared him to the wider political community. He went home to lunch with Máirín every day, even some days when the Dáil was sitting. Legend had it that one day she phoned the Taoiseach's office to tell him to pick up lamb chops on the way home. I had my own experience of Máirín's influence in an incident with an injured dog. The Lynchs were on the road when their official car clipped a particularly persistent car-chasing bitch. On Máirín's insistence the car stopped and nothing would do her but to have the dog carried into the nearby farmhouse – as it happened, the dog-owners' home. The owners appeared somewhat disappointed that the old mongrel had not at last met her deserved fate and kept apologizing to Jack and his wife for the trouble she had caused them. The dog was duly laid out in front of the kitchen fire, and she gave every appearance of wishing that she was knocked down by the former Taoiseach's car every day, such was the attention being lavished on her by Máirín. She asked if a vet should be called and thankfully didn't see the look of horror on the poor farmer's face. Honour was satisfied at last with Máirín insisting that, when next he was passing, Jack would call in to inquire as to the dog's condition. A few months later Jack and I were on the same road very late one night, having been at one of those interminable political dinners where every Tom, Dick and Harry insists on subjecting the audience, and particularly the distinguished visitor from Dublin, to their long-winded speech-making. As we

approached the house, I couldn't resist. 'Maybe we should call in
and find out how the dog is?' I said. It was one of the few occasions
when Jack's response was unrepeatable, and I had to promise never
to tell Máirín that we had passed the house and not called in to ask
about the dog.

Everyone had a story like this about Jack and Máirín. They
helped Jack's popular image. But they were also useful in fuelling
the perception that he shouldn't be taken that seriously as party
leader or Taoiseach. In the years between 1966 and 1972 Lynch
was portrayed, sometimes pilloried, by political commentators –
John Healy of the *Irish Times* in particular – as a stopgap leader and
Taoiseach. This arose out of the impasse that developed in 1966,
after Lemass retired and Charlie Haughey and George Colley were
locked in battle to succeed him. A lot of people in the party thought
it a little cheeky of George Colley to contest the leadership after
only a few years in the Dáil, but the truth was that the older
generation – men like Frank Aiken, Paddy Smith, Seán McEntee
and Jim Ryan – were caught unawares by Lemass's resignation and
did not want Charlie Haughey to succeed. To the old guard he
epitomized all that they regarded as wrong with Fianna Fáil under
Lemass. Yes, Lemass had done wonders in the short time left to
him after de Valera's long reign. His industrialization programme,
the attraction of foreign investment, his partnership with the
brilliant civil servant T. K. (Ken) Whitaker – these had all brought
a new vibrancy to the country. But his administration had also
produced brash young men like Charlie Haughey, Donogh
O'Malley, Neil Blaney and Brian Lenihan, who had no time for
the old shibboleths and introduced new slogans of their own.

For all his loyalty to his daughter's husband, Lemass knew that if
Charlie persisted with his candidacy for the leadership of the party,
and won, there would be mayhem. Hence his approach to Jack
Lynch to run as a 'compromise' candidate. Hence Charlie's with-
drawal from the election and Jack's comprehensive victory over
George. Hence the belief amongst the new blood that Lynch was
a caretaker and matters would be sorted out appropriately in a year
or two. But, as with all caretakers, the agenda didn't quite run as

expected, and Lynch went on to win the 1969 general election and to consolidate his position as leader.

If the elders of the party thought the brashness of the party's high-profile young deputies unseemly, they were appalled by Taca, a fund-raising scheme run by Neil Blaney. They thought that it brought unnecessary and unhelpful attention on the party, as well as introducing into Fianna Fáil a new, moneyed class that had no real sympathy with the party's founding ideals and would eventually lead to its demise. They found it difficult, impossible even, to accept that their day was done, and that, rightly or wrongly, there were to be new ways of doing things, including funding the party and its operations. And there was no doubt that Fianna Fáil was receiving substantial sums of money. Taca was formed in 1966 and it encouraged contributions to party coffers from individual businessmen and companies in order to fund the running costs associated with elections. In return for an annual contribution of £100, businessmen could enjoy monthly dinners with senior Fianna Fáilers at the Gresham Hotel. The cocktail of money and politics had indeed arrived in Fianna Fáil. Oil and water. Dangerous. The old hands recognized the perils involved, but the new era was unstoppable. As was Charlie Haughey, who came to epitomize the 'mohair suit man', though I doubt whether Charlie was ever so crass as to wear a mohair suit.

Taca (the name is the Irish word for 'support') was the forerunner of many subsequent inventive schemes that allowed business people to buy their way into the decision-making process, to gain access and to put their case forcefully in circumstances where others, who had not contributed, were denied an audience. Because it attracted such opprobrium, Taca faded away after a couple of years. But the goal of raising money from the business community didn't; the party just found more discreet ways of doing it. After Taca's demise Des Hanafin, a businessman who was a prominent party member, was recruited to bring a new respectability to the party's fund-raising activities. He had a highly secret list of donors, assiduously built up over a number of years. The operation had all the elements of Masonic intrigue and secrecy about it. It was run from an office in the Burlington Hotel in Dublin, where in plush surroundings Des received those who were willing to support the party in a tangible way. Nobody, other than Des, knew who these generous people were. It was never clear whether he told his party leader who they were either, but occasional exclusive dinner parties were held, in great secrecy, at which these unidentified benefactors met with the leader and in some instances senior members of the party's front bench. These genteel and well-mannered events afforded the bene-factors an opportunity to outline, without the possibility of inter-ruption or contradiction, their 'concerns' about public policy as it affected them personally or in their businesses. Of course, the thing that always clinched any argument being made by a potential donor was the possibility of providing employment. If the policy being pursued by the party, in either opposition or in government, could be shown to be a disincentive to creating jobs or, alternatively, a serious threat to those already in existence, then the issue was settled. Then, as now, there was no greater weapon to instil fear into a politician than the threat of the loss of jobs. Indeed there is no greater elixir in political life than the promise of mass job creation, particularly in a politician's own constituency. In both instances the politicians cave in. That a substantial donation to the party's coffers is forthcoming, immediately or at the next electoral contest, is regarded as merely coincidental.

In recent years, much has been made of Charlie's alleged attempt to consolidate all fund-raising to himself or to those who would be closer to him than Des Hanafin after he became leader in 1979. In those days there were no rules of disclosure. Therefore nobody knew who was giving and nobody knew how much had been donated. This was the nub of the problem when Charlie took over. He wanted to know who gave and how much. Des Hanafin disagreed and said that the confidentiality between the benefactor and the party would be breached if he were to disclose the identity of the donors. But, if that was the case, why had Jack Lynch been invited to attend exclusive, secret dinners with selected donors? Who attended? What transpired at these meetings? And what effect, if any, had these political trysts on public policy? Would anybody care even to admit that such encounters occurred? Of course not. And, presumably, in keeping with the tradition of not disturbing the accepted balance of recent political history, which follows the predictable and very comfortable – to say nothing of intellectually non-challenging – line that Jack and his cohorts were the good guys and Charlie and his pals were the baddies, I suppose it would be churlish to disagree with, let alone question, this palpably thin contention. But it's certainly worth considering.

But, returning to the Fianna Fáil I came to know in 1974, it was obvious that even before the arms crisis Jack had not liked Charlie Haughey. Neither had he liked Neil Blaney or Brian Lenihan. I once asked him what he thought of Donogh O'Malley – the man who introduced free education, and the man once described by Lemass as the type who came to you every day with a whacky idea until one day he suggested something that you knew was a winner (like free education) – and Jack replied dismissively that he wore pink shirts. Jack was never a member of the new Fianna Fáil circle. He was regarded as a journeyman politician who, because of a pleasant personality, combined with a sporting reputation and reasonable ability, fell on his feet when appointed a Parliamentary Secretary – the forerunner of a junior minister – by Eamon de Valera. His political career was a progression from his career as a sports hero. He had no political background whatever prior to his being approached by the Fianna Fáil organization in Cork to run for the party. That he was a barrister was irrelevant. That he was electable was the key point. At that time Cork was a Fine Gael city, and Jack, according to himself, deliberately set out, as somebody from the other side of the tracks, to infiltrate the social and sporting haunts of the merchant princes and impress them with his undoubted charm.

Jack's advance through the ministerial ranks was as much due to the fact that he was regarded as having a safe pair of hands as to any particular ideological commitment or overweening ambition. Eventually he arrived in the Department of Finance under Ken Whitaker. It was generally recognized at the time that Jack knew very little about finance and, just like most Ministers for Finance, he was a cipher. The department devised the policy and wrote it, and the minister read it or spoke it. It was said in the fifties and sixties – and may have been true with some ministers since then – that the civil service loved Fianna Fáil administrations: all you had to do was tell them what to do and they did it, what to say and they said it. Jack was an intelligent and articulate barrister, but a man with something of an inferiority complex, and he depended on Ken Whitaker, who had become the leading policy guru in the Lemass era and on whom the Fianna Fáil governments relied almost exclusively for policy initiatives and advice.

If Jack had ambition he concealed it well. After all, he was in the shadow of political giants like de Valera and Lemass. He certainly had none of their drive. But, while Lynch was not a member of the so-called mohair suit brigade and did not frequent the Russell Hotel or the Royal Hibernian for long public lunches, he did possess the one trait that was to stand him in good stead throughout his political career: cuteness. Others might be less kind and call it cunning, but Lynch, as he had on the football and hurling fields, marked his man and kept his eye on the ball. Most of all he waited. To him timing was crucial, and he moved only when he knew he could score. This characteristic became very evident during the first stirrings for a change of leadership in Fianna Fáil.

I vividly recall the night in November 1974 that President Erskine Childers died suddenly while attending a function in the Royal College of Surgeons. Jack was attending another function, something to do with the Bar Library. I managed to make contact with him and we drove to RTÉ, where, with the cooperation of Mike Burns, Jack did an impromptu tribute for broadcast on radio the next morning. When the recording was over, Mike Burns, Jack and I sat down for an hour or so while we had a glass of his favourite tipple, Paddy Whiskey. Mike Burns could not resist asking Jack if he would consider running for the presidency. Jack became quite animated and said very clearly, almost fiercely, 'I will never allow myself to be buried for seven or fourteen years in that mausoleum in the park.'

However, in the days that followed I had my first of many experiences of the power of political whispering. A campaign began suggesting that this would be an ideal opportunity for Jack to retire; he had made his contribution to Irish politics, he was popular, he would make a great President, and he and Máirín could relax after the hectic events of the late sixties and early seventies. These campaigns follow a pattern: some stooge journalist is set up with a story suggesting that such and such an event might occur and unnamed sources within the party murmur appreciative noises as to the desirability of such an outcome. Next, a patsy back bencher raises his or her head above the parapet and opines along the same lines. Soon the whole thing takes on a momentum of its own. Jack knew this and did not let the matter get that far.

After Childers died his family assumed responsibility for funeral arrangements with the government. These discussions were conducted mainly with the Department of the Taoiseach by Erskine's son, who worked with the United Nations. But it began to emerge, or at least it became obvious to those of us with a political brain, that a small problem had arisen. Rita, Erskine's widow, was hoping that she would be allowed to assume the office; or that the politicians would find it very convenient to avoid an election and her 'popularity' would guarantee that the matter would be acceptable both politically and electorally. Jack Lynch, who knew Rita as Erskine's wife prior to the presidential election of 1973, was appalled. The decision to run Erskine as a candidate to succeed de Valera had been a risk. Many in Fianna Fáil thought it a mistake. Erskine was detached, even remote. There were legions of stories of how he did not even know his own back benchers when he was a minister. For instance, when a cross-party delegation from Laois–Offaly went to see him at his office, one of the TDs present was the popular young Fianna Fáil deputy Ger Connolly. When the meeting concluded, Ger thanked the minister and said that his constituents were extremely grateful to him for giving them some of his valuable time to listen to their concerns – the usual guff that TDs indulge in when their more impressionable constituents are within earshot – only to be met with a quizzical look from Erskine and the question, 'Which party are you from, Deputy?' The language used in Ger's subsequent recounting of the story is unprintable.

Similar stories about the presidential campaign were quickly forgotten in the immediate flush of success. Jim Gibbons collected a good many of them together and at one time threatened to publish a book. Had he done so, there would have been red faces all round amongst the party hierarchy. They couldn't get over how the public took to Erskine, who, up to that time, was not known for his common touch. Quite the contrary. Gibbons took great delight in recalling one particular incident from the candidate's tour of his own Carlow–Kilkenny constituency. Erskine and Rita had developed a code that prevented him from going over his allotted speaking time at each stop of the tour. She sat in the front seat of the bus while Erskine stood on a specially designed, retractable platform within inches of her. After he had spoken for three minutes she tugged his jacket once, twice after five minutes, and when she delivered the third tug he knew it was time to conclude. According to Gibbons, two elderly farmers in Clogh, a village a few miles from Castlecomer, noticed the stratagem. When Erskine kept speaking after she had given the third tug, she reached out and gave his jacket a pull that was even more forceful than the previous three. With that, one of the farmers leant into the bus and said to her, 'For fuck's sake, woman, will you let the man talk!'

During that election for the very first time a political party made use of a bus while electioneering. Michael O'Leary of the Labour Party christened it the 'Wanderly Wagon' after the popular children's television programme. Sometimes Jack Lynch, then the leader of the opposition – Fianna Fáil having been defeated in the preceding general election – joined Erskine in the bus. Jack was very popular and there were large crowds wherever he went. As the bus proceeded through the main thoroughfare in Cork – Jack's own bailiwick – he noticed that Erskine was sitting po-faced and unmoving, not paying any attention to the onlookers. 'Wave, Erskine, wave,' said Jack. 'But Jack,' said Erskine, 'I don't know those people.'

Erskine couldn't shed the hauteur conferred by his Anglo-Irish ancestry, and this added to the sense of somebody who was not quite in tune with the grubby world of Fianna Fáil politics. But, by some mysterious fusion of emotions, or by some extraordinary connection with Erskine's rather other-worldly views about youth, the campaign took off and he was elected over Tom O'Higgins of Fine Gael. O'Higgins was appointed Chief Justice by the Taoiseach, Liam Cosgrave, a short time later. Everything was right with the world: Fianna Fáil had the presidency and Fine Gael the office of Chief Justice.

Now Rita – or 'Reeter', as some of the Fianna Fáilers mockingly referred to her – seemed to be attempting to take control of the succession, much to the chagrin of the career politicians, both those in the coalition government and those in Fianna Fáil, most of all Jack Lynch. A front bench meeting was held to discuss tactics, and it was decided – after the funeral – that Michael O'Kennedy and David Andrews would call on Áras an Uachtaráin and try to ascertain Rita's intentions. They duly travelled to the Park and were received by Erskine's son. They did not meet Rita, who, conveniently, was not available to see them. But the son made it absolutely clear to O'Kennedy and Andrews that both Rita and he were negotiating with the government to ensure that a smooth transfer to Rita would take place to the satisfaction of everybody, many of whom did not want another election.

O'Kennedy and Andrews were offended by the tenor of the meeting but had the good grace to share in their colleagues' mirth at their discomfiture. Lynch set about letting Liam Cosgrave know that under no circumstances whatsoever would Rita Childers be acceptable as an 'agreed' candidate.

The President's funeral gave me a small insight into the lingering bitterness over the arms crisis. The public element of the funeral concluded when the cortège arrived at Government Buildings in Merrion Street. Thereafter it was to be a private affair and the interment in County Wicklow was to be exclusively non-political. As I watched the proceedings from the car park of Leinster House, I noticed a sleek royal blue Daimler moving in behind the cortège. As it passed me, a window was lowered and a hand beckoned me over. I was slightly disconcerted to see the solicitor and great pal of Charlie Haughey, Pat O'Connor, behind the wheel. Then I realized that it was Charlie's car and that there were a number of people in it, including Charlie himself in the front passenger seat. I squeezed in and asked where we were going. 'We're going down to Wicklow to make sure this fucker is planted,' Charlie said. This comment was not lost on others but it puzzled me: why would Charlie be so crude about a former cabinet colleague who had amazed everybody by being elected President after an exciting election campaign? But I had missed the point. The searing malice of the remark went back to all that had occurred in late 1969 and early 1970. Erskine had taken Lynch's side during the arms crisis. Worse, in Charlie's view, he had gone on national television and spoken about 'felon-setting' – and had, by inference, included Charlie in this description, the worst possible accusation that could be laid at the door of an Irish politician, most of all a Fianna Fáil politician. The wounds of 1970 went deep with Charlie. Anybody who had sided with Lynch during the arms crisis was *persona non grata*. Even when he succeeded Jack, and felt obliged to appoint some of those who had been strong supporters of Lynch, such as George Colley and Gerry Collins, he never ever trusted them.

When the funeral was over, Lynch announced that he was nominating Cearbhall Ó Dálaigh, a member of the European Court of Justice and a former member of the Supreme Court, for the post of President. He had obviously been in contact with Ó Dálaigh, who had given permission for his name to be put forward. The coalition government was very sniffy about the idea – shades of things to come – but Jack persisted and eventually the coalition agreed that Ó Dálaigh would be nominated as President, without the necessity of an election. I remember Jack becoming irritated that he did not hear back from Ó Dálaigh or the government prior to the actual announcement. Lynch, like the rest of the country, had to wait for the public announcement to hear that his nominee had been accepted. This was another insight into his character: he was a stickler for protocol.

★

In no time at all there was another presidential crisis, and another attempt to shift Jack. After defence minister Paddy Donegan called President Ó Dálaigh a 'thundering disgrace' at a ceremony in Mullingar barracks, because of the President's stated intention to refer the government's Emergency Powers bill to the Supreme Court to test its constitutionality, another, and much more concerted, attempt was made to get Jack to resign. I heard what Paddy Donegan had said in the late afternoon and was contacted for an official Fianna Fáil comment by RTÉ. Jack was on his way home and until I could reach him I drafted a statement to the effect that it was totally unacceptable for a cabinet minister, particularly the Minister for Defence, to describe the President, the Commander-in-Chief of the Army, albeit in name only, in the terms reported. The statement called for an immediate retraction and, at the very least, a statement of censure of the minister by the Taoiseach. When Jack returned my call, I read this draft to him and after a number of amendments he agreed that it should be issued but, interestingly, not in his name or in the name of Deputy Joe Dowling, the front bench spokesman on defence. We agreed to issue it in the party's name and I ended up reading the statement during a teatime current affairs programme. (Paddy Donegan obviously heard the programme or was told about it subsequently. Some time later, when I was head of the Government Information Service, Michael Mills and I were getting out of the lift in Leinster House and Paddy was getting in. Though he was now an ordinary back bencher, because of the deference due to a former minister I stood back to allow him to enter. Paddy stood there, resplendent in a bespoke pinstripe suit, and loudly declaimed, leaving nobody in doubt as to who he was addressing, 'There y'are, ya little bollix, ya!')

Neither Paddy Donegan nor the government of which he was a member seemed to realize what he had started. This was a full-blown political crisis with constitutional overtones and Jack knew it. Again, he wanted to see how events would unfold. Fine Gael, the party of law and order and high-flown commitments to the institutions of the state, handled things very badly. Of course the whole matter was a mess, compounded by what seemed to be a stubborn and intransigent approach by Liam Cosgrave, who, according to Jack, had been reluctant to agree to Ó Dálaigh's nomination and had treated him, as President, somewhat cavalierly. Cosgrave did not, for instance, maintain as faithfully as he should have the practice of keeping the President informed, through regular visits, of what the government's intentions were; so, when the coalition announced that it was introducing new security legislation, it was gob-smacked when Ó Dálaigh said that he would refer it to the Supreme Court to test its constitutionality. Had Cosgrave maintained even minimal contact with Ó Dálaigh, the latter might never have decided to take the action he did.

Because it disliked Ó Dálaigh, who had had a Fianna Fáil background in his earlier career and had, it believed, been foisted on them by Jack Lynch, Fine Gael dug in its heels and the situation became almost farcical, culminating in the Taoiseach, Liam Cosgrave, ringing the President from a coin-box phone on the side of the street in Dun Laoghaire. Ó Dálaigh required a public apology for Donegan's shocking behaviour, either from the government or from Donegan himself, and in its absence would resign. It is generally believed that Cosgrave instructed Donegan not to apologize. The matter was further compounded when Liam Cosgrave moved Paddy Donegan out of Defence and into the Department of Lands – a clear demotion but with a subtle message attached: Donegan was one of his men at cabinet and under no circumstance was he going to sack him and offer him up as a scapegoat in a scenario that he knew was highly damaging to the reputation of the government. The inevitable occurred. Ó Dálaigh resigned and the coalition government was left with considerable egg on its face. Meanwhile, the other party in government, Labour, seemed to be carrying on blithely as if nothing had happened or as if these events had nothing to do with it.

While this quasi-constitutional crisis was being played out in the full glare of publicity, another game was played, surreptitiously but cleverly, by certain elements in the Fianna Fáil parliamentary party.

It was a reprise of the events that followed Erskine Childers's death. The country had no President. There was a vacancy at Áras an Uachtaráin, and nobody, least of all the coalition government, wanted an election in which it would be portrayed as having trampled over constitutional niceties and allowed party political considerations to interfere with the relationship between the government and the presidency. A glorious opportunity now presented itself to usher Jack Lynch into the Park. Again the usual arguments were made: popular, great democrat, significant contribution to the maintenance of democratic institutions. The old tune of what he had done to save the country from civil war in 1970 was replayed a thousand times. And there would be no need to have an election because the government was bound to agree to Jack's nomination to the position. Those whose interests Jack's departure to the Park would serve firmly believed that, in the circumstances that prevailed, and with the danger of the presidency being further reduced in public esteem, there was no way that Jack Lynch could refuse the opportunity, much as he might dislike the prospect of retirement to the Áras.

Jack knew a campaign to get him to go for the presidency was being cleverly orchestrated. He announced that a special parliamentary party meeting was to be held to consider the issue. Those who did not know him thought that this was merely a front to allow himself to be persuaded that he ought to step into the breach and that ultimately, after due consideration, he would reluctantly agree – with Máirín's blessing. The meeting was scheduled for 11.30 a.m. Immediately prior to it, Lynch arrived in my office across the corridor from the party room. His instructions were specific. I was not to leave the office for any reason until he returned, no matter how long it took. I busied myself with telephone calls to journalists, all of whom were convinced that this was the denouement and that Jack would announce his intention, depending on the agreement of the government, to become President. Michael Mills, who had first-class access to the coalition government, had assured me that if the Fianna Fáil parliamentary party announced the nomination of Jack Lynch the government would accept it publicly within hours. I had not passed this on to Lynch. Knowing the man as I did, I understood that this was not a time to be asking him about his intentions or passing on messages from the government via a journalist. He might have seen this as an attempt to ascertain information without having the courage to ask for it out straight. Had I asked him what he was going to do, he would have told me to wait and see what happened.

I later found out from many of those who were present at this parliamentary party meeting that Jack Lynch opened it by saying that there were no rules, anybody could speak and say what they wanted. Quite a few fell straight into the trap. The meeting continued until 1.15 p.m. and was scheduled to resume at three o'clock. Lynch came into my room and handed me a written statement with the terse instruction: 'Get that on the news.' At that time the lunchtime news on radio was at 1.30 p.m. I rang the programme and spoke to Gerald Barry, who immediately transferred me to a copy-taker. Lynch returned to my office as the news started and we both listened to the statement, which was the first item. In effect Jack Lynch had told his parliamentary party that under no circumstances whatever would he be a candidate, agreed or otherwise, for the presidency. Jack puffed contentedly on his pipe while listening and said at its conclusion, 'Your job is safe for another week. I'm going home for lunch with Máirín.' The twinkle in Jack's eye told me that he had outsmarted the parliamentary party and I was left wondering what would happen when the meeting resumed at three.

When I arrived in the Dáil restaurant for my lunch I was hailed loudly by both Charlie Haughey and Ray MacSharry and asked 'who the fuck' had issued the statement. When I said that I had, on the instructions of Jack Lynch, I was told that I had been hoodwinked, that nothing had been decided, and that the meeting was resuming at three. I took some pleasure in telling them that I wasn't the one hoodwinked and that Jack had managed to con them all. In addition, having invited the members of the parliamentary party to be as open and frank as they wished, and having listened to them speak loudly in his praise for over two hours, Jack now knew at first-hand the identities of those who wanted him to quit the leadership. Charlie recognized, and admired, the stratagem. The meeting resumed at three o'clock, and for face-saving purposes it lasted until three thirty. It was effectively over at 3.01.

This was Jack at his best: weighing the options, looking for the weaknesses, taking the advantage, however slight, when it presented itself. Little was said between us afterwards about the incident and when I raised it with him a considerable time later, he merely said, 'I hope you learned something.'

Jack now moved to the second front. The coalition was stranded. Jack was refusing to run for the job and the government had nobody in mind. Fine Gael also recognized that it was somewhat hoist on its own petard because of its treatment of Cearbhall Ó Dálaigh; even amongst the ranks of its party supporters, which would normally provide a fertile source of candidates − barristers, judges, former ministers and the like − not too many, if any at all, would be willing to go forward in circumstances in which they might receive the same dismissive treatment. But they didn't take account of Jack Lynch's cunning. Even before the parliamentary party meeting Jack had contacted Paddy Hillery, who was a European Commissioner − the first, from Ireland − and had been Minister for Foreign Affairs at the time Ireland acceded to the European Economic Community. Hillery lived in Brussels and he was reluctant. But he did not know if the coalition government would reappoint him as Commissioner − it seemed unlikely − so he might be leaving Brussels anyway. Hillery told Jack that he would think about it and get back to him.

I believe that at the time of the parliamentary party meeting Jack knew that Hillery would say yes but he remained silent. He announced after the meeting that he was nominating Hillery, and the government, with as much grace as it could muster, agreed. And so Paddy Hillery became President of Ireland, a position he was to occupy until 1990.

Thus the attempts to remove Jack Lynch, albeit in circumstances where he would have been elevated to the presidency by acclamation, failed. He was not for moving. The presidency was not on his political radar. And, more importantly, he was not going to be forced out. He would follow his own plan, however obscure that appeared to others.

2. Bringing back Charlie

I first met Charlie Haughey within three months of taking up the job as Press Officer of the party and I liked him instantly. There is no doubt that he went out of his way to be friendly. I vividly recall how impressed I was when he knocked on my door and wondered if he could come in for a chat. This was the man who had been Minister for Justice, for Agriculture and for Finance and who had been on the national stage for the best part of twenty years asking if I would have time for him. No wonder I was impressed. So would anybody else have been in the same circumstances. But that was the real Haughey – the charmer, getting people on his side. After that he frequently called to see me in my office on the third floor of Leinster House, beside the whips' office. I don't know whether he liked me or not, but this never concerned me. He was highly organized, full of ideas, deeply critical of certain stances adopted by the parliamentary party and evinced an abiding hatred for a few named individuals, including Jim Gibbons and Martin O'Donoghue. He regarded George Colley with contempt and believed firmly that George knew absolutely nothing about economics or finance.

From the outset Charlie was different from the run-of-the-mill TD. Though his first forays into electoral politics ended in failure, the trajectory of his career was to the Taoiseach's office. He believed, as did many others, but not with the same intense fervour, that there was little point in being in politics if you weren't in power. Being a TD brought a certain cachet in local constituency terms, but, as far as achieving anything of real substance, it was a thankless, pointless occupation. He had married the daughter of a Taoiseach and was in awe of his father-in-law, one of the most dynamic, pragmatic and far-seeing leaders that the country has ever produced. There are those who still believe that Charlie imitated everything that Seán Lemass did, including his mannerisms and particularly his mode of speech. It was inevitable that the combination of his marriage to Lemass's daughter, his intelligence and his innate cunning would ultimately lead him into front-line politics. Though there were others who could have laid claim to promotion, Lemass, with accusations of nepotism ringing in his ears, appointed his son-in-law to the cabinet, and everything Charlie did subsequently was predicated on one ambition: that of ultimately becoming Taoiseach.

When Charlie Haughey was his Minister for Finance, Jack Lynch was quite content to bask in the glory of any decisions he made for the benefit of deprived sections of society while at the same time recognizing that Charlie himself was not slow to bank as much political credit as possible for himself for the future. Nobody, least of all Lynch, was in any doubt that Charlie's ambitions went further than the Department of Finance, and, while there may have been some residual resentment about the way Charlie had managed to work himself into the hierarchy of the party, nobody, then, resented his ambition. Were it not for events in Northern Ireland in 1969, Fianna Fáil politics, and national politics, would have been dramatically different – and considerably duller. Lynch would most likely have gone on and on, and in due course, because of the strength of his position as Minister for Finance, Charlie Haughey might well have 'inherited' the leadership (and we might never have heard of Dessie O'Malley or the Progressive Democrats). Instead the scene was set for decades of internecine battles within Fianna Fáil for what was grandiosely called the soul of the party but which was in reality access to the levers of power.

When Charlie Haughey found himself in the dock in the Four Courts, and subsequently in the wilderness after his acquittal, he did not act precipitately. He knew, as did everybody else, that he had been stitched up, and he was unwise enough to say that those who were responsible for 'this débâcle have no alternative but to take the honourable course that is open to them'. But he knew that he was out in the cold, that there would be no welcoming doors opening for him, and that he would have to claw his way back in.

Virtually the entire period of Fianna Fáil in opposition between 1973 and 1977 was consumed with the aftermath of the arms crisis. The new breed of ministers – Des O'Malley, Gerry Collins and so on – turned up their noses at the mention of Charlie Haughey's name but this was more out of deference to Lynch than to anything they knew about Haughey. O'Malley had stepped into Micheál Ó Móráin's shoes at the Department of Justice and revelled in the introduction of hard-hitting, anti-subversive legislation (including non-jury courts). The establishment of the party – for its own corporate good and for its members' individual reputations – bent over backwards in the canonization of Jack Lynch. They had very good material to work with. Jack was undoubtedly popular. He was also a modest man, lived simply and displayed a lack of antipathy to his political opponents that was atypical in a Fianna Fáil politician. The more the establishment burnished Lynch's image, the more Haughey was demonized.

Despite the glaring contradiction in his action, Haughey had voted confidence in Jim Gibbons as Minister for Defence in the Dáil during the arms crisis. But there was method in his madness: by doing so he avoided losing the party whip. Above all he avoided giving his enemies the chance to call for his expulsion for what was subsequently to become known as 'actions unbecoming' a member of the party. (Ironically, that fate would ultimately belong to his arch-rival, Des O'Malley.) And so he remained within the party fold. Nobody could seriously question his activities. He broke no rules. He maintained a dignified silence and spoke only in that circumlocutory way in which politicians who don't want to say anything become adept. On the surface everything was calm, and nothing was said or done to give his enemies ammunition against him. There were dangerous outbursts but all within the confines of a small circle of loyal supporters. And it was a very small circle. After 1970 Haughey was loath to allow anybody to get too close to him. He withheld his trust and few, if any, got to know him well. I gained a small insight into this wariness after he asked me to ghostwrite a review of Leon Uris's book on Northern Ireland for the *Sunday Independent*. I was pressured to give the copy to the

newspaper before Charlie saw it; it was before the era of faxes and
he was out of the country. The article was published without
controversy, but Haughey was apoplectic with rage and gave me a
dressing-down, pointing out, quite reasonably when I reflected on
it later, that there were many who would parse and analyse every
word for hidden meanings and might attribute motivations to him
that would be entirely false. It was the first occasion on which
I experienced the famous wrath and it wasn't to be the last. However, he did have the good grace to present me with the *Sunday
Independent*'s cheque afterwards.

From time to time, even though he resolutely refused to talk
about the events surrounding his dismissal and the arms trial itself
– 'all that ould shite' in P. J. Mara's inimitable words – Charlie
once or twice let the mask slip, particularly when it came to Jack
Lynch. He once asked me if I was aware that 'that bollix' had sent
out the Special Branch to his home to have him arrested in front
of his wife and children. Now the truth is that Jack Lynch had had
no hand, act or part in having the Special Branch arrest Charlie, let
alone in front of his family, but such was the depth of his resentment
and enmity that the facts were overlooked. What Charlie was really
getting at was that there would have been no need for the Special
Branch to arrest him if the Taoiseach had not sacked him and
accused him of being involved in an illicit act. Despite all public
appearances of unity and camaraderie after his recall to the front
bench, Charlie never, ever, forgave Lynch for what, in his view,
was an outrageous and gratuitous act of betrayal.

While Lynch and the rest of the party hierarchy looked on
in bemused fashion, Charlie maintained a fully staffed office at
Kinsaley, bought Inishvickillane for £100,000 in 1974, travelled by
Daimler, dined in the Royal Hibernian Hotel in Dawson Street
and availed himself of every photographic opportunity that arose.
While some adopted a disdainful attitude to what appeared to be
nouveau riche consumerism, few expressed any great interest in
the source of his wealth until he loomed larger than any of his
detractors had ever expected on the leadership stage in 1979. During
the 1969 general election campaign Conor Cruise O'Brien had

made something of the sale of Charlie's home and lands in Raheny to the property developer Matt Gallagher, and of his subsequent purchase of the Georgian mansion and estate, Abbeville, in Kinsaley; but during my early years working for Fianna Fáil I never heard any of his many detractors either inside or outside the party ever question the origins of his wealth. There were many who expressed envy. There were some who tried to avail themselves of his generosity, including some – latterly, morally correct – journalists. But all accepted that Charlie had made a killing in selling land that was subsequently used for building, and that this had been his big financial breakthrough.

As time moved on, and as Jack Lynch became increasingly popular, in terms of electoral success at any rate, Charlie began to wonder if he would ever achieve his goal. In the immediate aftermath of the arms trial he did not frequent the Dáil very often but when he did he was always surrounded by a group of supportive TDs and senators. A campaign began, and lasted for nearly four years, to have him restored to the front bench. Lynch began to be plagued with requests for Charlie's reinstatement. The argument ran something like this: here was a man who had been Minister for Justice, for Agriculture and for Finance, and who, in the absence of any discernible talent on the front bench, was languishing on the back benches amongst people who, in the main, did not know how to read, let alone, draft legislation. Jack ignored these demands and was strengthened in his resolve not to bring Charlie back by a number of things: first, the advice of other members of the front bench, motivated by fear of Charlie's power and intelligence and by cunning – the longer Charlie was kept away from the front bench the less chance there was for contrast in ability and style; and second, Jim Gibbons, urged on by the likes of Dessie O'Malley, Bobby Molloy and others, made it clear that if Haughey was brought back he would resign.

Of course it was known that this campaign was under way. Charlie had decided that he was going to work from the grass roots upwards and spent considerable time and effort travelling to any and every corner of the country to attend the humblest cumann meeting. Mostly P. J. Mara and Liam Lawlor accompanied him, but I went along on a few occasions. He would drive down and I would drive back. My purpose in doing so was pretty neutral. I was single at the time and it gave me a chance to meet units of the organization that I would not normally be in contact with. But it also provided Charlie with some cover, however thin. I was a party official and for me to be seen accompanying him gave him a patina of acceptability that he might not have had otherwise. I never flattered myself, however, that Charlie worried whether I was providing him with anything. He couldn't then (and never did subsequently) give a fig for what either the leadership or his fellow TDs thought. He was on a mission: a focused campaign that had only one objective and all else was irrelevant. Most of the encounters were embarrassing. The crowd was usually small; the personnel were known dissidents within the party; the discussion was stilted; and the food, if any, diabolical. But Haughey didn't mind. During a visit to a cumann meeting in Castlebar we were entertained by a local party big-wig, one Pádraig Flynn. Flynn was a publican and teacher. We ended up in his house after the meeting, where we were introduced to the intricacies of west Mayo politics and whiskey. 'Jaysus, Charlie, these fellas you bring with you are well able to down the whiskey', was the charming comment as he poured me another glass. Flynn's clownish bombast was evident even then, but he was also shrewd enough to be in awe of Charlie. He could see that he might be the man to link up with if there were to be a future in national politics.

There was an inevitability about the type of people or groups with whom Haughey met and socialized: they were those who always felt themselves to be on the margins of the party and would continue to feel on the margins regardless of who was leader or what the policy happened to be on any given subject. Yes, Haughey knew that to a certain extent he was demeaning himself by accepting invitations to address cumainn throughout the country that would never expect to be graced by a member of the party's front bench, let alone a former finance minister. That Charlie was manipulating the vanity of those on the lower rungs of the party is undeniable. Seeing as I was a young and fairly new employee of the party, he might have been manipulating me too, but I certainly didn't feel that was the case. I admired his skilful use of words and his stony determination in the face of high odds, and I valued his friendship. How did I reconcile this with what I knew to be the official attitude to him by the party hierarchy? Quite frankly, I think I was too young – still in my twenties – to give a damn. I knew that Lynch and the others were pleased with what I was doing for the party on a national level and that the likelihood was that they would not interfere. And so it was. Haughey traversed the country – north, south, east and west – and took his case to the grass roots, not in any overtly hostile way, but in a calm, cool and collected manner. Lynch knew what Haughey was at, but he was powerless to do anything about it. More importantly, Haughey knew that he was powerless. It would have been both churlish and politically silly for Lynch either to bar Haughey from accepting invitations to cumann meetings around the country, or to issue a diktat to cumainn not to invite him. Each man chose to ignore the other's situation.

The extent to which senior members of the front bench feared Haughey – or at least looked on his possible return with some trepidation, believing that it would provide him with a springboard to launch an assault on Lynch's leadership – manifested itself when, after a few occasions when I had travelled with Haughey, Jack's secretary, Lelia, summoned me to his office. Normally if Jack wanted me he called me himself; when he got Lelia to call, I knew that the agenda would be a little more formal. Jack was even more pleasant than some of his enemies would grudgingly accept was his normal demeanour and after a few minutes of small talk he got to the point.

'I'm told you are travelling around the country with Charlie,' he said. Jack had acquired this style from de Valera, who, reputedly, would never directly accuse you of anything. It was always in the form 'They tell me that . . .' without ever identifying who 'they' were. I admitted that that was so and listed the places and times of such visits. 'I know,' he said. And then, in an almost avuncular way, he said, 'Look, Frank, you can do whatever you wish as far as Charlie is concerned. I know that you have become friendly with him. But some of the party don't like it and I don't want to see you getting hurt.' I said I understood that Charlie was a member of the parliamentary party, that he received numerous invitations from units of the organization throughout the country to address them and that on the few occasions he had asked me to accompany him I had done so. Jack wasn't slow and he knew that he could not forbid me to be seen in Haughey's company without facing some repercussions, not least of which would be my possible refusal to accept any stricture as to who I might associate with in the party. He just nodded and said, 'Be careful and watch your back.' The wounds of the 1969/70 period were still raw.

Haughey's antipathy to Jim Gibbons was mutual, but it left Lynch with a dilemma as the argument for bringing him in from the cold became unanswerable. Jim was holding a gun to his head, and Lynch could do nothing unless Gibbons could be persuaded to change his mind and allow Haughey to partake in front bench politics, if only for the optics. For me this familial spat was complicated because I was from Kilkenny and I knew Jim as the local Fianna Fáil TD. He knew my father. Indeed I believe, but I never got round to questioning him about it, that Gibbons was consulted by Jack Lynch prior to my appointment: a simple precaution to make sure that the right political pedigree was involved. I had taken to visiting Jim at his home, the Pheasantry, in Dunmore, just outside Kilkenny, when I visited my parents at weekends. Much drinking and political gossip took place, and it was from meetings such as these, together with the occasional revealing comment from both Lynch and Haughey, that I formed my view as to the real happenings in 1969 and 1970.

Jim Gibbons was an extremely intelligent and well-read man with a particularly acerbic sense of humour. He was an avid crossword fanatic and, regardless of the location or circumstances, always carried that day's crossword, even into cabinet meetings. As well as being a good mimic he was also a very competent cartoonist, and it would be fascinating to find out if there is any record of the many sketches he made of his colleagues at both cabinet meetings and gatherings of the parliamentary party. It was said that he drew various personalities in the Four Courts while waiting to give evidence during the arms trial. He could read both Greek and Latin and revelled in military history. He was in his element during his time in the European Parliament. He travelled the battlefields of Europe and astonished his colleagues, particularly the French, with his detailed knowledge of the Napoleonic campaigns. His membership of the parliament put him in a tricky spot, though, when he was asked to accompany his parliamentary colleagues on a visit to Kinsaley. Tom Earlie, a former civil servant, was the Assistant Secretary General of the group to which Fianna Fáil belonged in the European Parliament, a group that included the French Gaullists. It had decided to hold what it grandly called a 'study week' in Ireland, and Earlie prevailed upon Charlie to open Kinsaley to the visitors. The Fianna Fáil members were agog to see what Gibbons would do: would he forgo the opportunity of socializing with his arch-enemy? Or would he show up and maintain an outward dignity for the sake of the image of the party in front of his French colleagues? Gibbons had enough political sense to realize that it would be infra dig for him to display discourtesy to the party's guests by refusing to attend a social function at the home of one of its high-profile personalities. But it didn't prevent him from making sure that his feelings were known, more for the benefit of Charlie than for any visitors. So he conducted something of a running commentary as Charlie told them about the history of the house and its Gandon features. When Charlie pointed out a sundial that he had made himself, Gibbons was openly derisive and passed a remark to the effect that such accoutrements were typical of the arriviste. Gibbons regarded the whole affair as so much pretentious nonsense and said as much loudly at every opportunity. Charlie was dressed casually and wore white shoes – a sight that caused Gibbons something akin to apoplexy. But Haughey was at his gracious best and the French were wowed. The other Fianna Fáil members of the group had some difficulty in accounting for Gibbons's attitude to the bemused Frenchmen, and the whole affair was explained away as a clash of personalities between two strong representatives of Ireland's major political party.

At first I imagined that because of the events of 1970 Lynch and Gibbons would be close friends, or at the least something approaching political allies. In fact the opposite was the case, and I was amazed on one or two occasions to discover that their attitude to one another was distinctly chilly, even glacial. Underneath Gibbons's antipathy to Haughey there lay an animus, bordering on contempt, against Lynch. Again, it clearly went back to the events of the arms crisis. Gibbons did not trust him and was downright dismissive of him in many of the conversations I had with him. This seems extraordinary in circumstances where Lynch, to all intents and purposes, stood by Gibbons in the white heat of the controversy. Sometimes Gibbons could show chilling disdain for his colleagues and Lynch did not escape his sharp tongue. Gibbons was the father of a large family, and one night, when we had stayed up drinking and talking until the early hours, he made it clear that he thought Lynch's childlessness made him less of a man and that it wasn't quite fitting that the Taoiseach and leader of the country's largest political party depended, or appeared to depend, on his wife for political advice.

Lynch's problem with Gibbons was more rationally grounded. Remember that Gibbons had been the chief state witness against Haughey. Much rode on his performance in the trial and it is fascinating to read the transcript of the court proceedings and to savour some of the language he used when he was giving evidence. When under pressure to acknowledge that he knew what Captain James Kelly was doing (in Captain Kelly's evidence he claimed that he was acting under orders and that he had met the Minister for Defence, Gibbons), Gibbons employed a curious phrase: 'I had vestigial knowledge.' 'Vestigial' is not a word in common usage and it always struck me as something that might have been carefully rehearsed to give credibility to the fact that while he could not deny that he had met Captain Kelly he could, plausibly, deny that he knew exactly what Captain Kelly's activities entailed as far as the government was concerned. I spoke to Jim about a lot of things, including the arms trial, but he refused to discuss that particular phrase. I am in no doubt whatsoever that Lynch regarded Gibbons as a bad witness. I fully believe that Lynch felt let down by Gibbons and that the trial result – the acquittal of the accused – would never have happened if Gibbons had been stronger in his evidence in the witness box. This would seem to have been a harsh judgement on Lynch's part and leads one to believe that there was predisposition on the part of the state as to the accused men's culpability, regardless of the evidence. It also raises the appalling possibility that the government expected the courts to endorse the political action already taken, namely the dismissal of the ministers and the virtual sacking from the army of Captain Kelly, a man who clearly believed that he had been acting on ministerial orders. Why would an army officer behave as he did otherwise? And if he had been acting contrary to orders, why did his superiors not take action? The army is not a place where maverick behaviour is condoned. But Lynch couldn't do anything about Gibbons. He had to be seen to support him politically. He did this by appointing him to the European Parliament and reappointing him to the cabinet as Minister for Agriculture after the 1977 general election. Jim's nemesis came when Charlie took over. Anybody with an IQ of more than one would have realized that once Charlie became leader, Jim Gibbons's future as a minister was over, no matter how competent he was.

Gibbons also took it upon himself to advise me about Haughey. He was less circumspect than Jack, and to this day I have never been able to satisfy myself as to the truth of the things he told me. As a politician he could see that Haughey was forcing Lynch's hand. Gradually, he came round to the belief that if Haughey's return to the front bench would somehow pacify the organization he would go along with it, but he warned that, ultimately, Charlie would destroy the party. In the end he knew that I had a job to do, and that the presentation of Haughey's return to the front bench was an important aspect, however peripheral, of Fianna Fáil's public and media profiles. He told me to tell Lynch that if Haughey was brought back to the front bench, he would remain resolutely silent. And so he did.

For my own part, I had already come to the conclusion that it was necessary to bring Haughey back into the fold; the party needed his considerable talents. The official line I took, which Fianna Fáil subsequently used, was that we had a situation in which politicians, including Jack Lynch, in the Republic were advocating that politicians in the North forget their tribal and historical differences, however deeply felt, and get together to provide a peaceful platform for the future; yet here was an internal party situation in which a former senior minister was in effect being blackballed because of his alleged role in events regarding the North and in truth – notwithstanding the black propaganda indulged in by those who wanted to appear to be loyal Lynch men – events that a significant proportion of the public agreed with, namely the relief of Northern Nationalists' distress. The public might appear naive from time to time, but when the government opened field hospitals in border counties and also put troops there on standby, people could be forgiven for having thought that the government was going to take a proactive stance to prevent further bloodshed in the North. People wanted something done, and the fact that senior cabinet ministers seemed to be involved in organizing the means of actual defence for the Nationalist community would not surprise anybody.

As the question of Charlie's restoration to the front bench was being quietly considered by Jack and his advisers, George Colley remained silent and kept his own counsel. Whatever he may have been suspected of saying in private – and I believe that he didn't allow himself even this luxury – he never broke his silence in public. Remember that George Colley represented a Dublin constituency, and on the northside, not a million miles from Charlie's own constituency. He undoubtedly came under considerable pressure from time to time to speak out on whether Haughey should be rehabilitated. But he didn't. Yes, Jack Lynch consulted him prior to actually inviting Haughey back. According to Jack, Colley was against the move, mainly because of what he feared the effect would be as far as Jim Gibbons was concerned. Colley was friendly with Gibbons and supported him in cabinet at the time of the 1970 débâcle as well as subsequently, even though Jim's testimony in the arms trial had tested people's resolve. So Colley had given Lynch his view. He was afraid that Haughey's return would result in Gibbons's departure and the creation of a new rift. But George may not have known, and I had no reason to believe that Jack ever told him, that I had had lengthy discussions with Gibbons on the matter.

Eventually, Lynch asked me directly for my opinion. I was open and frank and highlighted the pros and cons of the argument. I recommended that Charlie be brought back to mainstream Fianna Fáil politics and given a front bench position. Lynch asked if I had Gibbons onside and when I said I had he was very surprised. That Gibbons's reaction worried him told me volumes about their relationship. I was then deputed to go to Kinsaley and ask Charlie if, should he be called upon, he would serve. I did so with my tongue firmly in my cheek. Charlie then decided to play a game and said yes, but it depended on the job he would be asked to do. In other words, his return was conditional. I refrained from asking either what he would like or what he would refuse, and undertook to inform Lynch.

Lynch's response was immediate: Health and Social Welfare or nothing. Amazing as it may now seem, these two portfolios were combined and the post was regarded as something of a backwater. It certainly did not carry some of the baggage, or the public contumely, that it does today, and Brian Cowen's famous comparison of the Department of Health to Angola would not have been understood, let alone appreciated, then. Lynch told me Charlie had twenty-four hours to make up his mind and that with or without him he was announcing a new front bench in two days' time. When I rang Charlie his response was simple. He didn't want the portfolio. 'Fuck him, he's trying to humiliate me again.' But he said he would get back to me, which he did after consulting some of his advisers, most notably the former head of the Government Information Service, Pádraig Ó hAnnracháin, who was then working in the Department of Education with Dick Burke. Ó hAnnracháin told me later that he reminded Charlie of Lyndon

Johnson's dictum that it was better to be inside the tent pissing out than outside trying to piss in. Charlie said, 'OK. I'll piss out.'

And so in January 1975, after nearly five years in the political wilderness, Charlie Haughey was brought in from the cold. What followed went along the lines of 'forgive and forget', 'a new dawn for Fianna Fáil' and the line I had worked out: that Lynch would not refuse to reconcile himself with Haughey while at the same time calling on Nationalists and Unionists in the North to bury their differences and work together for the good of their collective community. The display of unity by both sides belied the reality. Haughey admitted to me later that the bile sometimes rose in his throat, but he was prepared to bide his time. Both sides – Haughey's and Lynch's – knew that a watershed had arrived.

Long after Charlie's reinstatement to the front bench, I could see that his colleagues were keeping a wary eye on what he was doing. In November 1975 there was a by-election in Mayo West after the death of the popular Fine Gael TD Henry Kenny. The cute Fianna Fáilers in the constituency knew that no matter who they put forward as a candidate and no matter how hard they tried, his son Enda could not be beaten. In these circumstances Pádraig Flynn declined the invitation to stand – he thought it would be better if he didn't have an electoral failure on his report card – and decided to take his chances at the next general election.

Even though he was still in the wilderness, albeit back on the front bench, Charlie asked what he could do and was allocated after-Mass speaking engagements one Sunday. Charlie asked me if I would travel to Castlebar with him and I did so on the Saturday afternoon. Jack Lynch and Gerry Collins were eating together in the Travellers Friend Hotel when Charlie and I walked into the dining room early that evening. There was a noticeable chill in the air and after polite exchanges Charlie went to another table, leaving me with Lynch and Collins. Jack was too much of a gentleman to get down and dirty in a public place, but he did inquire as to why no speeches had been sent to the Sunday newspapers. To allow for inclusion in the early, country editions of the Sunday newspapers, which went to print early Saturday evening, speeches scheduled for delivery at political functions on a Saturday night were delivered to the newspapers' offices before lunch that day. Prior to leaving Dublin, I had followed the standard procedure and arranged for the evening's speeches to be delivered in the usual way. But while I was on the road with Charlie some reporter from one of the Sundays' newsdesks rang the Fianna Fáil election headquarters in Castlebar to complain that the speeches hadn't arrived. I couldn't be contacted – remember, it was long before the era of mobile phones – and unfortunately Collins, the Director of Elections, got the message from the irate journalist. He was his usual critical self. As Director of Elections on a number of occasions, he attempted to emulate Neil Blaney's famous ability to manage and run campaigns. This involved the adoption of a gruff, overbearing style – admittedly something he didn't have to work too hard on. However, he bore no comparison to the original. (Collins mellowed subsequently and became avuncular in style, especially after his election to the European Parliament.)

When I told Lynch that I had checked with the news editor as soon as we had arrived in the town, and that they had the speeches and everything was in order, he appeared satisfied. But Collins, who was not known for his ability to tiptoe through a tulip field delicately, couldn't resist a jibe to the effect that it would be better if I had made sure of things before travelling with Charlie. This, of course, was the nub of the matter – I was fraternizing with Charlie.

Obviously the Lynch side knew that the die was cast and that battle had been entered for control of the party, whenever the opportunity would arise. The Lynch men watched in sullen silence, a silence that cloaked a fear – fear of Haughey's magnetism, his charisma, his intelligence and his determination. They never stopped distrusting him. They continued to be suspicious of his every word and deed, and they waited for the inevitable clash that would not only decide the future direction of the party but also their own careers. With Charlie Haughey's return to the national stage came the start of a new chapter in Fianna Fáil's internecine warfare, one where the knives were rarely out of sight and the only sounds were of blades being sharpened for use. Still, the party presented a united front. No matter what crisis arose, it always seemed to come out of it unscathed. No wonder its opponents felt that Fianna Fáil was indestructible.

3. Hit and miss opposition

You could be forgiven for believing that in its four years in opposition the only thing that absorbed Fianna Fáil was Charlie Haughey. While it is true that, regardless of what else was occurring, the Charlie question permeated the thinking of every Fianna Fáil man and woman throughout the organization (for instance, at Ard Fheiseanna the media concentration would be on what Charlie was going to do or say and the party hierarchy would be watching to see if he, or any of his supporters, was up to anything), there were, none the less, many other issues with which the party grappled on a daily basis, the main one being the Northern question.

From 1969 onwards every nuance of every utterance by anybody of note, in all parties in the South, but especially in Fianna Fáil, was analysed for the minutest divergence from stated policy on the North. Any inconsistency led to an avalanche of publicity, followed by another avalanche of restatements of official policy by virtually everybody concerned; there was then relative calm until the next occurrence. Along with the Taoiseach, the Department of Foreign Affairs had overall responsibility for Northern issues, but the Minister for Foreign Affairs, Garret FitzGerald, spent much of his time abroad (much to the satisfaction of some of his own cabinet colleagues, according to one of my sources in the Department of the Taoiseach), so Conor Cruise O'Brien was given a free run at Fianna Fáil. He seemed to have Liam Cosgrave's permission to badger the party about its Northern policy and could not resist stirring the pot from time to time.

O'Brien was a curious phenomenon. He was highly intelligent and articulate and seemed to have a deep hatred of all things Fianna Fáil, notwithstanding the fact that he was married to Máire Mhac an tSaoi, the daughter of one of the party's famous stalwarts, Seán McEntee, a former senior minister and confidant of de Valera. In the early sixties O'Brien had served in the Department of External Affairs, as Foreign Affairs was then known, and had been involved in a much publicized international spat while working in Africa. There is no doubt that he aroused the basest of emotions in Fianna Fáil people. Much of this reaction was frustration at an inability to articulate, rationally and logically, the intellectual reasoning behind their Republican position. Most of them had a passing knowledge of Wolfe Tone – they commemorated him each year at a special ceremony at his grave in Bodenstown Graveyard – but to expect that they would have anything other than a slight familiarity with his writings, if that, let alone a thorough grounding in his political philosophy, was a step too far, and O'Brien relentlessly taunted Fianna Fáilers that they were mere gunmen in suits, with no clear view on what ought to happen in Northern Ireland. He particularly incensed people with his apparent sympathy for the Unionist cause over that of the Nationalist community. Of course, there were those who believed that O'Brien cleverly intervened on the issue to divert attention from some of his own government's deficiencies. Be that as it may, he still became a convenient bogeyman for Fianna Fáilers. He aroused the most visceral of emotions amongst those one would normally expect to have more sense, and he did considerable collateral damage with Fianna Fáil by provoking its more Republican elements to predictable extremism, much to the chagrin of Jack Lynch, who held absolute control over the Northern issue.

Fianna Fáil generally, and the Fianna Fáil government in particular, had been totally unprepared for the outbreak of violence in the North. The late sixties had been a time when even the most senior members – Aiken, McEntee, Ryan, Smith, veterans of the War of Independence – were still happy to spout well-worn party shibboleths along the lines that the unification of Ireland had been one of the party's founding principles in 1926 and was still its main aim. No leader's speech at an Ard Fheis would be complete without a rousing restatement of this aim. Very few Fianna Fáilers expected to be challenged to do anything about this objective. After de Valera's departure to Áras an Uachtaráin, Lemass had taken a pragmatic view of it, and, with the able assistance of Ken Whitaker, he turned the key in a process – building practical relationships with the North – that was to take over thirty years to come to fruition. However, when fighting broke out on the streets of Belfast and Derry, suddenly the old slogans took on a new life. On top of that, since some of the party's leading personalities hardly hid their view of Lynch as a 'caretaker' Taoiseach, its famous discipline slipped. The result was that while its leader had a clear mantra, 'unity by consent', Fianna Fáil's approach to the developing situation in the North, prior to the arms crisis, was characterized by incoherence and ambiguity. It was the trauma of the arms crisis that finally gave Lynch's line authority and force.

Nobody was allowed to speak publicly on the North without the Taoiseach's permission and then only after a careful analysis of the script. Things became unstable after the collapse of the Sunningdale power-sharing arrangement in May 1974, and Lynch, as well as other party leaders in the Republic, had difficult moments in trying to hold the line. In the end he succeeded, but there was an air of contingency about the party's attitude, with its critics waiting for some event that would prove conclusively that the apparent unity was a sham and that there were as many IRA supporters among Fianna Fáil TDs as there were thoughtful, peace-loving Republicans.

Ironically, Jack himself then landed the party in controversy. He was always reluctant to give live interviews on RTÉ's Sunday lunchtime radio show, *This Week*, which, in those days, provided fodder for the following day's papers. Other than sport nothing much happened on a Sunday, so reporters fed off the programme's political interviews. There was a standing request for Jack Lynch, as leader of the opposition, to go on the show. While he complied about once a year, he never enjoyed the experience, and after each one he would say that that was his last. During one such interview, Lynch said that granting an amnesty to those involved in IRA terrorism should be considered to give them an incentive to lay down their arms and to give the organization the impetus to follow a more peaceful, democratic method of achieving its objectives. In these post-Good Friday Agreement days, this proposal may not seem revolutionary, but circumstances were very different when Jack made his comments. After the interview was over he took me aside and, before I could make any comment, he said that the amnesty issue would cause trouble. But the programme was live and the damage was done. (Even if it had been a recording, I'm sure the programme team would have been unwilling to delete such juicy material.) Lynch knew he had made a mistake but decided to let the inevitable furore develop without issuing any clarification.

There was outrage from other political parties, blanket analysis of his 'real' agenda in the media and confusion amongst party members who had faithfully followed his anti-violence, unity-by-consent line since 1969. I was besieged for an explanation from all quarters – including the most senior members of the front bench. Some of them were less than kind, and one suggested that going into the interview Jack must have had a few 'Paddies' on board, a reference to his favourite tipple, Paddy Whiskey. When I assured the less-than-teetotal front bencher that that had not been the case, he became even angrier and said that Jack had obviously lost his marbles. The reaction amongst Unionists was predictably virulent. And members of the SDLP were taken aback that a man so experienced in the weighing of his words when it came to Northern politics could have used such infelicitous language, and also endangered their delicate wooing of Nationalist opinion away from the IRA.

There were two schools of thought about what had happened. The first was the one favoured by Jack's opponents in the party: he was losing his touch and he wasn't in tune with political reality, or aware of the impact such remarks would have on a public that consistently expressed its contempt for the IRA's campaign. If he had really understood the impact of his suggestion, he would never have spoken as he had, no matter how strongly he believed that an amnesty might be helpful. The second school of thought was that Jack knew something was afoot – British government talks with the IRA, possible moves by the IRA itself, or whatever – and that he was attempting to prepare public opinion in the Republic for the eventuality that, at some stage, perhaps well into the future, the only way to achieve progress would be for all the parties, including terrorists, to cease fire and engage in talks.

However comforting it might be to credit Jack Lynch with the political imagination to envisage the peace process of the 1990s, the fact of the matter is that he fluffed it. He was inveigled into the comments simply as a result of the interviewer's questioning. There was no plan for him to make such comments. They did not reflect either his own or the parliamentary party's policy, and the idea had never been discussed at any level in the party. The view, therefore, that Jack had lost touch was coming dangerously close to the truth: he was well known for his careful use of language, he knew the dangers of a misplaced nuance in talking about Northern Ireland, and he had taken sole responsibility for party policy regarding the North on himself. The buck stopped with him. The incident was symptomatic of a certain nonchalance that was creeping into his approach to weighty political issues. Occasionally his thinking seemed a little woolly and he didn't seem to consider the effect of his words as seriously as he once would have. The consequences were always dire.

The surprising thing about Jack making such an error of judgement was that it was on the basis of their attitude to the North, or their adherence or otherwise to his stated policy, that he measured the soundness of members of his parliamentary party. His front bench was made up largely of those he had appointed in the aftermath of the arms crisis. Consequently, they were Lynchmen, people who would unquestioningly follow his policy. Most never gave the matter any serious thought, or at least that is how it appeared to me. Ruairí Brugha, who unexpectedly had been elected to the Dáil in the 1973 general election in one of the south Dublin constituencies, was given nominal responsibility for Northern matters. Ruairí was a son of Cathal Brugha, who had been shot dead outside the Gresham Hotel by Free State forces during the Civil War in 1922, and his wife was the daughter of Terence MacSwiney, the Lord Mayor of Cork who had died on hunger strike in England. Brugha was completely under Lynch's control, and he was not given any leeway whatsoever in expressing the party's stance. This was a classic Lynch, and Fianna Fáil, ploy: to keep the party rank and file happy by letting the optics of the situation suggest one thing – in this case, appointing as Northern spokesman someone whose name would evoke staunch and unyielding Republicanism – while quietly pursuing a more sophisticated agenda. Lynch used Brugha as a type of roving ambassador to attend seminars and meetings, to discreetly carry messages between various parties, and to be seen at occasions (such as SDLP conferences and the many 'think-ins' about the conflict) for which Jack either didn't have time or where he thought it inappropriate, as a former Taoiseach and the leader of the main opposition party, to be seen. I don't believe that Ruairí Brugha ever met any representatives of the Official or Provisional IRA. The lines of contact with these organ- izations had long since been severed, and it would have been madness for anybody representing Lynch, or Fianna Fáil, to take such a risk.

SDLP delegations that were in Dublin to meet the government would then come to see Jack and those front bench members he would have selected in advance. These meetings were basically to exchange information and to reaffirm Fianna Fáil's strong support for the SDLP. There was an excellent rapport between Jack and John Hume, although Jack thought that Hume sometimes adopted an intellectual approach that – deliberately or otherwise – tended to put the other members of his party, particularly Gerry Fitt and Paddy Devlin, at a disadvantage. Hume always wanted to bring matters to a higher plane, whereas Fitt and Devlin were essentially street politicians with enormous amounts of personal courage who were content to discuss mundane, but crucial, day-to-day issues such as policing. On one visit, as Paddy Devlin was taking off his jacket, a pistol fell to the floor. Everyone froze. Jack was furious, but Paddy just laughed it off.

Ruairí Brugha was extremely well meaning, but he was not overly articulate and there was no contest between him and 'the Cruiser' (as Conor Cruise O'Brien was not so affectionately known). However, in the way of many other unrecognized and forgotten politicians, he performed a useful function in that he was a trusted intermediary between more powerful masters. Apart from Northern politicians and interest groups, another authority with which he liaised for Jack was the Catholic hierarchy. On one occasion, having met the Archbishop of Armagh, Cardinal William Conway, Brugha reported that Conway was upset by Lynch's support, in principle, for multi-denominational schooling in the Republic. Conway's message was to the point: 'Tell Jack Lynch to keep his hands off our schools.' Lynch's response was equally to the point. After discussing the cardinal's message, we decided that he would show his independence by making a gesture of support to a multi-denominational school project in Dalkey, and he made a speech welcoming its establishment. Conway read the signal exactly as intended and he got back on to Brugha. Around the same time I noticed that a priest from Archbishop's House in Drumcondra began to call us fairly frequently to acquire a copy of Fianna Fáil's education policy. Of course, no such document existed and we used to fob him off with vague promises to root it out and get back to him. It was obvious that the timing of the request, coinciding with the cardinal's complaint that Jack Lynch was endangering the Church's role in education by espousing the cause of multi-denominational education, was no accident. Lynch's line was pretty straightforward and followed the same logic – cynical and all as it had been when he restored Charlie to the front bench – that he could hardly expect reconciliation in the North without making gestures of reconciliation in the South. Eventually he and Conway met at a dinner and agreed to differ.

Lynch never got on with Conway. In fact, contrary to appearances (he was punctiliously polite to those members of the Catholic hierarchy whom he met on social and sporting occasions, and wasn't averse to being photographed with them – these were still the days when being pictured with a bishop gave a politician some electoral advantage), Lynch never really seemed to pay too much attention to the bishops' statements on public affairs and seldom, if ever, considered their position when developing or announcing any party policy. He was critical of certain elements of the Church, both at hierarchical levels and on the ground, for its ambivalent attitude to the IRA.

In theory the north Tipperary TD, Michael O'Kennedy, Fianna Fáil's spokesman on foreign affairs and a loyal supporter of the party's Northern policy, should also have had a high profile on Northern matters. But Michael wasn't close to Lynch. He spent most of his time in the Law Library and resurfaced on a Friday afternoon with great intentions of getting positive headlines with some speech or other to be delivered in Nenagh, or elsewhere in his constituency, that evening. These speeches were never written before four o'clock, so it was impossible to forewarn news editors about their content, a basic requirement for actually getting coverage. Michael's main interest – and this was true of others on the front bench – was media exposure over the weekend to show his constituents that he was about national business and to show his party that his position on the front bench was justified. This approach was then typical among politicians – and not just Fianna Fáil politicians. Michael and I were very friendly – and some years later he and I discussed the possibility of his becoming leader of the party in the right circumstances – but he couldn't understand my exasperation with him at this time. He operated on the basis that a press officer existed to disseminate a speech hastily prepared at the conclusion of work at the bar and to make sure it got reported. Michael believed that once he spoke the media would drop everything and listen. Apart from the fact that Michael wasn't the greatest speaker in Leinster House – he himself would not have claimed such a status – or particularly adept when it came to expressing the subtleties of Northern policy, his expectation displayed complete ignorance about how the media worked. Again, he wasn't alone in that. In the beginning I put myself out to get him the coverage he required, but when I realized that this would be his standard modus operandi I spoke to Jack Lynch and things improved.

Eventually, inevitably, Michael's individualistic approach to publicity got him into trouble. During 1976 Michael made a hawkish speech that appeared to question the party's stated policy on the North and caused mayhem in front bench circles. Lynch demanded to know if I had written the speech, but, while I sometimes wrote scripts or prepared background material for members of the front bench, I never ventured into the difficult waters of Northern policy. I had not seen the speech in advance and it had not been issued through my office. O'Kennedy was summoned to explain himself. A nervous man went in to see Lynch and a chastened man came out afterwards; because the unleashing of Jack Lynch's anger wasn't often seen, it made an impression. O'Kennedy was still on the front bench but he was marked as somebody to watch. There were those at the time who suggested that Michael was a stalking horse for Charlie Haughey, but in my view this was so remote as to be totally discountable. Though he sometimes got himself into positions where his motives were open to question, Michael, a former clerical student at Maynooth, was unquestionably decent and honest.

Meanwhile, away from the life and death matters of the North, many Fianna Fáil TDs were just as worried – more, if truth be told – about their futures. The Minister for Local Government, Jimmy Tully, had decided, much to the glee of both Fine Gael and Labour supporters, to outdo Fianna Fáil at constituency gerrymandering. The notion that an independent body would review constituencies based on population trends was completely alien to the culture of the time. Instead it was left to politicians, and during previous reviews Fianna Fáil had earned a well-deserved reputation for identifying even the smallest pockets of support in the most unlikely locations and incorporating them into their candidates' bailiwicks. Now the Fine Gael minister, Tully, announced drastic alterations to the constituency boundaries and the number of seats in each. There were howls of outrage from Fianna Fáil and the whole operation became known as the Tullymander.

It appeared that Tully had snookered Fianna Fáil. The party couldn't see how it could be elected: the figures didn't add up. While nobody in Fianna Fáil would publicly admit it, this was secretly accepted by senior figures in the party and a sense of futility became pervasive. For the first time in the history of the state it seemed as if a coalition government would be re-elected. Senior

front bench members were looking at the carve-up of their own
constituencies and some had to move to new ones in order to
follow their traditional support base. One was George Colley, who
came to me and asked if I would be interested in moving into his
old constituency on Dublin's northside. I told him I would think
about it but asked if there was nobody at local level who could step
into his shoes. 'There's a young fellow there called Ahern,' he said,
'but I don't think he'll amount to much.'

I went so far as to discuss the idea with Jack Lynch. His attitude
was benign but he remarked that I had been in Leinster House long
enough to know what a bear-pit it was and he asked if I really
wanted to spend the rest of my life constantly looking over my
shoulder to see where the next bullet was coming from. I thought
the advice said far more about Jack's attitude to politics than it did
about how I might get on. I put the idea out of my head. I didn't
fancy the lifestyle and, much as I enjoyed political intrigue, I
thought there was more to life. I told George Colley that I wasn't
interested. However, some months later I discovered that George
must have discussed it with his local party organization. I met Tom
Stafford, a member of the prominent family of undertakers, a Fianna
Fáil councillor on Dublin Corporation and a party officer in the
constituency, in the Dáil bar. Rather belligerently he said that he
had heard that I was thinking of running in 'his' constituency.
When I told him that I wasn't, he became very amiable and said,
'Sure come in anyway and we'll bury you cheap!'

Another issue that gripped a handful of politicos, although it was
too turgid in its detail to hold public attention for very long, was a
controversy over the Bula ore body in County Meath, and what
should be done with it in terms of state receipts, in which Justin
Keating, the Minister for Industry and Commerce, and Des
O'Malley became embroiled. It was my first opportunity to watch
O'Malley at close quarters in parliamentary debate, and there was
no doubt that when he set his mind to something, having been
briefed comprehensively, he could be devastating. Just like Michael
O'Kennedy, Dessie would decide, sometimes at very short notice,
that he was going to deliver a keynote speech on some topic or

other that he regarded as of importance and would virtually demand that his opinions be given widespread publicity. In fairness, given the quality of much of his material, publicity did follow.

O'Malley and I became tentative friends and met from time to time for dinner, including in his home in Rathmines. It is virtually impossible – or at least it was then, when he was still very much at the centre of things in Fianna Fáil – to relax in O'Malley's company. He unnerved people, mainly I think because he himself was constantly on edge. He chain-smoked, and he was didactic and bossy. He brooked little criticism of his views and they seemed unalterable. Many of his colleagues believed, as I did, that O'Malley had a sense of intellectual superiority. No doubt that had been given free rein when he became a very young Minister for Justice after the arms crisis blew up. He could be rude and offensive, and was to many people, except for those who knew him well enough to challenge him in argument and debate.

While Lynch had come around to the idea that it was better to bring Charlie Haughey back into the fold rather than have him as a focus of discontent outside, O'Malley disagreed. He believed Haughey had caused monumental upheaval both inside and outside the party and should be left in limbo. But O'Malley and Haughey had a complicated relationship that has never been properly analysed. For instance, O'Malley has never satisfactorily explained why he and Haughey had a private meeting in September 1970 in the run-up to the arms trial. In fact, both men have maintained total silence on this meeting, which was revealed only when the diaries of the late Secretary of the Department of Justice, Peter Berry, were published ten years later. O'Malley was the Minister for Justice, and Charlie had been sacked from the cabinet and was charged with conspiring to import arms illegally. Both men had legal backgrounds and should have realized that their meeting was open to interpretations that would do neither of them any good were it to become known prior to or during the subsequent trial – a trial that was held in almost exemplary haste. So why the risk? What was the purpose of the meeting? And why no explanation? In any discussions I had with him he ranged from total silence to absolute virulence with

regard to Haughey. And when Lynch finally announced that he
was restoring Haughey to the front bench, O'Malley became sullen.
For a while I believe that his respect for Jack Lynch diminished –
it certainly did not stay at the heights it had reached when I first
met him in 1974. But Dessie was like a child who sulks when
reprimanded and then, when he realizes he is not getting his own
way, ingratiates himself once again as if nothing had occurred.

Apart from dissecting government legislation and concentrating
on the Bula affair, O'Malley played little or no overt role in Fianna
Fáil's politics. He appeared to regard the great mass of party activists
and supporters with disdain, and it was obvious that he would have
preferred a system in which TDs could operate as they did in
the UK, concentrating on parliamentary matters and leaving the
tedious and petty constituency work to an agent. Those with
long-enough memories remembered Neil Blaney's comment during the by-election following the death of Dessie's uncle, Donogh
O'Malley, in which Dessie was the Fianna Fáil candidate and Blaney
was the Director of Elections. There had been an unseemly flurry
within the local organization in Limerick when Donogh's widow,
Hilda, indicated that she would like to be the candidate in the
by-election. This was not acceptable to the powers that be and
Dessie, who would not have been the automatic choice at the time,
was selected. Blaney said he didn't see why he should be breaking
out in a sweat on behalf of somebody that wasn't really a Fianna
Fáiler in the first place but a 'Blueshirt' at heart. It was a typically
blunt Blaney remark, but it indicated the brittle nature of
O'Malley's relationship with his party colleagues.

When O'Malley became suddenly ill on one occasion it was the
only time when I saw Lynch despair. Lynch idolized O'Malley and
in a different order of things would have regarded him as his natural
successor, but he could not be seen to be taking a hand in the
matter. Jack's only contribution towards deciding his successor was
the timing and in the end he got that disastrously wrong. I know
that O'Malley thought about succeeding Jack Lynch because we
spoke about it on a number of occasions and, much to my chagrin
now, I must admit that I tried to persuade him to think more

actively about it. However, notwithstanding his ability, and even with Lynch's backing, O'Malley would never have made it. A significant core of the parliamentary party detested him and he himself was contemptuous of a great number of his colleagues, with the possible exception of Lynch himself.

In fairness to O'Malley, whatever ambitions he harboured about the leadership were subsumed into an acceptance that it was Colley's right. This always intrigued me, because, in truth, George Colley had no claim whatsoever on the leadership. He had challenged for the job in 1966, as had Haughey and Blaney, and when these two withdrew he stayed in the contest with Jack Lynch and was soundly beaten. He had been in the Dáil for only seven years then, but, admittedly, he had put down a few markers that he was somewhat at odds with the new, ascendant, mohair-suited brigade. He was a very pleasant, upstanding, moral individual who did not mix either well or frequently with many of his colleagues, and certainly not with the back benchers, although he was always extremely polite. He smoked the odd cheroot or a pipe and did not drink too often in the Dáil. He had no regard for money and practised as an ordinary solicitor in an unspectacular fashion, doing well enough to look after his family but little more. His old-fashioned style appealed to the older generation, who had spurred him on in 1966. But the very fact that he had challenged then was virtually the only basis on which he could claim to be the natural successor to Jack Lynch.

Des O'Malley knew, as did virtually everybody else, apart from those few Colley supporters who were blinkered to the truth, that George had none of Lynch's charisma and none of Haughey's ability to evoke grass-roots passions. There were no fanatical followers. There were no spin-doctors. Few, if any, of the Fianna Fáil parliamentary party were avid supporters. Yes, they respected him for his honesty, his decency and his modesty, but they didn't feel comfortable about his ability to restore their fortunes. He made no rousing speeches, rarely if ever said anything controversial and lived politically on the kudos of the famous phrase 'low standards in high places' that he had used in an Ard Fheis speech in the late sixties. That was generally regarded as a coded indication of distaste for

Haughey's and Blaney's activities. George never clarified whether this interpretation was accurate, but, deliberately or otherwise, he basked in the limelight of the comment for quite a long time. However tentative and cloaked it was, it was the only public statement he ever made that could be construed as an indication of enmity with Haughey. To George's irritation, Charlie constantly referred to him as 'my old school pal'.

It was inordinately difficult to get George to fulfil radio or television engagements, and this, together with the lassitude of other members of the front bench, led to increasing criticism of the performance of the party's most prominent personalities. They were a sorry contrast to those government ministers who had brought political articulation to a new height. George fought a lonely battle on each budget day when he was expected to respond, without the benefit of any prior knowledge, to detailed financial announcements. And as the coalition's term wore on, because the Fianna Fáil front bench vetoed publication of the new policies its backroom committees were developing, for fear of alerting the government to the party's real thinking, he was further inhibited in his comments. Not being privy to this strategy, back benchers, who were coming under critical fire from grass-roots supporters who wanted the party to look as if it was about its business in a meaningful way, became increasingly frustrated. This led to mutterings to the effect that Charlie Haughey ought to be allowed to respond to budgets on behalf of Fianna Fáil.

Not only was George reluctant to appear on television, but there were those in Fianna Fáil HQ, and at senior levels in the parliamentary party, who were worried about his ability to slug it out on camera. It was increasingly accepted that TV would play an important role in any future election, and the performances up to that point had not been very encouraging. His bruising experience with Garret FitzGerald in the 1973 general election was still fresh in people's minds. The general view – and the truth – was that Garret had beaten George hands down. George appeared wooden, did not seem to be in control of his brief and was not quick enough verbally to compete with Garret's apparent mastery of figures.

There were those who even went so far as to blame the loss of the election on that particular performance, but that was an unfair and excessively harsh judgement. The anxiety about his TV profile reached such a pitch that we conducted research on the matter and discovered that George, sadly, was one of those people who, for whatever reason, does not engender trust amongst television viewers. George's stoicism in the face of this criticism – and he knew about it – did little to inspire confidence in those who wanted to support him, and thus the seeds of disaffection and disillusionment, which would eventually have catastrophic results for George himself, were sown.

From January 1975 onwards George was in the odd position of seeing his arch-rival rebuilding his political career from a seat beside him on the front bench. His genteel approach to politics – which, while the party was in opposition, took second place to his legal practice – never stood a chance. Charlie had nothing else to do and was consumed by ambition. Every waking moment was devoted to one thing: the ousting of Jack Lynch and his own installation as leader. And while both sides maintained a dignified posture, both knew what was in train.

By the end of 1976 those TDs who had wanted to remove Jack or get him to retire to the Áras now accepted that he was immovable before the election. They settled down to the inevitability of fighting the election under him, not realizing that he was the party's greatest electoral asset. In every other sense, the prospects were not good. The front bench had no apparent unity of purpose, other than a desire to dislodge the incumbents in office. This alternative government was made up of part-timers, men – and it was only men – who devoted very little time to policy issues, regarding this as the responsibility of others. While nobody believed that Fianna Fáil had any great chance, that some would actively encourage a defeat was something else entirely. Astonishingly, though, there were quite a few in the parliamentary party who contented them-selves with the belief – the hope, even – that Fianna Fáil would lose the upcoming general election and that Lynch would be forced to resign as a consequence of having lost two successive general elections, something that had never happened previously. Then, they believed, in the general disillusion that would follow, Charlie would be proclaimed leader and no government would be able to withstand the force of his parliamentary opposition.

They were all in for a surprise, because behind closed doors Fianna Fáil had been in election mode for over a year. While phoney public battles about media bias, propaganda and other issues were raging, the formulation of new, attractive policies – the real thrust of what the party ought to have been about – was being carried out by a backroom committee of experts. But their proposals were kept top secret for fear the government would cherry-pick the best ideas, leaving the party in a worse state than when it had entered opposition in 1973 with nothing by way of policies. And in party headquarters Séamus Brennan had been trying to get the organization into some sort of manageable shape. A youth movement had been established to bring in new blood (a move that paid off with the eventual election – though not in 1977 – of people like Micheál Martin and Dermot Ahern). In preparation for the election, Brennan had to guarantee that each constituency would have a panel of candidates that contained at least one new name. We had to guarantee that all of the candidates were vetted and that none would turn out to be mavericks during the campaign or after they were elected. With the exception of one candidate, we succeeded in the former objective and I will maintain a diplomatic silence on the success or otherwise of the latter. From these disparate efforts came the Fianna Fáil organization's belief that it was ready for an election, while its front bench faced the prospect with barely hidden trepidation.

In the summer of 1976 Jack established an election strategy committee under the chairmanship of Senator Eoin Ryan, a businessman and company director of some renown, the son of Jim Ryan, a party founder and former Minister for Finance under de Valera and Lemass. The committee was to ensure that when the election was called everything would be ready to go within twenty-four hours. Ryan was a brilliant chairman. Everybody understood exactly what had to be done, and a deadline was set for each task. Professionals were hired to advise on advertising, print, music, polling, photography, media relations, scheduling of the party leader's national tour, radio and TV broadcasts and appearances. Nothing was left to chance. I found membership of the election strategy committee the most rewarding and exciting aspect of my job at that time. Probably because it had no politicians as members – except Ryan, but he was not running for the Dáil – the committee worked extremely well, and none of its deliberations, decisions or strategies ever leaked out. The parliamentary party and most of the front bench knew little, if anything, about our plans – which didn't help the frustrations of TDs and candidates – but the party hierarchy was paranoid about being pre-empted and we were all sworn to secrecy.

The election strategy committee knew that however organized it was, however professional its deliberations and plans, it could not second-guess the contents of the manifesto. We were shooting in the dark, and our only consolation was that Eoin Ryan repeatedly told us that the contents of the manifesto would dovetail with all our other plans and strategies. (It was only after the election, at a celebratory party in his home in Ballsbridge, that I learnt that, just like the rest of us on the committee, he had not known any of the policy proposals contained in the manifesto until the day of its publication, less than twenty-four hours after the election was called.) And so, after almost five years in opposition, Fianna Fáil was now, hopefully, prepared for an election campaign that would decide far more than the next government. The careers of many, not least my own, rested on the outcome.

4. 'The greatest comeback since Lazarus'

In early May 1977 Jack told me that the bulk of the election manifesto was ready and that it would shortly be considered at a special front bench meeting. I asked for a copy, but he refused, saying it was preferable that nobody, other than the front bench, should know its contents prior to publication. I mentioned this to Charlie Haughey in the course of conversation one day. He was contemptuous in his attitude; mind you, O'Donoghue's involvement predisposed him to be negative from the start. His view was – and this was before he knew the manifesto's contents – that the party, if elected, might be landed with policies that would immediately have to be disowned as either impractical or impossible to implement. Those formulating the manifesto would probably have agreed; they were operating in the belief that, because of the Tullymander and the generally negative feeling about Fianna Fáil's prospects, the party wouldn't get elected. This is crucial for understanding the manifesto's origins and content.

Charlie had his own backroom committee on health. The issues weren't major, but Charlie knew that if Fianna Fáil were to be elected the likelihood was that he would end up with the health portfolio, and so in anything he said he was extremely careful to avoid giving unnecessary hostages to fortune. His attitude to Fianna Fáil's policy-making was clear from his hostility to a front bench proposal to introduce food subsidies for social welfare recipients. Charlie went ballistic and said that Martin O'Donoghue, who had been responsible for the suggestion, should be ostracized. He rightly pointed out that Fianna Fáil had eschewed subsidies as a policy back in the sixties. This little spat was just a foretaste of what was to come between these two men who had diametrically opposing views on how the economy should be run.

In Fianna Fáil we did not know that the coalition had decided to run for as long as possible – the actual term of office under the constitution is five years – in order to recover as much economic ground as possible. The economy was in a downturn after the oil crisis of 1975, but Richie Ryan, the Minister for Finance, believed that the country could borrow its way out of debt. He wasn't the first politician, and doubtless won't be the last, to suddenly discover a belief in voodoo economics. After 1975 he found that there was little option but to revert to established nostrums, including increasing direct and indirect taxation, politically fatal as that was. Ryan came in for virulent criticism, not only from Fianna Fáil (which, it was pointed out, had invented deficit budgeting), but also from economists who would normally have been expected to support a Fine Gael minister. When the long-awaited announcement of the general election came on 25 May, it was a relief to everybody, including, I suspect, the members of the government itself. Polling day was set for 16 June.

Fianna Fáil's election strategy committee had decided that the only way to gain the initiative was to strike first and in such a way that others would find it difficult to either match us or beat us. We didn't know what the government had up its sleeve. We might be wrong-footed by some electorally appealing announcement or promises that we hadn't thought of. As per the strategy committee's blueprint, Fianna Fáil issued its manifesto less than twenty-four hours after the election was called. At a time when people were used to vague promises at general election time, its very specific and generous provisions – including the abolition of car tax and domestic rates, and a £1,000 grant to first-time house buyers – had a phenomenal impact. There was immediate mayhem. The government, the media and indeed large sections of the party organization itself were stunned. Literally minutes after the manifesto had been launched I met Labour's Frank Cluskey outside the bar in Leinster House. Frank had obviously been tipped off about the juicier aspects of the document. This wasn't surprising: those of us who worked in the Dáil knew which journalists had Labour Party leanings and it was fairly predictable that a gregarious politician like Frank would get an early account of what was happening.

He greeted me with the words: 'Fuck ya, Frank!' It was a pithy and honest representation of the reaction to the manifesto amongst the coalition parties and certain sections of the media. While fully appreciating the attractiveness of the manifesto's promises, they adopted an immediate and fiercely hostile stance to try to diminish its favourable impact on the electorate.

One of its greatest critics – though obviously he didn't say anything publicly – was Charlie Haughey. When he read it he just raised his eyes to heaven, looked at me with a pained expression and said, 'Oh dear, oh dear, oh dear!' There were other scathing comments, to the effect that the document had been produced by Máirín, Jack's wife, or that it was an amalgam of the thoughts of some drunken economists in Doheny & Nesbitt's, the well-known watering hole in Baggot Street beloved of the chattering classes.

But no criticism could touch us. We had seized the initiative and we had the advantage: the manifesto and its contents dominated the press coverage for the best part of a week. However well we had prepared for events, we couldn't in our wildest imaginings have hoped for the free run we got for the first seven days of the campaign. In politics the general expectation is that the party (or parties) in power manipulates events to its own electoral advantage – or at least tries to do so. In this instance the opposite seemed to happen. The coalition seemed to be in shock; it had decided on the timing of the election but appeared to be totally unprepared for the event. There was no press conference; indeed there was no press office. There was no manifesto or programme. Fianna Fáil was allowed to dictate the agenda for the first week of the campaign. Each day Fianna Fáil made a new announcement. It unveiled a youth policy, accompanied by a special election song, 'Your Kind of Country', sung by Colm C. T. Wilkinson. We had tested the lyrics and the music on focus groups around the country before recording it and the approval rating was enormous. (Wilkinson went on to have a huge career in musical theatre, one that continues to this day, and the recording, which doesn't even feature his name on the label, is a collectors' item.)

One of the major elements of the strategy committee's preparatory work was scheduling a nationwide tour by Jack Lynch. He would make a major speech each day, and this would be complemented by a series of policy announcements by the various front bench spokesmen. Each day was tightly mapped out and, regardless of what controversy occurred, the schedule was followed religiously. Where possible every radio and TV talk show would have a senior Fianna Fáil TD participating. Nothing was left to chance. My contacts with the media were such that I got almost hourly reports of the reactions – or lack of them – from senior ministers, and we were able to turn up the heat accordingly.

The actual election campaign was a killer. The pressure was enormous and those of us in the front line had to spread ourselves very thinly – keeping an eye on what was happening in Dublin, watching as best we could the campaign throughout the country and, in my case particularly, keeping tabs on what was going on in the media. I made a number of forays out of Dublin to meet up with Jack and Máirín and to exchange notes about what was happening. On one such trip, to my hometown, Kilkenny, there was a mix-up in the scheduling, and Jack and I were left sitting on the platform for the best part of half an hour waiting for Jim Gibbons and his troupe of supporters to arrive. Jack was an experienced campaigner and he knew that the welcome that he was getting around the country wasn't just personal, but when we had time to talk, and he teased out various scenarios, he was clearly wary of predicting victory, a position he maintained until the very end. After the last rally in Cork I returned to Dublin with him and Máirín in the official car. 'I think we might be lucky,' he said. His thought was that Fianna Fáil might just scrape in. Even then, after three weeks of campaigning and with unrivalled support and enthusiasm for the manifesto and for Jack himself, he still wasn't sure of the outcome. But then neither was anybody else in the party, and, from what some of the political correspondents were telling me, the coalition parties were quite convinced that they would be re-elected on the basis of their record in office.

Such was the level of preparation that hairy moments during the campaign were few and far between. People had nightmares about what had happened in the 1973 election when the party had, after the campaign was under way for five or six days, spotted the popularity of the coalition's proposal to abolish domestic rates and decided to change its previous tack. It announced that if elected it would also abolish rates. But nobody told Gerry Collins. Gerry had taken out a very large advertisement in the *Limerick Leader*, his local newspaper, ridiculing the coalition parties for promising the abolition of rates, on the basis that the country couldn't afford it. It was too late to have the advertisement pulled. Gerry was mercilessly lampooned in the media, particularly by RTÉ, which had no love for him since the time he had sacked the RTÉ Authority over the Seán MacStiofáin interview.

It was obvious that Fianna Fáil was doing well when certain civil servants began to make themselves known to members of the campaign team. I recall being asked to meet two of them and being presented with a draft report on prices compiled in the Department of Industry and Commerce; this, according to the men who came to see me (whose identities I will not reveal, because they are still in the service), was being deliberately withheld during the election because it showed a dramatic increase in inflation and the coalition's campaign managers were afraid of its impact on voters. I consulted with Séamus Brennan and the Director of Elections, Eoin Ryan, and, having satisfied ourselves as to its authenticity, we decided to publish the document with as much fanfare as we could.

The effect was devastating. The Minister for Industry and Commerce, Justin Keating, was very angry. There were mutterings from the direction of Industry and Commerce about nefarious acts of treachery and national sabotage and so on, but, in the white-hot heat of an election campaign, nobody paid the slightest attention. Subsequently I appeared with Justin on RTÉ's election results programme, and the look on his face suggested that he was still furious with us.

If the tactics we adopted during the 1977 election were used today, there would be an outcry. Those few journalists who were sympathetic to Fianna Fáil, or who had Fianna Fáil connections, were given special access and treatment, and the maximum coverage was extracted from the papers in the *Press* group. Eoin Ryan told me that one of my tasks was to ensure that when the campaign began, Jack Lynch's photograph appeared in every national newspaper every day, up to and including polling day. That I succeeded was as much of a surprise to myself as it was to others. To achieve the necessary result I made an arrangement with the *Irish Times* and the *Irish Independent* that their photographers – both selected by me – would be given special treatment, driven after Jack by a party volunteer and driven back to their labs in time for the films to be processed and the pictures printed. Better still, on those occasions when I managed to be with the leader, the photographers and I selected the poses thought most suitable for publication. We exploited to the full the adage that a picture is worth a thousand words, and there must be many flattering and sympathetic images of Jack Lynch in both papers' archives.

The one area where we knew we would have problems, and did, was RTÉ. There was a well-founded belief that Fianna Fáil could not get sympathetic – or even fair – coverage from the station because most of its producers, those who actually controlled the content of programmes, were from the far left, and they were determined not only to frustrate Fianna Fáil (and, in certain instances, Fine Gael) but to enhance the profiles of those on the left in general and those with anti-Republican sympathies in particular. In recent years I have read various articles by Eoghan Harris, then a producer in RTÉ, which lend some weight to the belief that managers in RTÉ were either complicit in the appointment of a certain type of person to the job of producer, which seems unlikely, or so incompetent as not to recognize that they were being manipulated by outside political forces. Despite the difficulties we got the coverage we needed, and it was amusing, if somewhat nauseating, to watch the sycophantic grovelling of some of them after the election result became known.

Polling day is always something of a nerve-racking experience. There is the nagging feeling that more could have been done. Party HQ goes quiet for the first half of the day and everybody waits, as tension mounts, for indications of turnout throughout the country.

Invariably, party workers tell fibs to the party managers about the level of support that exists in a particular area. But this time the indications from the country were that there was a high turnout, and, as in all elections, we could only wait for the boxes to be opened the following morning and for the famous tallymen to do their thing. I would like to be able to say that we all went out and got roaring drunk the night before the count, but the truth is more prosaic: we were so exhausted that we went home to bed for a good night's sleep, something that we had not had for over three weeks.

There was a huge sense of anxious anticipation on my part the following morning. After all, this was the first general election in which I had been directly involved and for which I would carry some of the responsibility. Yes, I had worked on by-elections, but by and large these had been relatively timid affairs and their impact was minimal except for those immediately concerned. I went into Fianna Fáil HQ in Upper Mount Street, from where we had run the campaign for nearly a month and which was like a second home. To my surprise the place was almost deserted. It wasn't until about ten o'clock that most of the key people began to arrive. By then I had received a telephone call from Michael Mills of the *Irish Press*. I knew that Michael had had a small private wager with one or two of his colleagues on the outcome of the election, and he had opted for success for the coalition. So, when he called me at HQ on the morning of the count, he sounded somewhat deflated when he inquired if I knew what was happening. I was cautious because I didn't want to say anything that might end up as a quotation for the *Evening Press*. To my astonishment Michael said, 'It's all over, it's a landslide. How did this happen?' I found myself in the odd position of consoling the doyen of Irish political correspondents about the apparent result of a general election only an hour or so after the count had begun. This was a sort of reversal of roles. Michael was a decent man whom I had come to know very well after becoming Fianna Fáil's Press Officer. He adopted something of a fatherly interest in me and from time to time would console me when I thought the whole world was trying to do me down in my efforts to bring both sense and order to Fianna Fáil operations.

Of course Michael was right. It was a landslide, and, as the counts came in, it became patently clear that the government had been routed and that Fianna Fáil was set for the greatest electoral success in the history of the state, much to its own, as well as to everybody else's, astonishment, particularly the media's. It should have been more predictable. Apart from the economic difficulties as a result of the oil crisis, there was the débâcle over the presidency and considerable angst amongst Labour supporters because the party was participating in a government that was causing more difficulties for Labour than for the senior party. Yet nobody had had any confidence in Fianna Fáil either as an opposition – least of all its own supporters – or as an alternative government. I think it was Seán Duignan of RTÉ who joked, 'Everybody hates Fianna Fáil, except the voters.' He famously described the party's success as the 'greatest comeback since Lazarus'.

As the day wore on, various radio and TV commitments had to be fulfilled. I went to collect Séamus Brennan from his house in Goatstown to bring him to RTÉ to participate in an election results programme. Séamus spent the best part of an hour pacing up and down his sitting room in his underpants declaiming what a wonderful new world had opened up for 'us pair of young fellas'. Having persuaded Séamus to put on his trousers, I brought him to the studios, where he put in a masterful performance for which, even if he had done nothing during the previous five years as General Secretary of the party, he would have deserved the bouquets he got that day. In our excitement Séamus and I believed that we were now powers in the land and that we could do anything that we wished with impunity. How innocent we were.

For years after the election both Jack Lynch, and subsequently Charlie Haughey, were accused of buying the people's votes with the manifesto. Charlie used to smile wryly when this particular canard was flung at him, given that he had taken an especially jaundiced view of much of its contents. The reality was that at the time of its publication, apart from the predictable reactions of the usual anti-Fianna Fáil sources, there was little, if any, negative comment about it from established commentators, or indeed economists. Moore McDowell, an economics lecturer in UCD, was belatedly appointed Press Officer for Fine Gael for the duration of the election campaign. (Being the grandson of the patriot and minister in the first Free State government, Eoin MacNeill, he had an impressive Fine Gael pedigree.) I remember meeting Moore at the time of his appointment and he gave every impression, without actually saying so, that his was a futile exercise. But he had been asked to do a job and he duly obliged. Happily for Fianna Fáil, his was a solitary sane voice and few other economists tackled the document forensically. Instead, Moore was drowned out by the cacophony from those who just hated Fianna Fáil on principle. He was a gracious opponent and, as far as I know, he got little thanks for his efforts.

The public seemed to regard most of those attacking Fianna Fáil's 'pump-priming' antics as spoilsports. People felt that something dramatic was required if the economy were to be revived, and they seemed to think — or chose to think — that Fianna Fáil's radical and generous proposals might do the trick. After assimilating what was on offer, people were not in the mood for an objective critique; they just couldn't wait to get their hands on the loot. I vividly recall a woman coming to see me regarding the £1,000 first-time buyer's grant. She was building a new house, and her brother, a priest who lived abroad, was retiring and coming to live with her and her family. She wondered if she installed two front doors, one for the family's use and the other for her retired brother's, she would be entitled to two grants. I am sometimes amazed to hear commentators who were around then — and who told me privately how clever we had been to read the minds of the public and how accurately we had done so — now adopting poses of moral outrage at the 1977 manifesto. At the time I didn't hear anybody refusing the free lunch.

The man most surprised by the result of the election — a twenty-seat majority — was Jack Lynch himself. I spent most of the afternoon of the count with him. The plan was for him to go to RTÉ to be interviewed by Brian Farrell on the election special programme late in the evening when most of the results were in. The protocol and the courtesies began to click in quickly, and we were met at the door of RTÉ by the Director General, accompanied by an army of senior station personnel, many of whom would not have been seen dead with Jack Lynch, or his press officer, in the previous four years.

As we were about to enter the hospitality suite, we were told that a third Fianna Fáil TD had been elected in the Louth constituency – something unheard of in a four-seater. It was then that Jack said that the result was too good. Remember that he had thought that Fianna Fáil would barely make it, getting a two- or three-seat majority at best. The prospect of a minority situation, even if it were seen as less than desirable in terms of a vote of confidence, would not have frightened him. In fact, it might have been better than the actual result. Having such a big majority was a wonderful personal endorsement, but Jack knew that inevitably, as political life moved on, there would be unrest and unease amongst the back benchers, especially the newly elected ones, as they wondered if they would hold their seats. His political instincts were right: that twenty-seat majority was his downfall. From comments he had made to me I knew that he did not intend to stay on as leader, and consequently as Taoiseach, for the full five-year term. Though it crossed my mind, I did not feel it was my place to allude to this on election night. In retrospect, it was a big mistake not to make this clear, even in his moment of greatest success. Saying it would have lanced a boil that had already begun to fester.

As the party organization celebrated the election victory, its high-profile TDs were already locked into a new contest: the one for a seat in the cabinet. I was fascinated by the almost feral intensity with which they went about ensuring that their names were kept in contention. TDs knew that I was close to Jack Lynch and I have yet to meet a politician who suffers any embarrassment about promoting his or her own interests, so my telephone never stopped ringing. Of course, there were guaranteed positions. Nobody could envisage a situation where George Colley was not appointed as Minister for Finance. But Martin O'Donoghue, the architect of the manifesto, had been elected too, and as he would without question be in the cabinet, there was intense speculation about which job he would get. To further complicate matters, O'Donoghue's constituency colleague in Dun Laoghaire, David Andrews, was a former Parliamentary Secretary and government Chief Whip and could also legitimately expect promotion. But it was unusual to have two cabinet ministers in the same constituency. This was just one of the many dilemmas facing Jack.

While all the speculation was going on, Jack invited me to spend the weekend with Máirín and himself at their holiday cottage at Roaring Water Bay, just outside Skibbereen in west Cork. This was the last relaxed break that we had prior to the resumption of the Dáil and his election as Taoiseach. Needless to say there were many discussions about party colleagues and the suitability or otherwise of various people for a variety of jobs. In none of these discussions did Jack disclose his final choices, but, mellowed by a few glasses of Paddy, he did let his guard down about some of the less attractive characteristics of colleagues with whom he was forced to work. He knew well that there would be problems, sooner or later, as a result of the friction between Charlie Haughey and Jim Gibbons. After Charlie had returned to the front bench he had managed the tension between them relatively well. But government was different, and the competition for funding was known to have a cathartic effect on most relationships in cabinet, no matter how friendly ministers felt they were with one another. He knew also that the only thing that O'Malley and Haughey had in common was a hatred of each other, and that this would lead to difficulties. And that wasn't to speak of the animus between himself and Haughey. Likewise there was the problem of Bobby Molloy. Bobby had been forced to resign as spokesman on local government when he had falsely accused Jimmy Tully of accepting inducements from a builder in his constituency in relation to a planning permission that, at the time, was still within the purview of the Minister for Local Government. Should this error of judgement be held against him now? If all the people who were expecting cabinet posts were to be satisfied, the constitution would have to be changed to allow for more than the permitted number.

During the weekend Jack broached the subject of my own career prospects with the inimitable words: 'I suppose you will be wanting the big job yourself?' I professed not to know what he was talking about, but of course I knew exactly what was coming and was prepared. While I had not taken anything for granted, I had guessed that Jack would offer me a senior job. And so, in the immediate aftermath of the election, wanting to be as prepared as possible for a discussion about the most effective way of carrying out the task, I had sought out the coalition's GIS head, Muiris MacConghail. MacConghail told me he had experienced problems in accessing information from the civil service. This just confirmed what I already knew: the natural tendency of the civil service was towards secrecy, and, if the 'permanent government' (as John Healy of the *Irish Times* had dubbed the civil service) was so minded, it could make impossible the job of someone it considered an interloper, simply by withholding or delaying access to essential information. The obvious solution was to become one of them: to get myself appointed to the civil service at a relatively senior level and thus obviate the necessity to go through ministers or senior civil servants to find out what was going on. Of course, getting into the civil service at this level would be of huge personal benefit to me. I was getting married later in the summer and this would set me up in a well-paid, permanent and pensionable job. And when Fianna Fáil left office, though I would probably be moved out of whatever work I might be doing then, I would not lose my job or my rank. So, when Jack said that the position of head of the Government Information Service was mine if I wanted it, I struck while the iron was hot. I said that though I would very much like to say yes, I felt that to do the job effectively I would need to be made an Assistant Secretary in the civil service. This was the most senior rank I could hope for and it would give me automatic access to any information I needed to do the job. Jack knew the magnitude of what I was asking and he asked me to justify my request. When I did so, he agreed without further hesitation.

I discovered afterwards that when Jack got back to Dublin he consulted the Secretary to the Government, Dan O'Sullivan, about the appropriateness of such a promotion. O'Sullivan assured him that as Taoiseach he could make any appointment he wished 'in the public interest'. He rang me to say that my appointment would be on the government's agenda at the first cabinet meeting of the new administration. And so it came about that in June 1977 I was appointed head of the Government Information Service with the rank of Assistant Secretary at the Department of the Taoiseach. I have the distinction of being the last person appointed to the civil service in the public interest.

5. Getting to grips with government

When the Dáil assembled on 5 July 1977 very few, if any, of those to be appointed to the cabinet knew in advance what departments they were going to get and consequently there was a greater sense of excitement than normal. Denis Gallagher, who was to be appointed Minister for the Gaeltacht, was alerted to his impending post only when Jack passed him on the stairway in the Dáil chamber on his way out to be given his seal of office as Taoiseach by the President. The normal procedure is that the newly appointed Taoiseach comes back from Áras an Uachtaráin and names his cabinet. As he passed him, Lynch whispered to Gallagher *be reidh* – 'be ready'. And thus a cabinet minister was appointed. Similarly, Bobby Molloy was obviously not expecting anything because he turned up in a red check shirt that day – not the most dignified attire for such an occasion – and the man most surprised to hear of his appointment was Molloy himself. Along with the Secretary to the Government I accompanied Jack when he went to get his seal. He and Paddy Hillery had a relaxed chat, the ceremony was over in minutes, and after the photographs we headed back to the Dáil, Garda outriders escorting us, their sirens blaring for some unknown reason because there was no immediate hurry. The tension mounted considerably when Jack arrived back in Leinster House and the chamber was full to capacity, with every available seat in the Visitors' Gallery and the Distinguished Visitors' Gallery occupied by wives, parents and family members of the ministerial aspirants.

The only appointment that caused any surprise was that of Martin O'Donoghue as Minister for Economic Planning and Development. This was the first time in the history of the state that there was to be a minister with sole responsibility for economic planning. The closest Ireland had ever come to having anything similar was in the late fifties and early sixties, when Ken Whitaker and Seán

Lemass worked together on the *Programmes for Economic Expansion*
that had been the basis of Ireland's economic regeneration. (As
for David Andrews, who had helped get O'Donoghue elected in
Dun Laoghaire, he was to be disappointed by Lynch. He was rele-
gated to the somewhat pedestrian post of junior minister at the
Department of Foreign Affairs.)

The trouble about the announcement of this new ministry was
that nobody knew about it, including the new Minister for Finance,
George Colley, and his department. The truth was that it was a
political decision and the new department was established to provide a berth for the man to whom Jack believed he was most
indebted. O'Donoghue had played a key role for Lynch during the
previous five years in opposition. He had removed the day-to-day
burdens of running the backroom policy committees and looked
after the mundane details of hiring and paying staff in the leader's
office. But his influence had been far deeper than that. He had
successfully understood that Lynch couldn't really be bothered with
policy issues. Of course, Lynch regarded policy as important, but
he believed that the thinking regarding policy for the country as a
whole wasn't for the politicians. In Jack's vocabulary – and in
fairness, in the lexicon of most Fianna Fáil politicians – policy
meant any proposal or scheme that would help the party's political
profile. But if formulating policy meant generating ideas about
managing the economy, then that was for those who were paid to
do it, namely the civil servants, particularly those in the Department
of Finance. In short, Martin O'Donoghue was rewarded for his
services by being appointed to a newly created ministry but with
no clear thought by anybody, himself included, about how its
activities might dovetail with the existing departments of state, the
Department of Finance in particular. Those who had had any
experience of government, which did not include myself at that
time, knew that the new department spelt impending disaster.
There was no way that a Secretary of the Department of Finance
worth his salt would allow a new department to usurp any of the
powers of Finance, no matter how trivial. A few days after the
formation of the government I had lunch with Charlie Haughey

in the Dáil restaurant and he was scathing about the move. In his opinion the mandarins in the Department of Finance would take a long view and gradually strangle O'Donoghue's ministry to death.

Among Jack's other notable appointments were three to the senate: Séamus Brennan, who got a just reward for his work in reorganizing the party and dragging it into the seventies; Mary Harney, a young Trinity graduate who had impressed Lynch with her debating skills but who had failed to take a Dáil seat; and Ken Whitaker, the economics guru, who had become a friend when advising him in the Department of Finance.

Brian Lenihan's appointment was significant for negative rather than positive reasons. Jack didn't particularly like Brian and thought long and hard about dropping him from the cabinet altogether. He kept his dislike well hidden, but when he gave Brian Fisheries – an important ministry, but not one that you would automatically associate with a man who had previously served in Education and in Justice – Brian's family and supporters were not best pleased.

Brian was delightfully indiscreet. He found it difficult to lie, and when confronted about some misdemeanour or other would disarmingly admit to whatever mistake had been made. I vividly recall Lynch's anger when he discovered that Lenihan had allowed an *Irish Times* journalist, Olivia O'Leary, to do a profile of him titled 'A Week in the Life of a Minister'. Fisheries was a sensitive enough post, with controversy raging about the failure of the government as well as its predecessors to ensure that the Irish fishing industry was insulated and protected against the ravages of competition, from the Spanish in particular. Brian had agreed to the project prior to telling me about it, but when he did I saw nothing wrong with it and regarded it as an opportunity to highlight both the workings of a government department and the demands made on a minister. Neither Brian nor I happened to mention it to Lynch, and when the first episode appeared there was pandemonium. It transpired that Brian, true to his word, granted O'Leary full access to all meetings and consultations, including those in which advice was given by senior civil servants.

The row that ensued highlighted a fundamental difference of

style between Lenihan and Lynch. Despite his popular image Lynch was deeply conservative and highly suspicious of giving any leeway to the media, whereas Lenihan had a completely transparent attitude when it came to dealing with the press. Some of his own supporters failed to come to terms with Lenihan's approach, particularly when they thought that the media was less than kind to his undoubted intelligence and portrayed him in a less than complimentary light. What these people failed to see was that it wasn't the media that were responsible for any misconceptions about Lenihan's intellect; it was his party, which, in times of crisis, ruthlessly put him forward to explain what was sometimes inexplicable and to defend the indefensible. He did this to such effect at the beginning that he was overused and eventually became a caricature of himself. He was extremely pleasant to deal with and had enormous resilience in the face of political and personal adversity. Behind a genial exterior there was an acute political brain at work, and those of us who knew him well respected him for his sound judgement and advice. There is no doubt in my mind that he was one of the most underrated politicians of his time, and had he exercised a little more discipline, and been driven by as much ambition as some of his colleagues, he would have gone much further in politics than he actually did.

Anyway, on this occasion Lynch gave me a rare dressing-down and Lenihan was ordered to bring the arrangement with Olivia O'Leary to a halt. When I pointed out to the Taoiseach that this would cause even greater publicity, all negative, and portray the government as being afraid of even the most benign scrutiny, he relented, though less than graciously. It all reinforced his dislike of Lenihan. Subsequently, when some problem or other arose, I heard him describe Lenihan as a fool. The profile in the *Irish Times* was highly successful, and the irony was that I was inundated with requests from other ministers to have a similar exercise done on their behalf. I don't know if Lynch ever heard of these requests, but if he did it wasn't from me.

Having made his appointments, Jack did nothing to harness – or direct – the energies of his expanded parliamentary party. It may seem odd that if, as he admitted on election night, his majority was too great, he didn't try to do something to manage his back benchers' predictable restlessness. The explanation is simple: he hardly knew the new TDs. I recall running into him coming out of the library in Leinster House on the day the Dáil returned. The library is located to the left of the main lobby, so we stood watching the carnival atmosphere on the front steps as the new TDs arrived with their families and supporters. There was a particular hullabaloo as a man in a white suit and polka-dot shirt was shouldered to the front door. 'Who in the name of God is that?' asked an incredulous Lynch. 'That,' I said, 'is the one and only Pádraig Flynn from Mayo.' Jack should have recognized him. He was the man who, knowing that he couldn't take the seat, had refused to run for Fianna Fáil in the by-election to replace Fine Gael's Henry Kenny nearly two years previously. Though he would never have believed it that day, Jack was looking at one of those who would go on to change the profile, and in some instances the nature, of Fianna Fáil politics for ever.

Even if he didn't see the need to do so himself, Lynch should have advised Colley to make sure that he got to know the new intake. He should have seen the benefit that support from this new quarter would be to whoever had leadership ambitions. And, as time passed, seeing the inroads Haughey was making in wooing the new back benchers, he should have alerted those by whom he believed the party's best interests would be served. But, effectively, he – and they – left the field open to Charlie. In truth, his lack of action was simply another example of his laissez-faire attitude: he hoped for the best.

As the new government took control, the ministers disappeared to various offices throughout the city; they met collectively once a week but operated in isolation otherwise. This was a shock. I had been used to meeting members of the front bench, or at least talking to them by telephone, almost daily. Now they were removed from the centre of operations – the Department of the Taoiseach – and contact was minimal, and only then through the Private Secretaries (they alone knew where their particular minister might be found). This was before the era of mobile phones: it sometimes took hours before a minister could be contacted.

The problem of the disappearing minister was highlighted by an entertaining incident when Jack was Taoiseach during the previous Fianna Fáil government and wanted to speak to Brian Lenihan urgently. The minister's private office told the Taoiseach that the minister had left Athlone, his hometown, and could not be contacted for a number of hours. A quick-thinking civil servant in the Taoiseach's private office decided to ring some well-known watering holes on the road between Athlone and Dublin. After a few unsuccessful attempts he tried Harry's in Kinnegad and was amazed to hear what sounded like a familiar voice: Brian Lenihan was the only customer sitting at the counter and when nobody else picked up the ringing phone he did. Showing typical delicacy, the civil servant went through the motions of inquiring whether Minister Lenihan was about, but, without any bashfulness at all, Brian replied, 'Speaking!' Sadly what took place between the Taoiseach and Brian Lenihan when they spoke to one another a few minutes later is not recorded.

On another occasion, when I was working for a Fine Gael–Labour coalition, there was a panic when it was realized that the junior minister in Education, Michael Keating, was on his way to Limerick to buy Adare Manor, which he intended to turn into a sporting and conference centre. However, the purchase had not been sanctioned by either the Minister for Finance or the government as a whole, so he had to be stopped. The problem was that he had left Dublin and could not be contacted. The Minister for Defence, Jimmy Tully, was asked to get the army to set up a roadblock on the minister's route and to order him to ring the Taoiseach before proceeding further. I'm sure that the other motorists on the Dublin–Limerick road thought that a breakout from Portlaoise Prison, or something of that magnitude, had brought the army out. Thankfully, the minister was halted in his tracks and an announcement that would have caused considerable difficulties was averted.

Those who had never served as ministers before were somewhat shocked by how their lives changed. Politicians who had become accustomed to meeting each other and socializing together in the comfortable ambience of opposition found themselves constrained by the demands of their particular office and losing touch. And keeping in touch is one of the cardinal rules of political survival: being in the know means a politician senses which way to jump when the going gets rough; being out of the loop makes him nervous and ridiculous in the eyes of his colleagues. In effect ministers become managers of huge entities, sometimes employing thousands of people scattered in offices throughout the country. Men who a short time previously had followed a relatively leisurely political life now found themselves being consulted on an hourly basis about the most detailed and complicated of issues.

An individual minister becomes, in the terms of the arcane language of the public service, the *corporation sole* – in other words he is responsible for virtually everything that happens in the department over which he presides. A clever departmental Secretary can, if of a mind to do so, frustrate a minister's particular intentions and objectives by snowing him under with the minutiae of administrative detail. I have seen highly intelligent politicians, one in particular, being driven demented by the tactics of a departmental Secretary who knew that if he gave the minister free rein he would cause havoc with the traditional and accepted methods of doing things. The reality is far nearer to *Yes Minister*, the classic BBC comedy depicting the relationship between a bumbling politician and his scheming civil servants, than most democrats would like to think. In fact, when I worked with John Boland in the Department of the Public Service, he scheduled reruns of *Yes Minister* in his private office for the senior management of the department, and accompanied the screenings with cryptic and caustic comments about the strategies of individual officers, who were sitting there, vis-à-vis particular terms of departmental policy. The mandarins were not amused.

This was the snake pit of intrigue and Machiavellian tactics that I entered as head of the Government Information Service. My first port of call was to the office of the Secretary to the Government, Dan O'Sullivan, who was also Secretary of the Department of the Taoiseach. At that time, the two jobs were combined and performed by the same person. It was Charlie Haughey who created two posts. Kerryman Dan O'Sullivan was an old-style civil servant – full of innate shrewdness and courtesy – and had been over the course a number of times with various taoisigh, including Jack Lynch (previously) and Liam Cosgrave. Nothing could faze him. His immediate greeting was somewhat disconcerting. 'Good morning, Mr Dunlop. I'm afraid I can't talk to you until you sign this' – 'this' being a copy of the Official Secrets Act, which at the time was widely used by the government collectively and by individual departments to refuse to release even the most pedestrian items of information. (I recall a terrible row some months later when the Department of Justice, which was notorious for invoking the Act, refused to provide the menus used in prisons. But then, the Department of Justice was to give me more than a few headaches in my time in government service. It didn't matter what party or parties were in power: the officials in St Stephen's Green seemed to operate according to a completely different set of rules from anybody else. I recall one Secretary of the department, Andy Ward, refusing to speak to me unless I would do so on the scrambler phones that had been installed in my office and my home within hours of my taking up the job with the GIS. The department feared that the IRA, amongst others, was able to tap into its phones. No matter how innocuous the conversation, he would precede it by asking, 'Have you your button pressed?' and would not continue until so assured. Given his worries about being overheard, I often wondered afterwards what, if anything, he did know about official or unofficial eavesdropping activities.) Having been advised to sign the Official Secrets Act by Dan O'Sullivan – 'If you don't, Mr Dunlop, I will not be able to speak to you about anything to do with the government, no matter how long you are in the job' – I duly did so and promptly, like many others who have subscribed to its terms, forgot about it and probably broke its stringent provisions within hours.

Once the paperwork was out of the way Dan O'Sullivan became his affable self and talked freely about the operation of the government, and we established a rapport that served me well in the time that he remained as Secretary. Notwithstanding the circumstances in which Dan found himself – I had not come up through the ranks of the service, but I was, none the less, now an officer of his department with the second-highest rank in the service, and he was obliged to provide me with as much information as I deemed necessary for the proper conduct of my job – we got on fairly well together. I have no doubt whatsoever that he viewed the new media-friendly dimension of government as distasteful and unwholesome. I imagine that if he had ever even suspected what I was telling the political correspondents about matters being discussed by the cabinet or scheduled for discussion, more than likely he would have sought my arrest for breach of the infamous Official Secrets Act. But he was an intelligent man and probably preferred not to scrutinize my activities too closely and so avoided finding out something he didn't want to confront.

He explained the mechanics of cabinet to me: how the cabinet agenda was drawn up, how ministers scheduled matters for discussion and how decisions were arrived at and recorded. At first I found the entire process Byzantine and totally incomprehensible. When he sent me my first cabinet agenda I looked at it in amazement. It contained nothing more than requests for the government to authorize the publication of various Annual Reports of state and semi-state bodies and attached these huge wordy reports as addenda. There was nothing relating to government policy on anything, no matter how innocuous. When I brought this to his attention, he merely laughed and said that I would learn in due course that the more important matters were never put on the agenda and that in some instances the most important issues of all were never recorded.

I did indeed learn that there was absolutely nothing on an agenda to indicate what might actually happen at a cabinet meeting. The items listed would be dealt with in a very short time, and it was then that the real business of government took place. And I was to learn in due course, as Dan O'Sullivan had said I would, that from time to time the Secretary to the Cabinet (that was another of Dan's hats) left the cabinet meeting at the request of the Taoiseach and that the subsequent discussions, political or otherwise, were never recorded and therefore were never publicly acknowledged as ever having taken place. This was crucial to understanding how the cabinet really worked. (The lack of a detailed written record explains a lot about the fallout from the arms crisis. After the outbreak of violence in Northern Ireland the cabinet decided to allocate £100,000 for the 'relief of distress' of the Nationalist population – a proposal that the Dáil subsequently debated, voted upon and passed. But that is the entire record of what took place. There is no indication of the arguments expressed and the differing positions of cabinet members. A few of those who attended these crucial meetings are still alive – including Charlie Haughey and Pádraig Faulkner, both of whom were ministers, and Dessie O'Malley, who was the Chief Whip – and unless they intend speaking about those meetings or leaving something in their papers, it is doubtful that we will ever know the truth of what actually happened.)

There was then, and perhaps still is, a certain mystique about what happens at cabinet meetings, and politicians love to give the impression that momentous discussions take place before decisions are arrived at. The theory is that they read the voluminous material circulated by the cabinet secretariat and then have informed debate. In my experience, for the simple reason that there just aren't enough hours in the day to read everything, most of this material was ignored. When a particular issue was raised at cabinet, everybody looked to the relevant minister for his or her view – or, more accurately, the view of his or her department – and voted accordingly. The cabinet merely gives its imprimatur to decisions that have already been taken in principle elsewhere, mainly in the line departments, after consultation with the relevant minister, who then brings them as faits accomplis to his or her colleagues. Rarely does it happen that a minister would find himself or herself in a position where the cabinet would overturn a decision already approved. Rarely are there major rows. Everything is usually smoothed out in advance between the departmental secretaries, and any compromises are signalled well in advance. Most rows that occur are the result of the incompetence of the minister involved, his or her department, or both.

Many of the procedures leading to the making of cabinet decisions are arcane and would not be tolerated in any self-respecting business or professional organization, and certainly not one that has the budget and staff numbers of the government. Each department has to circulate all material relating to an impending decision to all other departments for what are quaintly referred to as 'observations', a requirement that is tantamount to inviting a dilution of the original proposal. This, in fact, is what happens on occasion, and the end result bears no comparison with the original intention. This is particularly the case after the Department of Finance finishes with matters. The *raison d'être* of that department is to control, and to be seen to control, any new policy departure, particularly if it involves extra expenditure, and it takes a strong department in the first instance, and a strong minister also, to counteract the scrutiny of the mandarins in Finance. It is something of a shattering experience for a new minister to discover that whatever the relationship he or she may have or have had with the Minister for Finance, it is the civil servants in the Department of Finance who, ultimately, decide whether the proposal will succeed. Those of us who served ministers got used to hearing a rather plaintive cry from time to time: 'But I thought we were the government!'

An understanding of how government really worked was crucial to my gradual realization that, while I was being sent out to inform the media, and consequently the public, about what had taken place at a particular meeting, I might not necessarily know what had actually occurred. First, the Secretary to the Cabinet might not have been present for the whole meeting; and secondly, for political reasons, the ministers, including the Taoiseach with whom I consulted after every cabinet meeting, might not tell me the details of any discussion or decision that had been arrived at. Since the very business of briefing the political correspondents after cabinet meetings was a matter of some contention between certain ministers and myself, none of them were unduly concerned about whether I felt I was properly informed.

It is perfectly understandable that a cabinet, which after all is made up of party-political men and women, takes time to discuss political issues that are not relevant to the official agenda. It is also understandable that they, being human, try to maximize their own political advantage arising from the information available to them as ministers. But I am often amazed at how politicians ask us to suspend our natural instincts, attribute to them only the noblest of motives and take their word for it that, no matter how unlikely it seems, their version of how they arrive at decisions happens to be the truth. There are myriad examples of the scenario. No administration, no matter how high-minded, is immune from managing events to suit its own political agenda and then trying to portray itself as acting solely in the national interest.

I was, to a small extent, the victim of this exasperating mix of pomposity and hypocrisy when the government decided to sack the Garda Commissioner, Ned Garvey, in January 1978. Though ministers had undoubtedly been discussing Garvey's position for some time, I was completely unaware of it. My first inkling that something was afoot was when, at the end of a regular briefing of the political correspondents, Denis Coghlan of the *Irish Times* asked me what I thought the government's reaction would be if the Garda Commissioner resigned. I thought it an odd question and I said that if the Garda Commissioner wished to resign I was sure it would be for genuine and sincere reasons and that the government would respond accordingly. After the briefing Michael Mills took me aside and warned me to be careful. I was puzzled and asked what he knew. He said that he did not know precisely what was going on, but that something earth-shattering was about to occur and that I had better get the facts and not look foolish when the story broke.

I could not get hold of Jack Lynch that evening and decided to leave the matter to the following morning, when I would ask him if there was anything I ought to know about the Garda

Commissioner and his intentions, or indeed the intentions of the government. Delaying was a mistake and one from which I learnt a hard lesson. Instead of calling the Taoiseach the following morning, I received an irate call from him asking me to explain a front-page story in the *Irish Times* in which I was quoted as saying that the government would consider the resignation of the Garda Commissioner. I was flabbergasted and outlined the circumstances of what had happened in the political correspondents' room the previous evening. Lynch was not mollified and asked me to meet him in his office within the hour.

When I arrived I found him with the Minister for Justice, Gerry Collins. The atmosphere was poisonous. Collins went on the offensive and accused me of jeopardizing the government's intentions and said that I ought to tender my resignation there and then. But I wasn't going to stand for treatment of this sort. I again outlined what had happened and told the minister that I had no intention of resigning and that if the Taoiseach had lost confidence in my ability he could fire me. I asked about the government's intentions regarding the Commissioner and Jack Lynch said that it was better if I knew nothing for the time being, that I would be kept informed, and that he was happy with my performance in my job.

As far as I was concerned, it was clear that a serious situation – the forced resignation of the Garda Commissioner, or his sacking – was in the offing. I said as much, though without spelling out that this would have huge media ramifications; I hoped the implication was clear. The *Irish Times* article was only the tip of the iceberg. Collins went ballistic, and said that I would be wise to keep such speculation to myself. It took Lynch some moments to calm down his Minister for Justice, and then he gave me a nod to leave the room. That evening I issued a statement on behalf of the government to say that it had lost confidence in the Garda Commissioner, Edward Garvey, and was terminating his employment with immediate effect.

The same evening the Texaco Sports Awards were on in the Burlington Hotel and, because of the massive media interest in the story, my wife and I were the last to arrive for the dinner. Jack

Lynch beckoned me over to his table and I briefed him on how the matter was being received by the political correspondents, together with the reactions I had picked up from the opposition parties. With a typically mischievous glint in his eye, he asked if Collins and myself had kissed and made up. I told him we would get over it. The truth was that we never really did. Collins and I never trusted one another after that episode, notwithstanding the fact that Collins knew that I had been ambushed by the *Irish Times*. The paper was obviously aware that something was afoot, but couldn't run with it unless it had something, however tenuous, on the record. It was the first and only time that I got caught in such an ambush.

Later that night I ran into Máire Geoghegan-Quinn, with whom I had always had a very close association arising out of the fact that I had been friendly with her father and had been partly responsible for persuading her, on the day of his funeral, to stand for his Galway West seat. Naturally Garvey's sacking came up. 'I'm delighted that Jack and Collins got the message,' she said. 'The rest of us have been telling them for months that he should be sacked.' When I asked her why, she said that they were fed up with guards in their constituencies coming into their clinics every weekend complaining about Garvey and his modus operandi and asking the government to do something about him. And so a matter that was essentially one of Garda morale, arising from Garvey's determination to run the force in a particularly strict way, became an issue with major political and even constitutional consequences when enough gardaí managed to harass enough ministers. It shows how susceptible to lobbying politicians can be when they see that it is in their interests. In this case Ned Garvey was known to have Fine Gael sympathies, so it suited the Fianna Fáil administration to move him out of the position. Garvey subsequently took an action against the government in the courts, won it and was awarded damages. (Later there was speculation that Ned Garvey was sacked because he was too close to the British security forces in the North and too ready to facilitate their policing of the border, policing that he knew sometimes strayed into the South. However, I never heard this alluded to in public or in private at the time.)

It was the autumn of 1977 before I settled down in the new surroundings of Government Buildings. Sheila and I had married in August, six weeks after the general election, and our honeymoon was a welcome break from the day-to-day hassle of reorganizing the Government Information Service. I had not envisaged that part of my job would be the management of the staff of the service, and it took me some time to come to terms with the fact that while the job sounded very grand and important, it entailed very mundane, time-consuming tasks that had very little, if anything, to do with its real objective, which was to ensure that the most positive presentation – now known as spin – was put on every action of the government or of individual ministers. Eventually I sent a memo to the cabinet along the lines that I could not continue to juggle publicity responsibilities for each department, as well as looking after the broader picture. Staff were drafted into the various departments to deal with routine publicity matters, and early in 1978 I was appointed the first ever Government Press Secretary. When I took on this position the intention was to appoint a new head of the GIS who would be responsible for the smooth running of the service, allowing me to concentrate on the policy issues. It took time to get round to this and by that stage Jack had resigned and Charlie had taken over.

The government was barely a wet week in office when individual ministers began a series of announcements giving effect to the various promises that had been made in the manifesto. These ranged from the abolition of domestic rates – a hugely popular decision that was widely welcomed by all political parties, even though more thoughtful politicians knew that this was storing up enormous trouble for the future in terms of local authority financing – to arrangements for the paying of £1,000 to every first-time house-buyer.

The minister who presided over these giveaways, Sylvie Barrett, Minister for the Environment, was also responsible for a measure that seemed farcical at the time but that had potentially serious long-term consequences. He had to face a huge logistical issue: there weren't enough driving-test inspectors to clear the backlog of provisional driving-licence holders awaiting tests. The simple solution was to remove the necessity for those on the waiting list to pass a test before getting a full driving licence. Sylvie made the crucial decision and the relevant announcement (with or without the knowledge of the cabinet is a moot point) and the predictable mayhem followed. There was outrage amongst the driving public, particularly those who had gone through the system and viewed the proliferation of learner drivers on the road with scepticism and worry. Meanwhile the insurance companies looked askance at the sudden arrival of a plethora of newly 'qualified' – and mainly young – drivers on the roads and that had an inevitable impact on premiums. Arguably Sylvie Barrett's decision was the genesis of the debate about the quality of driving in Ireland, particularly since a new generation of drivers had been instructed by parents who never sat a driving test themselves. Sometimes ministers' apparently mundane decisions have greater long-term effects than those that appear far more momentous.

A raft of other manifesto promises was fulfilled, and the public appeared insatiable for more, regardless of cost to the exchequer. I didn't hear any objections from either the trade unions or the left-wing politicians about the alleged impropriety of a political party, now in government, fulfilling its election promises. The problem was that they didn't know what the government knew – that the kitty was bare and that drastic action would be needed to correct the public finances. The only way to do that – and the only way any government can correct a situation in which spending exceeds receipts – is to increase tax.

From time to time Jack Lynch and myself would relax together, in his office or at a discreet hostelry, and we used to talk about what was happening in terms of decisions to be taken and the probable effect on political support or otherwise. Six months after the general election I made some remark that we would have to find new morsels to satisfy the public appetite for pork-barrelling. Jack looked at me in that hang-dog way of his and said that the trouble was that the government had given away everything and that there was no more to give. Jack didn't say this regretfully, or with any sense of fear about the impact on the national economy or on his own or the government's reputation. It was said merely as a matter of fact. It would be up to George and Martin to devise policies to take account of these developments.

O'Donoghue was installed in his new ministry. Its lower and middle ranks were filled with personnel from a variety of departments, some of whom had been conveniently provided to him by Secretaries who had been vainly looking for berths for several of their less well-regarded staff. Martin was not a political animal. He was an academic and tended to treat all matters in the way that certain academics did: by looking at a problem from forty different viewpoints. This was not the way of Irish politics and anybody adopting such an approach would surely come a cropper in the jungle of national politics, where there are more man-eating carnivores than in the wildest reaches of the Serengeti.

When in opposition Jack had given a hostage to fortune during an interview on *This Week* one Sunday when he said that if unemployment got to 100,000 under a Fianna Fáil-led government the party would not deserve to be re-elected. It was a reasonable and courageous thing to say at the time. But when that figure was reached, and there seemed no end to the relentless increase in the monthly jobless figures, it looked like political suicide. While he was Taoiseach he was harassed on the issue week after week. O'Donoghue was commissioned by the government to produce a paper on employment. Other ministers hoped this would spell out a programme to deal with the single most important political issue in the country.

O'Donoghue's document on future prospects for the economy, *National Development 1977–1980*, was discussed and cleared by the cabinet and scheduled for launch amidst a fanfare of publicity. The only problem was that on the afternoon of the press conference the

Evening Herald carried virtually the full text. The press conference went ahead, but it was a shambles. O'Donoghue, Colley and even the Taoiseach were absolutely convinced that the new initiative had been leaked by Charlie Haughey. There was no basis for this belief, but they could not be convinced otherwise. Their argument was that Charlie had displayed a highly sceptical attitude to some of the document's provisions at cabinet, particularly one that promised zero unemployment by the year 2000. His argument was that there would always be an element of structural unemployment and that the government should not display ignorance of rudimentary principles familiar to any first-year economics undergraduate.

As the Government Press Secretary I considered it my duty to telephone the *Evening Herald*'s editor, Vincent Doyle, to remonstrate with him about the breaking of the embargo. In the course of a somewhat heated conversation he intimated that I would be very surprised if I knew the source of the leak. This was a common line from the media – they were hearing things from interesting sources – and I dismissed it at the time. But later, when I considered the very limited circulation of the document – just the cabinet – I often wondered whether it was a double sting: to get the information out in advance and thus provide the leaking politician (it was undoubtedly a politician) with credit in the bank with the *Evening Herald*, and also to cause a hue and cry for which the sceptic at the cabinet, Charlie Haughey, would inevitably be blamed.

Noel Whelan, the Secretary of Martin O'Donoghue's new department, and the other senior civil servant in the department, Pádraig Ó hUiginn, had been largely responsible for writing the document and were disgusted by its reception. Whelan had come from an obscure section of the Department of Finance, where he had written volumes and delivered well-meaning speeches at equally well-meaning conferences about the reform of the public service. Ó hUiginn, of course, would become a high-profile and influential civil servant. Neither man could understand how certain sections of the media, mainly the financial journalists, and Colm Rapple in particular, could not – or, more suspiciously, would not – appreciate the extent of their wisdom in being able to predict, and consequently plan for, the economic future of the country.

Added to this, they knew that the Department of Finance took a dim view of the Department of Economic Planning and Development usurping the role of economic forecaster. Senior officials in Finance knew that the new department was the brainchild of Martin O'Donoghue himself, and in their long-term view – and if the Department of Finance is good at anything, it is in taking the long view – neither the minister nor the department would last very long. Their reaction to the document was conditioned by this attitude. Officials had the good grace to keep their opinions private, but at the same time ensured that the department's views were disseminated amongst important opinion-formers such as stock-brokers and bankers to whom the media would turn for reaction and views. The paper went down in flames and was consigned to a vault somewhere in the bowels of the state's archives, along with many another green paper, and indeed white paper, before and since.

Watching all this from his eyrie in the Department of Health, Charlie Haughey was going about the business of buttressing his existing support amongst those back benchers who had been in opposition with him and gathering adherents amongst the new TDs. Charlie remained aloof from the economic woes of the government. At a cabinet meeting he offered to intervene in the Posts and Telegraphs dispute, which lasted for over six months and looked, for a time, insoluble. The minister involved, Pádraig Faulkner, was a decent man who stuck doggedly to the brief provided for him by his department. While it was necessary and advisable to have in the cabinet men like him who were solid in the face of adversity, it became something of a problem when they proved to have little capacity for lateral thinking. Charlie had developed very good relations with Michael Mullen of the Irish Transport and General Workers' Union, and offered to talk to him to see if some compromise could be reached. The dispute was crippling the country in terms of communications, and the longer it went on the more ridiculous the government appeared. But

Pádraig Faulkner was not for turning: he wanted to stand up to the unions. Eventually, as Haughey predicted, the government had to cave in and the unions drew blood.

Charlie spent most of his time making good-news announcements about health matters, from the distribution of free toothbrushes to every schoolchild in the country, to the decision to build a major hospital at Beaumont in his own constituency. It would have been politically foolish of Charlie not to avail himself of any opportunity for good publicity. This is where Charlie excelled and where his colleagues failed miserably. No matter how difficult the scenario, he always managed to find something positive in it. Other ministers seemed to keep digging the particular hole in which they found themselves. This, of course, led to jealousy. It is quite normal in any government, regardless of political hue, for tensions to arise regarding publicity. There will always be those who think they are being hard done by and that others, for some indefinable reason, are getting an easier ride. I had the devil's own job trying to explain to his colleagues that Charlie went out of his way to accommodate journalists and photographers, and that a gimmick like the free distribution of toothbrushes to all schoolchildren was something that caught the imagination of the voters and the media. Much to his amusement, I – or my office – was accused of favouring Haughey above the rest of the government. The truth is that Charlie didn't need assistance from me and would have regarded any involvement by my office as rank interference. There were those who thought that Charlie was buying publicity. He made sure that certain journalists received bottles of whiskey at Christmas, but, other than that, he did no more than any other politician with an eye to burnishing his own image. Back benchers mistook positive media coverage for popular support – a common error of politicians – and the more exposure Charlie got for his efforts in Health, the more of a potential leader he seemed to be. So began in government the same cancerous growth of suspicion that had bedevilled Fianna Fáil in opposition both before the restoration of Charlie Haughey to the front bench and afterwards.

It would be virtually impossible, save amongst those few remaining participants from the time, to reprise the sense of dread and foreboding that pervaded the back benches of Fianna Fáil in 1978. As the government's problems mounted – especially increasing unemployment and mass marches against the high levels of taxation – back bench TDs began to worry about their prospects for re-election. This anxiety afflicts all politicians, no matter how nonchalant their public demeanour, almost from the time they are elected, and it increases exponentially as the term of a government passes. But it is something that affects first-time TDs more than the hardened old dogs who look on elections as one of democracy's necessary evils. Barely a year after the new government came into office with the largest majority in the history of the state, the electoral prospects of some of the newer entrants to the Dáil, at least in their own minds, were beginning to look decidedly shaky. In this torrid and fearful atmosphere, every rumour became inflamed and anxieties were magnified out of all proportion. Much of the unrest was attributable to TDs who had been swept into office on the coat-tails of a populist election programme – the benefits of which were now dissipated and virtually forgotten. They were either unable or unwilling to face up to the reality of political life, which is that the good times don't last for ever. The growing unease was not helped by George Colley's laissez-faire attitude, epitomized in his view that little Ireland could not withstand the maelstrom of global economic upheaval. This attitude provided highly combustible material for a few articulate newcomers, particularly one Charlie McCreevy, who, with a few of his colleagues, argued that the manifesto was the cause of the government's problems and that pump-priming could be taken only so far. In his view Fianna Fáil should have announced, on taking office, that the financial situation didn't allow for the fulfilment of its generous election promises.

Undoubtedly there were those on the back benches whose main interest was to foment as much trouble as possible for the government and for the party leadership in particular. The spectacle of a senior minister – O'Donoghue – getting a public mauling on a matter as fundamental as employment did nothing to reduce the suspicion that their masters didn't know what they were about. A sense of drift developed — a condition that is fatal for any government unless it resolves things quickly and decisively. It didn't, and it was in these conditions that the opportunities for those who wanted to get rid of Jack Lynch were enhanced.

6. The beginning of the end for Jack

Though members of the Department of Foreign Affairs would deny engaging in anything as vulgar as lobbying for position – diplomats emerge organically, as it were, after gentlemanly consultations between men in grey suits – the truth is somewhat different, as I was to discover when the plum posting of Ambassador to Washington came up in 1978. All Lynch's instincts told him that a new broom was needed in the United States if the propaganda machines of the IRA-supporting Noraid and Fr Seán MacManus's Irish National Caucus were to be effectively challenged; but also that there would be more than the usual discommoding of self-regarding officials in the Department of Foreign Affairs if the normal run of ambassadorial appointments was not followed. When Jack Lynch went to New York for a session of the UN General Assembly, Eamon Kennedy, our Ambassador to the United Nations, invited him to lunch in the Windows of the World restaurant on top of one of the World Trade Center towers. An hour before this lunch Jack asked me to come along. 'It's not that I particularly want to have lunch with you,' he said, 'but if you're there Eamon Kennedy can't bring up the issue of the Washington embassy.' I realized that I would be a most unwelcome guest at the party and said as much to Lynch, but he just laughed and said this was amongst the sacrifices of the job. Eamon Kennedy, ever the diplomat, didn't give any overt indication of his surprise or annoyance on seeing me. However, my presence didn't have the desired effect and he blatantly made his pitch for the job. He wasn't slow in highlighting the alleged deficiencies of all other candidates for the post, including Seán Donlon, who was in charge of the Anglo-Irish division in Foreign Affairs and whom he must have known, or at least suspected, was odds-on favourite. Lynch was at his inscrutable best and deftly avoided any promises or undertakings. It was actually a very pleasant occasion, but, towards the end, as Jack was making signs that he wanted to conclude, Kennedy somehow managed to up-end a glass of red wine into my lap and on to my best suit. There were expressions of regret and so forth, but Jack couldn't stop laughing in the limousine on the way back to the hotel. 'That'll teach you not to interfere in another man's ambitions,' he said. The minute we arrived we were met by members of the Department of Foreign Affairs, who knew full well the purpose of their colleague's lunch invitation to the Taoiseach. Nothing would do Jack but to regale them all about my 'accident'.

Seán Donlon had taken over the Anglo-Irish post at the Department of Foreign Affairs from Éamon Gallagher, who had been a close confidant of Jack when he was Taoiseach in the late sixties and the early seventies and who was credited with keeping matters on an even keel with the British at a time when relations between the two countries were fragile. Donlon was from Meath and the son of an Inspector at the Department of Education. He was highly intelligent and ambitious and had worked closely with Garret FitzGerald when he was Minister for Foreign Affairs. Garret and Jack were socially, if not politically, close; their wives were friendly with each other and there was a noticeable absence of the political, and indeed personal, antipathy that was to characterize the relationship between Garret and Charlie Haughey. When Jack was in opposition there were consultations with Garret on Northern Ireland and I recall talking to Donlon a number of times between 1974 and 1977 about the coalition's approach to the Northern question. There was no doubt, therefore, that Donlon and Lynch got on well together and that they had a mutual respect for one another. At the time I suspected that Jack consulted Garret about the appointment: Garret's public reaction to the announcement was such as to give the distinct impression that he had been a party to the decision. Subsequently, in his autobiography, he actually claimed credit for suggesting it.

Donlon's appointment was an imaginative one and, as matters were to turn out, the proper one. He immediately established himself as a key power-broker on Capitol Hill and used his

undoubted communications and lobbying skills to bring the influence of a coalition of well-placed supporters of the Irish government's cause to bear on the White House in order to counter the
influence of the British government. Chief amongst these were
Congressman Tip O'Neill, Senators Ted Kennedy and Daniel
Patrick Moynihan, and Governor Hugh Carey of New York;
collectively they came to be known as 'The Four Horsemen'. The
strategy was spectacularly successful and therein lay the genesis of a
problem that provided a frightening insight into the role and
influence of those who were not in favour of the government's
policy on Northern Ireland. This came to a head when Charlie
became Taoiseach.

After Donlon had been in Washington for a few months he asked
Lynch to send me to America to tour the major media outlets as an
official government representative and to put on the record the
official policy with regard to Northern Ireland. I was very happy
to do this, and in January 1979 I took off for what amounted to a
month-long tour of the United States, from the East Coast to the
West, in the company of Ted Smyth, an official at the Irish Consulate in New York. On the night of my arrival Ted and I, accompanied by James Downey of the *Irish Times*, went to Eamon Doran's
Pub to meet Seán Donlon and Andy Mulligan, the former Irish
rugby international. Downey and I were staying at Ted Smyth's
apartment, and, as we walked back to it, James Downey became
involved in an altercation with three street ladies and eventually
found himself lying on the ground with one of them sitting on his
chest. Ted and I managed to remove her, and Downey's dignity
was more injured than his person. It was only when we reached
the apartment that he realized that his address book had been stolen.
The police were called, and Downey was at pains to tell them that
it contained the private telephone number of a former British
Prime Minister, Ted Heath. The cops were totally mystified by the
importance of this number (as, indeed, was I) but much to our
amazement they returned an hour or two later with the precious
address book.

The following day we were scheduled to meet the editorial

board of the *New York Times*. I did not tell Downey about this appointment, and it was with some surprise that Ambassador Donlon, Ted Smyth and I found him at the same lunch as ourselves; the paper's news editor, who was going to give Downey a tour of its new technology, had invited him along. Downey proceeded to tell of his experience the night before, and, much to our chagrin – Donlon's, Smyth's and mine, that is – he prefaced it by saying that he had been returning from a night out with me, the Irish government's Press Secretary. Donlon, Smyth and I felt that we acquitted ourselves reasonably well under the detailed questioning of some ten senior editorial staff, who had clearly been briefed by British officials, and we hoped that the lunch would lead to some favourable publicity.

Publicity – though not the sort we had hoped for – followed sooner than we expected. Smyth and I took the red-eye shuttle to Boston the following morning. We both read that morning's *New York Times* but failed to spot a small piece inside, headlined 'Editor Gets Slice of Life', detailing Downey's experience with the street ladies. Annoyingly, the story began by recounting how he had been 'returning from a night on the town with the Irish government Press Secretary, Mr Frank Dunlop'. Later that day I received a message that the Taoiseach wanted to talk to me urgently and I duly rang him at home. Máirín answered the phone and said, ominously, that I shouldn't mind anything Jack said to me and if he persisted to ask him about what had happened to him in Paris in 1954! When he came to the phone Jack was all officious and wanted to know what was going on 'over there'. Apparently the first edition of the *Evening Herald* that day carried the banner headline 'Lynch Man Mugged by Black Hooker in New York'. Despite the fact that he called Sheila – collect – from somewhere in the Midwest to apologize for the publicity that had followed, to this day I have not forgiven Downey for dragging me into his misfortune. For at least a week after the story, no matter where we went, Smyth and I were introduced as 'the two guys who were mugged by the hookers in NY'. Eventually we managed to turn the matter into a joke and got Pete Hamill to carry a story in the

New York Post that made something of a skit of the whole affair and gave us credit for our efforts in trying to provide a balanced picture of what was actually happening in Ireland and of what the government was trying to do with regard to Northern Ireland. There were some senior politicians at home who took delight in my predicament. In fairness to Donlon he reported back to Lynch that, notwithstanding its inauspicious beginning, the trip had been a success.

Another notable appointment – not for its suitability, which was unquestioned, but for the delicacy with which it was handled at cabinet, and the ripple of amusement that it created in political circles – was made to the High Court in July 1979. The procedure for dealing with vacancies in the judiciary was that the Minister for Justice brought a name to the cabinet for approval. On this occasion the name Gerry Collins put forward was Ronan Keane. At the cabinet table a carefully choreographed discussion then took place. Jack asked if anybody had anything to say with regard to the proposed appointment, and Brian Lenihan and Michael O'Kennedy, both barristers, recommended Ronan Keane highly. Nobody expected Charlie to say anything, and he didn't, but the irony of the situation was not lost on those who at least suspected, even if they were not certain of, the relationship that existed between Ronan Keane's wife and their colleague. Brian Lenihan told me the whole story afterwards, and he extracted the maximum of innocent fun from its retelling. The scene was re-enacted time and again in the Members' Bar in Leinster House, and the tale got more exaggerated each time. Sadly, the cabinet minutes will record only the fact of the appointment, not the discussion surrounding it. They will certainly make no reference to the 'knowing' looks that were exchanged between various members, including the Taoiseach Jack Lynch.

Nothing could have prepared anybody for the traumatic and potentially disastrous events surrounding the assassination of Lord Mountbatten at Classiebawn Castle in County Sligo on 27 August 1979. Sheila and I had been in Donegal with our baby daughter,

Sinéad, and had only just arrived home when I received a call from Dan O'Sullivan to tell me the news. I was appalled and my mind went into overdrive, thinking about the implications both for Anglo-Irish relations and, more bluntly, for Lynch's and the government's reputation. Ireland was once again in the international spotlight and for the most heinous of reasons. It was left to the government to take the heat of public fury that such an event could occur in Ireland. Jack and Máirín were on holiday in Portugal at the time, and I advised Dan O'Sullivan and the Tánaiste, George Colley, that Jack should return immediately and take personal control of the situation. To our horror, Jack said that he would not break his holiday and that he would be home on the day scheduled and not before. As it happened, his return and the removal of Mountbatten's body from Ireland coincided, and we ended up with a scenario in which the Taoiseach and his wife flew into Baldonnel, changed into funereal black in the officers' mess and attended the removal ceremony within an hour. The special representative of the Queen, sent over specially to bring Mountbatten's body back to England, was the epitome of military iciness and merely inclined his head fractionally when Jack offered his own and the government's condolences for what had occurred. The officer stared at Lynch expressionlessly and never spoke. Nor did he salute, which the Irish military present interpreted as an official indication of the fury with which Mountbatten's murder had been received in both royal and British government circles. However strong the feeling, the British are nothing if not proper, and Lynch duly received an official invitation to attend the funeral in Westminster Abbey. He had no option but to attend and to adopt as stiff an upper lip as the British would have done, and did, in similar circumstances.

It was just over three years since the assassination of the British Ambassador, Sir Christopher Ewart-Biggs, as he drove from his official residence at Glencairn in south Dublin. The Irish, as far as the British were concerned, were getting a pretty bad reputation for protecting VIPs, and Lynch knew that there would be an inevitable backlash in terms of relations with the British government: it would be all the harder to loosen the stranglehold that the

Unionists had on the UK government, whatever its political hue. He should have known better than to persist in his determination to organize a meeting with Mrs Thatcher immediately after the service. Nobody could persuade him of the impracticality, politically and otherwise, of such a meeting, but once the request was made there was no going back. Downing Street had agreed to it with alarming alacrity, so it was with a sense of foreboding that we changed from our morning dress into ordinary business suits at the Irish Embassy in Grosvenor Place prior to leaving for the meeting at No. 10.

Lynch had met Thatcher only once previously. She had become Prime Minister in May 1979. There was no special relationship between them, nor was there the remotest possibility of the two developing a rapport on anything to do with the North. As far as we knew, Thatcher was an out-and-out Unionist and the Irish Republic was alien territory. Lynch and Thatcher were complete opposites. She represented the new, somewhat brash face of Conservative politics, which was characterized by an insufferable arrogance; Jack was used to relationships between British and Irish governments – particularly those of Wilson and Callaghan – operating in a more gentlemanly fashion. Mind you, he had had very difficult moments with Ted Heath, Mrs Thatcher's predecessor as leader of the Tories, who had all the hallmarks of somebody who had striven long and hard to break into the upper reaches of British society and, in trying to copy their behaviour, succeeded only in coming across as arrogant and unsympathetic.

The intelligence from the Department of Foreign Affairs had been that the meeting would be frosty, but nothing could have prepared us for the onslaught that awaited us. She was incensed that Ireland was doing nothing, in her view, to police the border between the North and the Republic; that we were refusing to extradite terrorists for crimes committed in other jurisdictions, mainly the UK; and that we were in effect harbouring and providing safe haven for murderers. Nobody in the Irish delegation was expecting a tirade of such vehemence, and Lynch, who at this stage had lost the fire in his stomach on matters of this sort, was slow to reply. Thatcher saw his silence as agreement, tacit or otherwise, with her point of view. Jack Lynch did not speak or try to interrupt Thatcher as she ploughed on with the passion and fervour for which she was famous, and neither did George Colley or Gerry Collins. Officials from the Taoiseach's Office and the Department of Foreign Affairs looked on with as much dispassion as they could muster.

I think it was at this terrible encounter that I finally realized that Jack Lynch was coasting as Taoiseach. He was far too relaxed at a meeting that he had insisted on requesting and was allowing Thatcher to overwhelm him with questionable data – everything that we had come to expect from the British propaganda machine – and the unquestionable force of her personality. It was a saddening experience. I knew, having worked as closely as I did with him for over five years, that this was a changed man. A year earlier he would never have allowed himself to be caught in – or, more accurately, invited himself into – Thatcher's web, particularly in the emotional and politically febrile circumstances surrounding the assassination of a member of the royal family. However doubtful he might have been about the sincerity of the Prime Minister's devotion to the monarchy – and some of her own supporters believed that she regarded herself as the real Queen – it was both silly and stupid to put himself into the invidious position of having to defend his government's policy on matters of such wide-ranging import. One can imagine that at their weekly meeting Mrs Thatcher left the Queen in no doubt about what she would do to the 'Teeshock' when he came around; 'filleting' is the word that comes to mind.

However, Thatcher got more than she bargained for. George Colley, sensing that Jack was not going to intervene, eventually interrupted her and, in language that surprised his own delegation, told her bluntly that she didn't know what she was talking about. The Irish side felt like cheering but maintained the tight-lipped restraint one associates with such high-level meetings. In a snappy and uncharacteristically destructive fashion, Colley laid bare the false premises underlying her arguments about extradition, in particular her snide inferences about Ireland's failure to conform with international conventions. Yet nothing would gainsay her, least of all some guy called Colley of whom she had never heard. She instructed the Secretary of the Cabinet, Sir John Hunt, to summon the Attorney-General immediately and left us to cool our heels in the cabinet room for twenty minutes. The unfortunate Attorney-General, Sir Michael Havers, arrived and was instructed by Thatcher to give the Irish delegation what amounted to a lecture on extradition. It became clear within minutes that he and the Prime Minister were not singing from the same hymn-sheet. Obviously, he had not been briefed as to the circumstances of the meeting and his views on extradition mirrored Colley's exactly. Thatcher cut him short with the inimitable words, 'Attorney, I think it is time you returned to your chambers.' That ended the matter, and the meeting, and afterwards both sides gave a very sanitized version of what had occurred.

Nothing of major importance for Anglo-Irish relations turned on these events. They certainly did not have anything like the disastrous effect of Thatcher's famous 'Out . . . out . . . out' put-down at a press conference after a meeting with Garret FitzGerald some years later. But none the less the word spread, mainly within Fianna Fáil circles, that Jack had lost his bottle. That Colley had saved the day was mentioned, but not emphasized. The embarrassing circumstances of Jack requesting the meeting and his treatment at Thatcher's hands lost nothing in the telling.

On top of all that we were in the midst of one of the most time-consuming events during the lifetime of the administration: the Pope's visit at the end of September. This was a logistical nightmare and one that brought together every element of Irish society and all arms of the state, the government, the Garda and the army, together with the corporate Catholic hierarchy and the competing interests of individual Catholic bishops throughout the country. It was a momentous occasion with a number of farcical moments – not least of which was Archbishop Marcinkus, then in charge of the Pope's security and later, infamously, in charge of the Vatican bank, minutes before the Pope's plane landed, in tones more suited to his native Chicago than to the more refined corridors of the Vatican, asking that the 'broads' be moved back from the receiving line. The 'broads' were the wives of the members of the cabinet. In retrospect I am amazed that there wasn't a row about the incident, but I suppose that even in the late 1970s the word of an archbishop still carried the force of authority. On one of his evenings in Dublin the government was invited to the Papal Nunciature to meet the Pope privately. RTÉ cameras were there to relay the beginning and end of the event, but because the Pope was running so late the studio team had to fill out the time with a lot of padding, occasionally cutting away to the scenes at the Nunciature – which were mainly shots of ministers and other leading politicians enjoying the contents of the Nunciature's ample cellars. It was only by chance that some unprepossessing incidents were not transmitted or recorded.

In the weeks leading up to the Pope's visit I began to notice that Jack was becoming testier by the day and, unlike in the year after the election, I found it increasingly difficult to engage him in discussion about matters concerning the government. There was no apparent reason for this change of temper. Yes, I knew there were rumours about his drinking, but I ignored these on the grounds that I knew that he had a tolerance for whiskey that had never interfered with his capacity to do the job. From the time I had started working for him, whenever we went away we always made sure to bring a bottle or two of Paddy. As the conversation flowed and people joined us, Jack was wont to say, 'Let's see if we can get below Thurles' – a reference to the map of Ireland on the label. Any night he got below Thurles was a good night. It was obvious that a destabilization campaign of a very personal nature, which both of us had discussed and dismissed previously, was under way.

However understandable it was, it was still discomforting to experience Jack's new mood and it took me a while to adapt. While in the Nunciature awaiting the Pope's arrival from Drogheda, I was approached by a journalist requesting a comment from the Taoiseach about the Pope's plea to the IRA – 'on my knees' – to lay down its arms. I found Lynch, who was in the company of two other cabinet ministers, and put the journalist's request to him. Jack bared his teeth and told me not only to tell him to 'fuck off' but to 'fuck off yourself'. George Colley, one of the ministers present, looked as shocked as I felt. Thereafter I maintained a discreet distance from the man with whom I was supposed to be working closely, and with whom I reportedly had an almost father–son relationship.

When working with Jack you realized soon enough that nobody was indispensable, and I was ever conscious of the fact that this was the man who, in the middle of the night, had sacked two senior ministers and walked through a wall of fire for months afterwards in dealing with the consequences. Jack knew that I had developed a very good rapport with the press, and, despite occasional rows and a few own goals, he, and consequently the government, was held in as much regard by the media as any Taoiseach and government could be after two years in office. But I didn't take anything for granted. I discussed the matter with George Colley, who assured me that I was wrong to worry and that Jack had too much on his mind to be concerned with the niceties of our professional relationship. George said that I should just continue to do what I was doing and that the temporary difficulty would pass. To a large extent he was right. Jack was not one to hold a grudge – no more than the normal accepted standards of politicians, that is – and as time moved on the relationship became a little warmer. But somehow we never recovered the intimacy that had been there from 1974 onwards.

Shortly after the Pope's visit, Jack and I were thrown together in circumstances that neither of us could have imagined. He called me into his office one afternoon and told me that he had just got off the phone with the President, Paddy Hillery, who had sought his advice about going public regarding rumours circulating about his marriage. Neither Lynch nor I had heard anything about these rumours, although in retrospect both of us realized that we had been blindsided by our involvement in the preparations for the Pope's visit. Apparently, there was a story circulating in the British tabloid press about alleged difficulties in the President's marriage and the name of a female Italian Eurocrat, who had worked with

Hillery when he had been Ireland's Commissioner in Brussels, was being linked with his. The Irish media, in fairness to them, not only refused to touch it as a story but dismissed it completely as unworthy of their interest. Whatever happened between the Pope's visit and Hillery's call to Jack Lynch must have convinced the President that he had to act. I was appalled at the prospect of the President issuing a statement denying that there was a problem with his marriage. I strongly advised against any such initiative. Lynch tried Hillery on the secure private line to the Áras but it was engaged.

I went back to my office, and an hour or so later Lynch called me again to say that Hillery was determined and had already made arrangements for a press conference at the Áras that evening. An element of farce now entered into the situation. The President thought that if he was going to hold a press conference, the only appropriate people to do it with were the editors of the national dailies and the head of news at RTÉ. They were duly summoned and, to their amazement, were confronted by a President willing to talk about the strength of his marriage and to deny any rumours to the contrary. To buy time the editors went through the motions of asking what rumours he was talking about. They said that if the President wanted to persist with the story, the people he ought to speak to were the political correspondents. One of them rang me and asked if I knew anything about it. Off the record I confirmed that I knew what was afoot, as did the Taoiseach, and that both of us had strongly advised against Dr Hillery's course of action. So even before the press briefing began the detail of the story was in circulation, albeit on a restricted basis, and there was little, if anything, that the President could do other than to say that his marriage was stable.

The political correspondents duly arrived at the Áras and were briefed by the President. During the course of the meeting, he excused himself to take a call from his wife, Maeve, who was abroad at the time. Hardened as they were by the rough and tumble of political coverage, the 'pol corrs' (as they are colloquially known) none the less found the experience excruciatingly embarrassing and one of them tried to talk the President out of his course of action.

But it was to no avail and the country tuned into the nine o'clock news that evening to hear that the President, Dr Hillery, had announced that there was no difficulty with his marriage. The obvious response was 'Who said there was anything wrong with his marriage?' and even more ironically, 'What difficulties?' Only people whose taste ran to trash journalism would make any connection between the presidential statement and a story, 'The Crucifixion of Paddy Hillery', that had appeared some time before in a British Sunday tabloid. Members of Hillery's extended family were unaware of his intentions to make a statement and were as shocked and surprised as the rest of the country. The net result of the statement was that people, including members of the media, began paying more attention to the President and his wife than they would have welcomed. The incident was particularly surprising in that Hillery, when in government as Minister for Foreign Affairs and in Brussels as Commissioner, was considered to be a safe pair of hands and shrewd enough to know when to speak and when to stay silent. His isolation in the Áras, and his understandable desire to counteract a painful rumour, however limited its circulation, had obviously clouded his judgement in this instance.

While it is easy to see bad judgement in another, it is sometimes impossible to see it in oneself. So it was that Jack Lynch's final months were filled with anxiety. It is always difficult for a leader of a political party, particularly one who also happens to be head of government, to make the right call about his or her departure. They invariably get it wrong. Some attempt to influence the succession in the mistaken belief that their legacy can be preserved and protected only by somebody of their personal choice. Invariably they get this wrong too, and the usual outcome is chaos accompanied by bitterness and recriminations. Jack couldn't see this and I probably didn't see it in those clinical terms either. But I did know that groups of back benchers were meeting and discussing their futures under Jack. The identities of those gathering late at night in Dublin hotels were known. The fact that most, but by no means all, of them were from the new intake of TDs was also known.

Lynch asked me if I knew anything about these meetings, and, after I told him the little I knew, he asked me to keep my ear to the ground. Given that in the minds of TDs I was part of the Lynch entourage, the likelihood of my being told anything of importance was very remote. But I promised to report back if I heard anything of substance. However, I knew that he wouldn't like to hear the back benchers' views in graphic detail, and we never spoke about the matter again until he raised it at an important tête-à-tête in Boston in November.

In an attempt to keep up with what was happening, I spoke briefly to Charlie McCreevy, who was a fervent admirer of Charlie Haughey. McCreevy said, quite straightforwardly, that the Lynch era was over and that the only task remaining was to bury it. I had known McCreevy in UCD when he was doing accountancy at night, and he and I had mutual friends. He was then, and is now, very personable and likeable and it was probably these endearing characteristics that made him add a rider: 'But don't worry, Frank, we'll keep you.' When I inquired as to whom he meant by 'we' he just laughed and walked away. Unfortunately, in the autumn of '79 McCreevy did not display the courage he was to show subsequently in speaking out no matter how it might affect his own fortunes. It is to his shame he did not do the brave thing and say publicly that it was time for Jack to go. Apart from one man, Pádraig Flynn, none of the people who were conspiring with him at that time did so either, which is to their individual and collective shame. It was largely as a result of Jack Lynch's popularity and his public reputation that these new TDs had been elected. But, as is often said about political life, eaten bread is soon forgotten and this was certainly the case in this instance.

I approached Colley, to get his read on the situation. He told me that while he was worried that Jack was letting things slip, he had not spoken to him and would not speak to him, for fear of being suspected of trying to push matters beyond their natural political progression. I warned Colley that Jack was indeed letting things slip and that if someone didn't take matters in hand, there would be chaos in the government of the country. Colley knew what I was intimating, but he just smiled and said that he would prefer to let matters take their course. Meanwhile, Charlie Haughey and I had a number of discussions as to when Lynch might retire. Without having any particular insight into what Lynch was thinking, I knew that he was shrewd enough to know that whoever succeeded him would need a good two years to bed himself in and to stamp his authority and personality on the party before the next general election. Charlie said that the natives were getting very restless and that hardly a day passed when he wasn't asked to act. I cautioned restraint and Haughey agreed but said – ominously – that he could not be held responsible for the actions of others. Given the air of general unrest, both the timing and opportunity were right for a succession battle.

In November Jack went to the US in what was to become his last visit abroad as Taoiseach. The trip was an official one, at the invitation of the White House, and had been organized by Seán Donlon. It included a meeting in the Oval Office with President Jimmy Carter. One of the key considerations in Jack's act of faith in appointing Donlon was his belief that Donlon could access, infiltrate even, the senior ranks of the American administration and provide a counterbalance to the almost umbilical relationship between Pennsylvania Avenue and No. 10 Downing Street or, more crucially, between the State Department and the Foreign Office. That the visit was taking place at all was evidence enough for Lynch that Donlon had caused a welcome shift in the attitude of the Irish Embassy in Washington. Prior to his arrival it had been content to confine itself to a traditional and relatively superficial approach to Irish diplomacy. Its efforts were described, mockingly, both by the British and by the more forward-thinking young Turks recruited during Garret FitzGerald's tenure at the Department of Foreign Affairs, as 'St Patrick's Day syndrome'. They were dying to get their teeth into diplomacy of a more aggressive kind than had been practised heretofore.

As events turned out, the government was faced with two by-elections in Cork in the run-up to the trip and polling took place on the day we left for America. This meant of course that we would be out of the country when the results were announced, something that was to have a crucial bearing on what occurred in the following weeks. The Irish party arrived in Newport News in Connecticut for a one-night stopover prior to the official visit commencing in Washington the following day. At breakfast, American time, I received a phone call from the Taoiseach's Private Secretary, Brian McCarthy, to say that he had been in contact with his deputy, Seán Alyward, in Dublin and that the news about the by-elections was not good. This was civil service code language for disaster. I asked him to get more information and to call me back in ten minutes. Meanwhile I tracked down Michael Mills, who was amongst the political correspondents accompanying us, to find out what information he had on the results. My worst fears were confirmed. The government had lost both by-elections. This was bad in its own right. That both had been in Cork, the heartland of Jack Lynch's support base, had ominous implications not only for the government as a whole but for Jack Lynch's reputation and standing as Taoiseach in particular. The sands were beginning to move under our feet. Brian McCarthy was anxious to know who was going to tell the Taoiseach the bad news. I told him that I would talk to the Minister for Foreign Affairs, Michael O'Kennedy, who was travelling with us. Michael was not keen to be the messenger and eventually I rang the Taoiseach in his room and said that I wanted to speak to him immediately. Shrewd man that he was, he asked, 'How bad is it?' His instincts had told him during the campaigning that things were not right and he suspected that he might lose one of the by-elections. He never imagined that he would lose both.

As calmly as we could, we agreed a short statement to be issued on his behalf in Dublin and carried on with the preparation for the official welcoming ceremony at the White House scheduled for a few hours later. But we both knew that there was no turning back now and in effect the initiative had been wrenched from Lynch's hands. Until the by-elections he had had the opportunity of revealing his intentions about how much longer he was going to remain as Taoiseach and leader of Fianna Fáil. He passed on that opportunity, and from the moment of the results he was in a downward spiral that he could not control. Outwardly he maintained his characteristic bonhomie and gentlemanly demeanour, but privately he was seething. How he managed to carry on with the engagements scheduled, in the full knowledge that they were probably the last official functions that he would attend as Taoiseach, I don't know.

At the White House we were accorded the full ceremonial welcome on the White House lawn and proceeded from there for refreshments with the President, his wife Roslyn and members of his cabinet. Afterwards Máirín Lynch and Breda O'Kennedy accompanied the First Lady on a tour of the White House while I had a meeting with my counterpart, Jody Powell, the President's Press Secretary. When we had agreed on the text of what we would say to the media at the end of the meeting between the President and the Taoiseach, we indulged in a relaxed chat about the relative ups and downs of being a press secretary. Powell couldn't get over the fact that we only had six journalists travelling with us. By his reckoning, six reporters would accompany the town dog-catcher on his rounds back in his home state of Georgia. He thought I had a doddle of a job. I refrained from telling him that the six who were accompanying us would probably eat twenty American journalists for breakfast.

What he had to say next astounded me. Apparently the President was looking forward to impressing the Prime Minister – he couldn't pronounce 'Taoiseach' – and the Irish delegation with the depth of his knowledge and understanding of the situation in Northern Ireland. Being a Southerner, the President believed it was common courtesy to his guests to show as much knowledge as possible about his visitor's country, no matter how small. I knew that Donlon had flooded the White House with briefing material, but even Donlon couldn't have anticipated that the President would stay up half the night reading this, together with the documentation from the State Department, so as to present himself in the most informed light. Powell confirmed to me that this was normal practice for Carter and that he did this regularly in advance of meeting foreign heads of state and government. I managed to get a quiet word with Jack before the meeting began and told him that Carter was determined to show off his knowledge and therefore he should give him a free rein. Jack, showing an understandable scepticism, said that he would wait and see how knowledgeable the President actually was; previous American presidents had not been known for their grasp of Irish affairs.

But we were all in for a surprise. After the usual diplomatic courtesies were over, Carter began and gave a hugely detailed and knowledgeable overview of his understanding of the problems of Northern Ireland. He got the names right. He got the dates right. He got the history right. We could only marvel at his capacity to master such a complicated brief. We wondered what Jack could say in response that could add anything to this man's encyclopedic knowledge and the answer was nothing. Jack contented himself with complimenting the President on his comprehensive presentation and appealed to him to act in whatever way he could to curb the activities of Noraid, a front for the IRA. The President made the usual diplomatic noises – we didn't expect him to do anything else about Noraid – and we went on our merry way to the rest of our engagements on the trip, with the help of Air Force Two, which the President put at our disposal. Later, in New York, we would be confronted by Congressman Mario Biaggi, who was a Republican sympathizer and outspoken critic of both the British and Irish governments, and something of a thorn in the sides of Irish diplomats in America.

Whenever the Taoiseach or a senior minister visited America, it was normal for the heads of the semi-state organizations with offices in the US to meet him and brief him on whatever developments they thought of value to the employment prospects for Ireland. Such a meeting was organized for Chicago. It was to be followed immediately by a briefing session between the Taoiseach and senior editorial writers from some of the major media outlets in the region. A few of the heads of the US-based semi-state organizations remained on for the briefing session. There was some embarrassment when Jack became totally confused about several of the statistics that he had been provided with to highlight the positive elements of the Irish economy. This was completely out of character for him and he apologized afterwards for having to seek guidance in response to direct questions from already well-informed opinion writers. While it was unnecessary for him to do so, he apologized to me saying that he was exhausted and really ought not to have agreed to the arrangement in the first instance.

Matters, however, were to get far worse and once again it was proved, if proof was necessary, how difficult it is for the leader of a government to control events at home when on the other side of the world. We were to find out how important this was as we flew down to Texas. Word came through that Charlie Haughey had made a speech in which he had, by implication, praised Pádraic Pearse's belief in the nobility of the blood sacrifice and, by further implication, left his position on government policy hanging dangerously. Jack and Máirín, Michael and Breda O'Kennedy, Seán Donlon and his wife, and the American Ambassador to Ireland, Bill Shannon, and his wife, were sitting together in the forward cabin and Ted Smyth of the Irish Consulate and I were together some distance away. The political correspondents were also on the plane. Drafting a response to a speech made by a minister while flying at 32,000 feet above Texas was neither easy nor pleasant when realizing, as we all did, that the screw was being turned relentlessly and that regardless of the response the pressure would continue to mount on what was a dying leadership.

The response was robust and blunt: the sentiments expressed by the Minister for Health in his speech did not reflect government policy and the latter, in respect of matters to do with Northern Ireland, was the preserve of the Taoiseach. Crucially Charlie was asked to disavow the implications of what he allegedly had said and to publicly acknowledge that he supported the collective government's stand on Northern Irish policy.

The political correspondents were agog with a new controversy and when we landed in Austin everybody scurried to the nearest telephone. I rang Charlie and told him the contents of the Taoiseach's statement. His response was characteristic. 'Fuck him,

Frank, he's finished. Tell him to come home and see for himself the mess he's left the party in.' I asked what exactly Charlie was going to do and he told me that there was nothing in the speech that he had delivered that in any way contravened government policy and that he would say so publicly. 'After that, it's out of my hands.' I pleaded with him to wait before doing anything precipitous, but he said that things were moving too fast to stop and that neither he nor Lynch could control events any longer. I didn't believe this for one minute and said so. Charlie didn't like anybody crossing him, particularly in circumstances where he had set out on a particular course of action. I didn't know what he was up to, but I had a fairly good idea, and I said that my impression was that Jack would very shortly indicate his intentions. We finished the conversation with Charlie asking if I could ascertain a date for Lynch's departure and I undertook to do this – more in the hope of deterring him from doing anything in our absence than in providing him with further ammunition in furtherance of his campaign to become leader of Fianna Fáil and Taoiseach as quickly as possible.

There is no doubt that a campaign of destabilization was in train. But where were the Lynch men – Colley, Collins, Faulkner, O'Donoghue? They either knew what was going on and were refusing to take a stand, or they were so politically obtuse that they didn't, or couldn't, read the signals. The latter is an unimaginable scenario. In effect, they were in shock after the results of the by-elections. They didn't want to face up to the fact that the end-game was in play – it was too troublesome to contemplate – so they refused to take a position about what was happening. Had George Colley made a stand at the time of the by-election results, he could have rallied crucial support – support that would have reduced the margin of error significantly in any impending leadership battle. But Colley remained aloof and, tragically for him, took the size of his support base for granted. He should have known that he needed every vote if he was to come close to beating the relentless campaigning that Charlie had been conducting – or had had conducted on his behalf – over the previous twelve months.

In America a dangerous calm descended and the official visit proceeded without further incident until we arrived back in Washington, where Jack was due to speak at a lunchtime meeting of the National Press Club. This took the form of a brief address by the guest speaker, followed by half a dozen questions drawn at random from a box placed in front of the chairman of the event. Dermot Nally, his main adviser on the North as well as much else besides, who was an expert when it came to nuanced language, was sitting beside him and I sat beside Nally. By now Lynch could give a speech about Ireland, and particularly Northern Ireland, with his eyes shut; he had been doing it two or three times a day for the previous ten days. After his speech the first three questions drawn from the box were innocuous enough and were dealt with easily. There then followed a question that nobody, least of all Lynch, expected. Did Jack Lynch agree that the British Army should be allowed to indulge in 'hot pursuit' into the independent territory of the Republic of Ireland on the basis of suspicion of terrorist involvement of those being pursued? That was the question.

Now, it had been quietly agreed by the two governments that while the Irish Army and the Garda would patrol the Southern side of the border, the British Army would patrol from the air and would communicate with the Irish authorities if they suspected that an individual or vehicle had crossed from North to South in suspicious circumstances. The fact of the matter was that the British would operate an air patrol whether the Irish government agreed to it or not. Dermot Nally was taping the session, and when I replayed it immediately after the lunch Nally could clearly be heard saying 'Oh shit!' as Jack Lynch began to reply to the question. Jack confirmed that the Irish government had given its approval to the British authorities to fly over the border in circumstances where suspected terrorists were involved. Dermot Nally vainly attempted to pass a note to Lynch to help him put matters in context, but either Jack was too tired or couldn't care less, and he ignored the note and persisted with his answer. I can still see the expressions of shock and amazement on the faces of Michael Mills of the *Irish Press* and Chris Glennon of the *Irish Independent* as they listened to what, to them, was hot news.

As we travelled back to our hotel afterwards, there was total silence in the car until eventually Lynch looked at me and said, 'I think we're in a bit of trouble.' I agreed and advised that he ought to arrange to meet the journalists travelling with us immediately to try to recover matters as best we could. He refused.

The government was left in the sticky situation of admitting that either collectively or through the Taoiseach it had colluded with the British authorities regarding a fundamental issue of Republican ideology: the invasion of national territory in pursuit of those whom the *British* authorities believed to be involved in terrorist activities. The reality was that security services on both sides knew that there were hundreds and hundreds of incursions each year. But the crucially significant factor was that an Irish government had agreed to trust the British authorities and to accept their bona fides. The notion of 'hot pursuit' was alien to Fianna Fáil's Republican tenets and unsavoury in the eyes of the Irish public generally. (Less important politically, but probably equally humiliating for the departments of Foreign Affairs and Justice, was that the disclosure seriously undermined the British authorities' confidence in their Irish counterparts to maintain confidentiality regarding security issues.)

And so began a messy episode in Fianna Fáil's history when the back bencher Dr Bill Loughnane publicly called for the Taoiseach's resignation on foot of his admission that he and the government had given the British permission to enter Irish sovereign territory in hot pursuit of alleged terrorists. Lynch's supporters were slow to rouse themselves – which was a message in itself – and when they did express their outrage at Loughnane's audacity a motion was placed on the agenda of the parliamentary party to have the party whip removed from the Clare TD. The motion was instigated by Colley, who, belatedly, decided to show some leadership. It was defeated. Those who had any political instincts at all knew immediately that Jack's course was run and that the time to hand on the baton had finally come. All that was required was a decision as to the timing. The failure of the motion also threw the party's fault-lines into stark relief. That Colley, Lynch's putative successor, had been embarrassingly defeated in his attempts to discipline a back bench TD provided Haughey's supporters with a golden opportunity to highlight his supposed lack of fitness for the job. An earthquake was in the offing.

By this time I knew Lynch's intentions. Over late-night drinks in the Parker House Hotel in Boston, after Máirín had gone to bed, he had told me that he was going to resign early in the New Year. When I pressed him, he said that he would be announcing his resignation as Taoiseach and leader of Fianna Fáil in the first week of January. Without saying so directly, he intimated that the decision was as much Máirín's as his. He wanted me to know because he could not forecast what was going to happen and I might want to make arrangements for my future. I thanked him for telling me and we went on to discuss the various options available to the party after he resigned. He was wary of talking about Haughey's prospects, but it was obvious that he was fully aware of the challenge that George Colley faced. However, he believed that in the end Haughey would lose out and that that would put a stop to his leadership ambitions once and for all. While I had no special insight into what might happen, I knew that Charlie would move heaven and earth to win and I said as much to Jack. His only comment was 'We'll see.' We agreed to disagree. I had the distinct feeling that Jack believed – because of his innate decency – that what he saw as the forces for good within Fianna Fáil would ultimately triumph over what his more avid supporters seemed to regard as the forces of evil, and that when TDs came to vote for his successor they would resist the temptation to do what was in their own personal interest and vote for the greater good of the party and the country as a whole. I resisted the temptation to tell him that politics had moved on, that he was representative of a generation of politicians in danger of extinction, and that a new breed of political animal had come on the scene – one that would stop at nothing in the pursuit of ambition and for whom party allegiance meant far less than it had to those who had gone before them.

The morning after that conversation I phoned Charlie Haughey and tried to impress on him the need to wait for matters to take their course. I told him of Jack's impending announcement and imminent retirement. He wouldn't believe me. He thought it was a ruse on my part and, such was the level of suspicion that pervaded senior levels of government and Fianna Fáil, I can't say I blamed him.

We ended our American visit in New York. By then, because the reporting of the events at the National Press Club lunch had led directly to the political crisis at home, the relationship between the official party – Jack, Michael O'Kennedy, Seán Donlon and Dermot Nally – and the accompanying journalists had soured. It was a classic example of politicians in difficulty blaming the messenger. Once again, and, as it turned out, for the last time, Jack became vicious with me and took out all his frustrations in a vehement attack, witnessed by Michael O'Kennedy, in which he castigated my 'friends in the media'. The upshot was that the political correspondents – Michael Mills, Chris Glennon, Liam O'Neill, Dick Walsh and Seán Duignan of RTÉ – were invited to the Taoiseach's suite for an end-of-tour briefing. I knew what was in the offing and I warned both Mills and Glennon in advance. The spectacle that followed was not pleasant. Jack did his reputation no good by attacking the men for their reporting and virtually accused them of treasonous behaviour. They were incensed and their anger was further increased when they realized that I was taping the briefing. Matters deteriorated sharply and they left in high dudgeon. Jack was quite pleased with himself and remarked sarcastically that he had probably undone years of good work by me, adding, 'I couldn't care less, Frank. They deserve to be told a few unwelcome facts now and again.'

I knew that it would take me some time to repair matters with the pol corrs but I also knew that, deep down in himself, Jack was fully aware of how wrong he was and that he was merely attempting to transfer blame for his own shortcomings on to the press with whom he had had a love–hate relationship since returning to office in 1977. He viewed certain sections of the media as having sold their soul to the coalition in the 1973–7 period and believed that any criticism of him or his government – especially when all the pol corrs had predicted that the coalition would be returned to office – was tinged with an element of sour grapes. The issue was far more complicated than that, but Lynch was in no mood for any generous interpretation of the motives of the Irish media. We began the long journey home in the knowledge that a chapter was about to be closed.

7. Charlie takes over

Even though we had been away for only ten days, it seemed like a lifetime. Those who met us at Dublin Airport appeared nervous and did that thing that politicians do when their minds are elsewhere or they are not being entirely straightforward: talked at us incessantly without ever making eye contact. It was obvious that TDs and ministers were there only out of a sense of duty; and the sooner they could get away, the better. It was as if people weren't sure whether they should be seen with a man whose career they knew was over and whether their presence might adversely affect their prospects under a new regime. The scene was redolent of all that was hypocritical and hollow about political life. Here was a man who had led his party to historic victory in a general election two years previously but who, by virtue of infelicity of language and events over which he could not possibly have had complete control, was now injured. The law of the jungle applied: the wounded animal was deserted and left to die alone and in isolation. While some of the senior ministers were polite enough to go through the motions of asking me about the American trip, the remainder displayed no such sensitivity and plunged straight into demands for details about Jack's immediate intentions.

Like the rest of the returning party I was exhausted. All I wanted to do was go home to bed, recharge the batteries and enter the fray refreshed. Knowing the party as intimately as I did, over the previous few months I had come to the conclusion that Charlie Haughey had enough support amongst the back benchers to win a leadership race. Early on I had decided that I was going to adopt the attitude of the bystander: I knew nothing and I was saying nothing. But when it came to the crunch, I didn't have the willpower to stay out of it. When I had been talking with Charlie from the States, he asked me to go to see him in Kinsaley after I returned. In spite of my resolution not to become involved, I agreed – partly because I couldn't resist the opportunity for intrigue, but mainly because I wanted to maintain my good relations with the man I believed would be the next leader of Fianna Fáil. So, despite the exhaustion, within hours of arriving back I was lodged in Charlie's study in Kinsaley. He was in buoyant mood. He firmly believed he was on the cusp of success. He wanted to know everything. What was Lynch's mood? When exactly would he make the announcement? How did I think he would behave during the leadership election? Would he take sides publicly? Did he really think that Colley could make it? Wasn't O'Malley his real choice? And so on and so on. He was like a man possessed, but it was no more than I expected after getting to know him over the previous years. Once he set out to achieve something, nothing, but nothing, would stop him, and the level of detail that he went into was staggering – right down to individual back bench TDs' preferences in food and drink. Nothing was left to chance. I pitied the amateurish approach George Colley and his supporters had taken, but I imagined that when they saw what they were up against, once the leadership election was announced, they would change their tactics. I should have dreamt on.

After our arrival home, purely by force of circumstance, I had little contact with Lynch. There was a lot to catch up on and no need for either of us to bother the other with matters that were not crucial to the operation of government. I did wonder, fleetingly, if Lynch was shutting me out. Certainly the episode in the hotel in New York had been distressing, but, having considered it on the flight home, I realized that Lynch must have been under enormous pressure and was probably in turmoil as he reflected on how his place in Irish political life was ending. I was just a target in his sights and there was probably nothing personal in it. Frankly, I still felt a residual resentment, especially when I thought about the sacrifices I had made in his and the party's interests over the past five years. There was one compensation: since I had had the foresight to have myself appointed to the public service, no matter what happened I was an established civil servant and could not be sacked. However inequitable such a process was – and it is no longer possible to make a permanent appointment to the civil service in the public interest – it provided me, newly married and with a young daughter, with a certain comfort as I watched, part bystander, part participant, the convulsions within the ranks of Fianna Fáil.

My suspicion that Lynch had decided to freeze me out of his inner circle in the last days of his administration was increased when, on the Wednesday after our return, his Private Secretary, Brian McCarthy, called me to say that later that morning he would have a statement by the Taoiseach for me to issue to the media. This was the first time Lynch had behaved in this way; normally I would either draft statements for him or he would pass his own drafts to me for suggested amendments. Shortly after the parliamentary party meeting began, I issued the statement that Jack Lynch was resigning as leader of Fianna Fáil and as Taoiseach. The announcement began two of the most difficult and pressurized days of my life in politics. It also began a series of events – some of which I would prefer to blot completely from my mind – that would be seared into the consciousness of those involved and would indelibly colour the careers of certain politicians for ever.

Around the time I gave Jack's statement to the media, an announcement came out of the parliamentary party meeting that the election of the new leader, and consequently a new Taoiseach, would take place at noon the following Friday, 7 December 1979. And so after all the rumour, the conniving, the caucus meetings, the deliberate campaign of innuendo, the hopes, the fears, the intrigue, the ineptitude of some and the clever manipulation of others, it was over. There were no fancy speeches. No fanfares. No eulogies. The end was matter-of-fact, pedestrian even. Now there was other business to be done. *The King is dead, long live the King*, so to speak – except they had to choose the King. Realizing that their day had come, the back benchers couldn't get out of the room quickly enough, and each campaign manager – a grandiose title for some of those concerned – set about getting as many commitments as possible for his candidate. Given that everybody knew that there would be only two candidates, the task wasn't going to be all that difficult – or so some people thought. I was a civil servant and should have had nothing whatever to do with Fianna Fáil party matters, but it was hard to kill old habits. I maintained as discreet a profile as I could and kept out of the media spotlight as far as possible.

Charlie lost no time whatsoever. There was an immediate announcement that he would be a candidate and that his 'good friend' Ray MacSharry would be proposing him. This was a signal to the back benchers. Ray was a minister, albeit a junior one, and popular. For some of them he epitomized what could be achieved in political life: he left school in his early teens and had suffered financial difficulties in his business due to a combination of events in Northern Ireland and his involvement in politics. Now he was in a position to propose Charlie Haughey as the next leader of Fianna Fáil and to expect that if Haughey won he would be in a senior cabinet position. The corresponding announcement from George Colley's side said only that he would be a candidate.

Within minutes of the parliamentary party meeting breaking up, I met Dessie O'Malley on the main stairs leading to the Dáil chamber and he invited me to a party in his home in Rathmines that night. I thanked him and went about my business. Early in the evening I had a drink with the political correspondents, who were anxious to mend fences after the incident in the hotel in New York. Then I went home and found a note from Sheila telling me that Dessie had rung wondering where I was. I had completely forgotten about his party and I wasn't particularly anxious, having arrived home, to drive back into the city from County Meath. I phoned him to apologize for not turning up and told him I was home and probably wouldn't make it to Rathmines. I felt that I ought not to be there, but I didn't say that to him. My instinct seemed justified when, having urged me to change my mind, he ended the call by saying that if I decided to come after all I should be careful when I arrived because there were reporters outside. When I heard that the press were camped outside his house, I knew that Dessie's was definitely not the place for me that evening. I contented myself with returning the numerous phone calls from reporters doing stories about Jack's resignation and the leadership race. I went to bed early and forgot about the matter.

It was only as I listened to the early news bulletins the following morning that I realized how lucky I had been. A reporter from RTÉ had either been tipped off about Dessie's party or had heard about it by accident, and decided that there might be something newsworthy afoot. She drove to O'Malley's house and watched the arrival of a succession of senior politicians and party officials. When Sylvie Barrett started to go through the wrong gateway, the helpful reporter pointed him in the right direction. She asked how often he visited the O'Malley household. 'Regularly,' he said. She wondered why, then, he was going into the wrong house. The comedy continued as politicians, including George Colley, Séamus Brennan and John Wilson, arrived or left. They were asked what the meeting was about. All professed merely to be attending a very pleasant social get-together in their friend Dessie's house, and, as if to prove the point, Séamus presented himself to the RTÉ reporter while eating a canapé. She didn't buy the politicians' story and portrayed the gathering as a meeting of George Colley's campaign managers and chief supporters. It was a PR disaster. (Incidentally, the reporter was Yvonne Murphy, now a judge, who is married to another judge, Adrian Hardiman, a member of the Supreme Court, who was a major supporter of Dessie O'Malley's Progressive Democrats in the mid eighties – which just goes to show how small is the world of Irish media and politics.)

Had I attended this party, I would have been destroyed. Apart from the fact that there would have been serious questions asked about a senior civil servant, albeit one with a very distinct political background, attending what was in effect a party-political gathering, the mind boggles as to what the Haughey camp would have made of it. When he heard of the imbroglio, Haughey described it as the dead attending their own wake in advance of their deaths being announced. The intriguing thing about this somewhat innocuous incident is that afterwards O'Malley appeared to believe that not only had I snubbed his soirée but also, and even worse, that I might have had something to do with the media hearing about it and that I had, in the interests of the Haughey camp, tipped off Yvonne Murphy or had someone else tip her off. This was not the case. It was to colour our relationship for ever more.

As the rival campaigns started, the central issue was very basic: back benchers wanted a leader whose face they could use on election posters and who would give them some hope of being re-elected. While they had discarded Jack Lynch as yesterday's man, those who thought in any way deeply about the matter knew that Jack's face on the 1977 election literature had been as reassuring to voters as their wild promises had been alluring. They wanted to make sure that the new leader would have the same impact in their own constituencies. And that was their main concern: their individual prospects in their own backyards. Not those of their colleagues, no matter how close. Not whether the government would be re-elected. (Thus the notion put abroad subsequent to the election, that TDs voted for either Colley or Haughey because they thought one was more Republican than the other, is complete piffle.)

If they had only descended from the moral high ground for long enough to understand the back benchers' fears and their rather crude way of seeing things, then Colley and his team might have made a greater effort to win the leadership. There is no question but that his campaign was amateurish in the extreme. It epitomized an attitude then prevalent amongst some senior ministers – Colley himself, O'Malley, Gibbons, Faulkner and Collins – that back bench TDs would vote for Colley out of deference, almost from a sense of being honoured to do so. Nobody can say that if a different campaign had been conducted, the result would have been different, but certainly the margin of Charlie's win – six votes – might have been tighter if George had taken greater personal command of his campaign team and deployed some of them somewhat differently, or indeed, not deployed them at all. While there was sympathy for George's difficult task in managing the economy in difficult circumstances, there was none for his main canvasser, Martin O'Donoghue, who was blamed for creating those circumstances. There is no question but that O'Donoghue was demonized by the Haughey side. Admittedly this was relatively easy: he was not a natural politician and nothing proved this more conclusively than his attempts to get back bench TDs to vote for George.

While George may have found it difficult to empathize with the more elemental aspects of political life – he was never one to carouse in the Members' Bar – he should have known that a personal approach to the TDs would have been well received. Those who knew him found him extremely courteous and engaging but he didn't make conversation easily. He wasn't one for *bonhomie* nor someone who developed casual friendships. This wasn't because he was afraid to or because he was suspicious of those around him; he simply had a natural reserve that was slightly at odds with the hail-fellow-well-met rough and tumble of politics, especially Fianna Fáil politics. Notwithstanding this reserve, George was respected for his independence and integrity, and I rarely heard him indulge in any really critical remarks about his colleagues. Such was his personality, and his misunderstanding of the needs of back benchers, that he had decided that others would canvass on his behalf. It was a big mistake.

On the other hand, Charlie's campaign was carefully calibrated. I was in his ministerial room in Leinster House the evening before the vote. Johnny Callanan, a TD from Galway, knocked on his door and came in. Charlie put a forefinger to his lips to tell me to stay quiet and he listened as Johnny told him about his overtures to Máire Geoghegan-Quinn. This was fascinating to me because, as I have already mentioned, I had been amongst those who had encouraged Geoghegan-Quinn to run for her father's Galway West seat after he died in 1975. She had been active with her father in the constituency and was a fluent Irish speaker. Jack had heard her at meetings in the Gaeltacht during the previous general election and was greatly impressed. After the funeral there was lunch in the Geoghegan house and everybody was polite enough to avoid the question of who would stand in the impending by-election. Being young – barely out of her teens – at that time Máire was far more reserved than she subsequently became, but it was obvious that she was eager to stand and only needed the nod from the local organization and party HQ. As we made to leave, I said to her that we would be talking to her again very shortly and I wished her well. She was clearly pleased that somebody from Dublin would allude, however indirectly, to the possibility of her being the candidate. She was aware, however, that the main man in the constituency at the time was Bobby Molloy who had been Minister for Local Government in Jack's last administration. She knew that if he went against her she would have no chance. But Bobby got the message – Máire was Lynch's favoured candidate – and she was duly selected, and elected. Despite the fact that there was ample room in the constituency for two Fianna Fáil TDs, a strong rivalry developed between them and they were never very friendly, a condition that seems to afflict TDs who share a party and a constituency.

Callanan told Charlie that Geoghegan-Quinn was coming under severe pressure from some of the Colley supporters in the constituency, particularly Bobby Molloy's people, but wanted to vote for him. Johnny undertook to keep up the pressure on behalf of Charlie and to report with any further news. When Callanan left, Haughey said that Máire was only playing the odds to see if she would be offered anything. It was known that she was very ambitious and a highly capable infighter when it came to survival in a predominantly male bastion. She was odds-on for a senior post not only because of her undoubted ability but also because she was a woman; there were so few women in Fianna Fáil at a high level that one of any intelligence was virtually guaranteed preferment. I'm pretty certain that in the end Geoghegan-Quinn opted for George Colley, and, if she didn't, she made a good job of convincing his supporters that she had done so. That Charlie elevated her to full cabinet rank in a subsequent government revived the suspicions of those who were unsure of her loyalties, particularly her rival, the strongly anti-Haughey Bobby Molloy.

Around midnight the night before the leadership vote, Jack and I had a conversation during which we arranged to meet in Leinster House the next morning. Jack had rung me at home and the conversation was much in the spirit of the thousands of calls we had made to each other over the past five years – friendly, open and completely relaxed. He asked what I thought the outcome would be. I didn't tell him that I had a bet with some of the political correspondents that Charlie would win. I just said that it was going to be tight and that, at that stage, the advantage, however slight, was with the Haughey side. Jack said, in the classic de Valera mode of speech that he adopted from time to time, 'That's not what I'm being told.' I said that it depended on who was telling him and he replied, 'George and Martin.' I resisted the temptation to tell him about the reception Martin O'Donoghue had received from some back bench TDs in the party rooms on the fifth floor of Leinster House that very afternoon: they were politely silent while he was present but vocally dismissive as soon as he left the room. Jack became a little more insistent and wanted my actual call on the outcome. And so, twelve hours before the vote took place, I told the Taoiseach who his successor would be. His parting words were to the effect that we would both know in the morning.

Through that evening and night Haughey's team continued making phone calls, and votes were tied down and copper-fastened. Where there was doubt, TDs were visited at home. In at least two cases a wife and a girlfriend were recruited to stiffen the respective backs of their other halves.

On the morning of the vote I received an early – very early (I was still shaving) – telephone call from Charlie. There were no social niceties. 'Michael O'Kennedy is voting for me. Spread the word.' I imagine a few people got the same call that morning. And with that, he was gone. I was stunned. I had pored over the list of all the members of the parliamentary party, including members of the cabinet, and no matter how hard I tried I could not see how any of the ministers would vote for Charlie, apart from himself, that is. There was nobody beholden to him at the cabinet table. Each minister owed his position to Jack Lynch. Likewise each minister had been dependent on George Colley for the funding to run their departments and, no matter how straitened the public finances had become, they knew the efforts that he had made to accommodate their various problems. In the immediate aftermath of Charlie's call I thought that maybe I was being set up and used to promote something that might have been hoped for, rather than real. But I discounted this as paranoid.

My meeting with Jack was arranged for ten o'clock but I had arrived early and he wasn't in his office. As I made my way back down the ministerial corridor, Dessie O'Malley came out of his room and asked me if I had seen Michael O'Kennedy. I said that no, I hadn't, and, because I couldn't resist the temptation to stir things, I added, 'If you are looking for him for the reason I think you are, then you're wasting your time.' He asked me why. I told him that O'Kennedy was voting for Haughey and that it was futile trying to persuade him otherwise. I admit that I was chancing my arm, but O'Malley took the bait and, with the supercilious air that was unique to him when he was riled, asked how I would know what was happening. It was my turn to get riled, and I told him to check with me after the vote and we could settle any bet he was prepared to make at that stage. He turned on his heel and re-entered his room, slamming the door as he went. This was less than forty-eight hours after I had missed the now famous party at his home. O'Malley and I never had a friendly conversation after this incident; while both of us maintained an outer decorum, neither of us could really conceal the animus that had grown between us.

I met Jack a few minutes later and told him about the 'rumour' that O'Kennedy was going to vote for Haughey. He asked where I heard it but I didn't tell him; I just said something vague about 'the grapevine'. Lynch was totally dismissive and refused to believe it. To him it was only black propaganda, aimed at intimidating timid back benchers who had found it safe and comforting to bask in his reflected popularity down through the years but who were now on their own, making a decision that would likely determine their future careers.

Right up to the last minute, Haughey's team made every effort to maintain his support. This included having loyal aides stick like limpets to wavering TDs and, in one instance, making sure that a man who was fond of his alcohol not only had sufficient to drink the night before but was physically guided to the party rooms minutes before the vote took place, thus avoiding a last-minute change of heart as a result of any contact with canvassers for Colley.

Nobody knew about Michael O'Kennedy until the morning of the vote. And when the penny finally dropped with Colley's people that there might be some truth in the rumour that the north Tipperary man was about to 'defect', it was too late. Colley was contacted and decided to go to Michael O'Kennedy. But he made the mistake of bringing Martin O'Donoghue and Dessie O'Malley with him. Purely by accident – when I was still knocking around after bumping into O'Malley, waiting for my meeting with Jack – I had seen the three men enter O'Kennedy's room. I had also seen O'Donoghue and an incandescent O'Malley exit it quite quickly afterwards. Many years later I quizzed O'Kennedy about the events of that morning and when I told him what I knew he looked at me in amazement and asked, 'How the hell did you know that?' When I told him what had happened, he dropped his reserve and said that O'Malley had seemed to think that the vote was a matter of cabinet solidarity and that unless there was unanimity on the part of his ministerial colleagues in George Colley's favour it would be difficult for him to stamp his authority on the party in the future: any rebel would only have to point to the division amongst his cabinet colleagues at the time of his election as a defence for defiance of his leadership. Whatever backbone O'Kennedy had, he showed it when he told O'Donoghue and O'Malley to leave the room and said that he would speak to Colley alone or not at all. By then everybody knew what was about to happen and all that had to be discovered was what Haughey had promised O'Kennedy, if anything.

The rumour machine went into overdrive and the fact that Haughey subsequently appointed O'Kennedy as Ireland's European Commissioner did nothing to dampen the suspicions that he got a promise for his vote. I do not believe this to be true, but the fact that senior members of the Lynch cabinet believed it then, and that some of those who are still alive continue to believe it, indicates the hysteria that surrounded the events of that famous day.

O'Kennedy was obviously angered by the suggestion that he could be persuaded by Haughey, or that equally he could easily be talked out of his decision by Colley and the others. To underline his independence, and to indicate his defiance of the establishment wisdom that Colley was the man to opt for, O'Kennedy decided to perch on the arm of the leather armchair in which a relaxed-looking Haughey sat during the parliamentary party meeting. The Colley camp could only look on with gritted teeth.

Like many people, I don't believe O'Kennedy was the sole cabinet minister to break rank. It had been clear which back benchers were going to vote for Haughey. In the weeks leading up to Lynch's resignation, and certainly in the days after it, they lost no opportunity in making their views known. Therefore a reasonably accurate headcount was possible in advance of the vote. It was clear that another cabinet minister had supported Haughey, and the result of the immediate post-mortems was that the only other possible defector was Brian Lenihan, who had remained aloof when the leadership battle was at its height. That suspicion arose chiefly because Lenihan and Haughey were friendly. Indeed, Lenihan was his only friend in Jack Lynch's cabinet. There was a clear fracture in the cabinet that divided Charlie from the rest. While some of the others socialized together, it was rare for Charlie to be included. He maintained an air of privacy that was not easily invaded. He retired to Kinsaley when others indulged in senior politicians' normal extra-curricular activities, mainly drinking with one another, affirming each other's prejudices and scheming for their own futures within the government and the party. The only member of the cabinet who had any relationship with Haughey – and this arose from the Lemass period, when they had served together as young ministers – was Brian Lenihan. At the time of the arms crisis Brian was Minister for Transport and Power and his friend Paddy Hillery was Minister for External Affairs (as Foreign Affairs was then called). Brian walked a thin line. He maintained his friendship with Haughey, remained loyal to Lynch and, uncharacteristically, remained relatively silent. Their relationship was resilient. Without appearing to do so, Charlie relied on Lenihan for advice and respected his judgement. And Lenihan despaired of Charlie ever facing up to the reality that he would never be leader. He genuinely believed that Charlie would never succeed.

When the day came to choose a leader, Lenihan voted for Colley. Brian was challenged about this, in a friendly fashion, by some of his colleagues in the Dáil bar subsequently. He said that he had written Colley's name diagonally across the ballot papers and invited his critics to check the ballot papers and satisfy themselves that this was the case. This silenced people for a time until it was realized that the ballot papers had been destroyed, by agreement, a short time after the vote.

Charlie knew that Lenihan hadn't voted for him, but he didn't hold it against him and kept him close until the débâcle of the presidential election in 1990 when he had to sack him in humiliating circumstances. Lenihan, supremely intelligent, had always known that the party was in for a rough ride if Charlie took over, but when the decision was made he fell in behind him one hundred per cent and was often responsible for keeping some of his less than enthusiastic colleagues – erstwhile supporters of Charlie, like Ray Burke, who discovered that they did not always like his demanding style after he became party leader – in line. He rallied the troops, as it were.

I believe the defector was another cabinet minister who shrewdly anticipated Haughey's success and jumped his way, albeit without drawing attention to his decision or making anyone the wiser after the votes were counted. That the vast majority of the cabinet voted as they did indicated the depth of the rift that had developed between ministers and back benchers.

Even though I had no role in the events that were taking place, I wasn't about to leave the scene of the action and miss out on a small bit of history in the making. I arranged to meet Michael Mills for a cup of tea so that we could organize the quickest way of getting the result into an early edition of the *Evening Press*. I went back up to the fifth floor of Leinster House and I make no bones about the fact that I eavesdropped on the proceedings within the parliamentary party room. It was the only way to get an accurate account of what was happening. When the result was announced – Haughey forty-four votes, Colley, thirty-eight – I raced down the backstairs to deliver the news. On the way I ran into Senator Des Hanafin, an ardent Colley man. After I answered his anxious inquiry about the result of the vote, he upbraided me fiercely and said that it was no time for joking and that this was a serious matter. He just would not believe me when I told him that Charlie had won. He kept saying, 'Oh, my God, the party is ruined. Ruined.' Michael Mills was standing less than ten feet away, and when Hanafin heard me repeat the result to Mills, giving the actual vote, he had the good grace to apologize for doubting me, before repeating that the party was ruined. Des and I had to step aside smartly as an avalanche of TDs and supporters carried Haughey along towards the senate antechamber, where the new leader's first press conference was to be held. Since the two lifts could not hold all those wishing to make a beeline down to the ground floor, Charlie had opted for the stairs and was being followed by a band of his more ardent supporters. He was shepherded by the Chief Whip, Michael Woods, who, by some mystical process, managed to survive the serial upheavals that were part and parcel of Fianna Fáil for the next decade.

As he passed by, Charlie shouted over that he wanted to see me later in his old room in the ministerial corridor. I nodded and went back upstairs to see what Jack was up to. I found him sitting relaxed on the side of the top table, puffing on his pipe and chatting to Pearse Wyse, a fellow Cork TD. As I approached, Wyse said to me that what had happened was a shocking development and that he couldn't understand how it had come about. With a twinkle in his eye, Jack said, 'They had more votes than we did, Pearse; that's what happened.' He then turned to me and said, 'You were right.' And with that I accompanied him back to his office. On the way I inquired delicately about his plans. He said that he was going to take life a little easier, he wouldn't write his memoirs, he would never talk about 1970, and, if I didn't have any more questions, he was going to 'clean out his files'. I met him again the following Tuesday, prior to the debate on the nomination of the Taoiseach, and afterwards rarely saw him or spoke with him, except on one particular occasion when I was sent to meet him at the request of the new Taoiseach, Charlie Haughey. This was the end of what to me, at least, was an exciting and enormously enjoyable partnership from which I had learnt a great deal; I was going to have to draw heavily on what I had learnt in the coming months and years.

There can be no doubt but that Jack Lynch enhanced the image of Fianna Fáil through his innate decency and charisma. But he also had faults, serious faults, which were not all that apparent at the time of his leadership but which have been put into sharper focus with the passage of time. In Jack's case, however, there will be no dispassionate overview. The perspective will be uniform. The underlying thrust will be that he was a man of ineffable charm and good manners, thoughtful, shrewd, considerate and, above all, politically successful. All of this is indisputable. But the categorization of Jack Lynch as some sort of latter-day political saint is as silly as it is fatuous. I believe history will not be as kind to Jack Lynch as his contemporaneous observers and supporters have been. Any demythologization of his reputation will undoubtedly contain some substance, and his supporters would do well to remember that the nature of the political animal doesn't change. Just like now, back in the sixties it would have been impossible for a politician, regardless of how popular he was with the public and the media, to become leader of Fianna Fáil without having some cunning and artifice in his psyche. I have no doubt that Jack Lynch possessed those characteristics in abundance. I spent five and a half years working with him closely, on a daily basis, something you cannot do without getting an insight into your employer's make-up, so I believe I'm in a better position than most to evaluate his personality.

When future historians come to analyse the nature and extent of Jack Lynch's contribution to Irish politics, they will have to rely mainly on the views of those who either served with him or who lived through his periods in office. Amazingly, as far as I know, he left no papers other than sacks of routine constituency correspondence. The only documentation that will be available will be sterile civil servants' memoranda (albeit memoranda that may contain notes in the margins; nowadays, because of the Freedom of Information Act, civil servants write their comments on Post-it notes that can be removed if the main memorandum has to be made available for public viewing). But there will be none of Jack Lynch's personality in these papers and the only indication of his involvement with them will be his signature and the date. When he was leader of the opposition I once asked him if he would ever write his memoirs. He stood up from his desk, opened a cupboard and pointed to a big stack of black bags. I thought I was looking at the makings of a valuable future tome that would provide definitive answers to a lot of persistent questions about modern Irish politics. Jack must have detected my interest, because he opened one of the bags and showed me a sample of the material: ordinary representations by him in his capacity as a TD. 'There are no memoirs there,' he said, before advising me, in a fatherly way, not to keep too many records because they usually caused trouble.

When I left Jack Lynch in his office cleaning out his files, I decided I would go in search of George Colley to have a word with him. I can't really remember why I went to see him. I may have gone there because I thought he would expect me to do so. Or it may have been that I went along to see who would be commiserating with him. He wasn't alone: I was a little startled, though not terribly surprised, to find a sulphurous Dessie O'Malley, a reflective Bobby Molloy, a Gauloises-smoking Jim Gibbons and an incandescent Des Hanafin in the room. It was a relatively small room – it was long before any extension to Leinster House – and the office looked and felt crowded. There was an eerie silence when I entered the room. These were men that I was close to and had worked with for over five years. But there was a palpable air of hostility. I was an interloper in this private moment of grief amongst those who had just seen their role in Fianna Fáil reduced to that of mere spectators. I was the enemy. At that stage there was no indication on the part of the new leader as to what role, if any, I would play when he became Taoiseach the following Tuesday. I sympathized with George while O'Malley looked on with daggers in his eyes. Jim Gibbons laughed drily and said that I would have my work cut out now. According to Jim, life would not be as easy with Haughey as it had been with Lynch; little did he know that life under Jack had not been the doddle he imagined. O'Malley made a remark to the effect that I might not be kept. At that stage nobody knew what was going to happen and any speculation about who would be kept and who wouldn't reflected a very hostile attitude on his part. The comment was also a foretaste of a question he asked me years later, after he had departed from the cabinet, when he bluntly inquired why I continued to serve.

At his press conference Charlie was as cool as a cucumber. He deftly flicked away a few questions about his private finances, a matter I'm sure he knew would be raised as soon as he assumed the leadership. For some time Vincent Browne had been conducting a virtual one-man campaign about Charlie's finances. However, having been raised in this forum, it was an issue that entered into the general media agenda and never went away completely thereafter.

When I arrived at Charlie's office to wait for him to return from the press conference, I was surprised to see that, as well as a small group of his constituency men, Gene Fitzgerald was there. He was the only politician present.

Gene and I had always been friendly and I found him extremely affable, willing to seek advice and, as Minister for Labour, courageous in his efforts to come to grips with the power of the unions. There was a view – one with some substance – that the Department of Labour was a sub-office of the Irish Congress of Trade Unions and that whatever floor of the department you visited you were sure to meet with some union representative or other in consultation with its officials. As a former trade unionist himself, Gene knew the realities of life for the ordinary members of a union and he tried his very best, in difficult economic circumstances, to maintain as much industrial peace as possible, despite the job losses resulting from the downturn.

Gene was not known as a Haugheyite. But he hadn't been

known as being particularly anti-Haughey either. There was a general presumption that being a member of Lynch's cabinet meant that he was a Colley supporter. He seemed as surprised to see me arriving as I was to see him already there. We exchanged uneasy pleasantries, and he averred that life must go on. The slight embarrassment was overcome by Charlie's arrival, and whatever business Gene had with him was over and done with in a matter of minutes.

Charlie said that he wanted me to stay on as Press Secretary. I was both flattered and relieved. I had always got on well with him, both when he was in the political wilderness and after he had been restored to the front bench. He knew that my association with him had caused me some discomfort as far as Jack and other senior members of the front bench were concerned, and I think he respected the fact that I didn't allow that to inhibit my activities. I told him that I would stay on as Press Secretary on the same conditions that I had served under Lynch: all I required was to be kept informed on matters relevant to the government, and in sufficient detail to be able to judge how they might play out in public and advise accordingly. I remembered the débâcle over the announcement of the sacking of the Garda Commissioner shortly after Jack – a man with whom I believed I had an unrivalled and trusting relationship – came into office, and I did not want a repeat of that dangerous precedent. I was damned if I was going to allow myself to be put into a similar position under a new Taoiseach. Little did I know what the future held, but in the reasonably euphoric circumstances of December 1979 I was willing to accept the assurance of the man I believed to be best suited for the job at that time. Charlie was positive and encouraging, and said something to the effect that we would make a great team.

Before we concluded he invited Sheila and me to his home for drinks that evening. I said that we had a baby – Sinéad was then six months old – and it might be difficult for both of us to attend. 'Frank, just come and bring her – she's becoming part of history', was the reply. And so my young daughter attended her first political 'do' in the salubrious surroundings of the Gandon mansion that had been Charlie's home since 1969. She slept through it all.

Charlie's immediate family was celebrating, along with some notable figures from the business world, including the property developer Patrick Gallagher. Ray MacSharry was there also, but most of the other TDs who had voted for Charlie had left for their constituencies to bring the good news of a bright new economic and political era. During my time in politics I was constantly amazed at the naivety of politicians. They have an unrelenting hunger to trust somebody, to put their faith in one man, to latch on to the one outlook that they believe will immunize them against all of the ills – political, economic and otherwise – with which they are confronted daily. This hunger had been clearly evident during the 1977 general election campaign. Most of the Fianna Fáil candidates were happy to bask in the glow of Jack Lynch's undoubted popularity. It saved them from having to consider too carefully the implications of the party's manifesto and distracted from any problems there might be on the ground in their local constituencies. Time and again throughout that campaign nervous candidates asked me what I thought of their – as opposed to the party's – chances of success. And so it would be with Charlie. Those who had supported him knew that they had carried out a political deed of devastating magnitude for which they would ultimately be held accountable – particularly if it failed. It was therefore a time to reassure party workers that the right thing had been done and that the future was going to be even brighter than it had been under Jack Lynch.

And so the turbulent years of Charlie Haughey's leadership began. The clouds of dissent had already gathered and the long-term forecast was not good. These clouds never really cleared, and disaffection, intrigue and collusion were in the air almost on a daily basis. Prior to announcing his cabinet nominees Haughey had a secret meeting with Colley. The meeting was denied on a number of occasions subsequently, and I did not have it confirmed as a fact for quite some time afterwards. At the meeting Colley undertook to support Haughey as leader on two conditions: that he keep Gerry Collins in the Department of Justice and that Haughey's nominee as Minister for Defence would be acceptable to him. In effect, this was imposing a veto on Haughey's authority as Taoiseach to make appointments of his choice to departments that had proved to be of vital importance in the past and doubtless would prove so again in the future.

Lynch had regarded Collins as a safe pair of hands and, notwithstanding the general view of him as a cute and somewhat cold individual, his capacity to do the job was never in question. Neither was his support for George Colley. There had been some speculation as to the reasons for this request – or the exercise of the veto – by Colley. I'm not quite sure whether it was an unquestioning belief by Colley in Collins's ability to keep an eye on Haughey or in his capacity to do the job. I raised the topic with Colley later, but he did not want to talk about it.

There is no doubt that Charlie was in a difficult position. With the exception of Michael O'Kennedy and one other cabinet member, none of his ministerial colleagues had supported him in the leadership context. So what was he going to do? Sack them all and replace them with his own placemen, none of whom – with the exception of Ray MacSharry, who had served under Colley in Finance – were tested as either ministers or ministers of state? Therefore he had a dilemma. His supporters on the back benches were looking for new faces, new talent, new hope. They believed that the Lynch cabinet was moribund and bewitched by Martin O'Donoghue's economic voodoo. But now that he was in the driving seat the responsibilities of leadership came into play. He agreed to keep Collins in Justice and said that, while he would not be keeping Colley himself in Finance, he would not humiliate him with an appointment beneath his status. In the event he retained him as Tánaiste and made him Minister for Energy.

The Dáil debate on the nomination of a new Taoiseach is usually a matter of form in which the leaders of the opposition parties make fairly predictable remarks about the government party and its leader. However, this time it was an exceptional situation. This was the government changing its Taoiseach midstream. There was no general election to explain Charles Haughey's nomination as head of the government. I ran into Garret FitzGerald in the corridor outside the Ceann Comhairle's entrance to the Dáil chamber about half an hour before the debate commenced. He was unusually exercised and asked me if there was any way Charlie's election – or, more accurately, his nomination – in the Dáil could be stopped. I looked at him in amazement, but he went on like a man possessed and said what was happening was wrong and that it would be bad for the country. I asked him exactly what he had in mind and he outlined a situation in which, if all George Colley's supporters would join with Fine Gael and the Labour Party in voting against Charlie's nomination, he would fail to get the necessary majority and Fianna Fáil would therefore have to put forward another candidate, presumably Colley, whom the opposition parties would support.

To my mind, this was an unwarranted interference in Fianna Fáil's affairs. As gently as I could, I told him that what he was suggesting was completely unacceptable and could not be allowed to happen. It wouldn't occur anyway, because no matter how bitter or resentful George Colley might be – and he gave no outward signs of it – or how aggrieved his supporters felt, they were members of the Fianna Fáil parliamentary party, a body that had conducted a proper and democratic election of a new leader whom it wished to be the new Taoiseach, and it would stand by that decision. Garret nodded and muttered to the effect that he supposed I was right. I forgot about the incident in the aftermath of his actual remarks in the Dáil an hour or so later, which infuriated the Haughey family and the members of Fianna Fáil throughout the country. But I did tell Charlie subsequently. His response is unrepeatable.

In his speech on the nomination of the Taoiseach, Garret used the phrase 'flawed pedigree' about Charlie. Charlie's mother and wife were present in the Visitors' Gallery, and his family was deeply upset by that remark and particularly by the fact that Garret refused to withdraw it even though many senior people in Fine Gael acknowledged privately that it was a totally unjustified personal attack. Subsequently he admitted that he was wrong to use those words and said that he regretted them, mainly because he considered that they had been taken out of their intended context, which was a contrast of Haughey with his predecessors in the office of Taoiseach; they did not refer to his family or social background. But it is hard to believe that a man of Garret's vaunted intelligence and sophistication, someone whose abilities as a diplomat were legendary in fashionable circles, didn't grasp how the use of the words 'flawed' and 'pedigree' together would be received by Haughey's supporters and enemies alike. In his hard-hitting speech, Garret knew that he had a sympathetic audience amongst senior members of the Fianna Fáil parliamentary party. While unwilling to go public with their views about Charlie, his personality, his lifestyle and his policies, they were content enough to have Garret FitzGerald, somewhat of a media darling at the time, give expression, no matter how crassly, to their own true feelings. That there was no outcry by the media convinced Charlie that there was a concerted effort in at least one major newspaper to continue with the beatification of Garret FitzGerald, regardless of any errors of judgement, while simultaneously continuing with the demonization of Charles Haughey.

Much of the fury generated by Garret's remarks was forgotten in the aftermath of the announcement of Charlie's new cabinet. There was some surprise when only three members of the Lynch cabinet were dropped – Bobby Molloy, Jim Gibbons and Martin O'Donoghue. There was little sympathy, if any, for O'Donoghue, and Gibbons's exclusion was completely predictable. However, few could understand the dropping of Molloy. Those in the know were not surprised: Molloy was a fierce opponent of Haughey in his Galway West constituency and lost no opportunity in putting forth the view that Jack Lynch had been wrong to bring him back to the front bench, that he was untrustworthy and that unless people like Molloy himself spoke out regularly against Haughey no good would come of his presence in front-line politics. Molloy was clever enough to keep to his own bailiwick, so the media did not know about this. But Haughey knew and this was his revenge. Ultimately Molloy, who was a good minister and is a good man, repaid this act of treachery by leaving Fianna Fáil and joining the Progressive Democrats.

The new ministers were Ray MacSharry, Albert Reynolds and Máire Geoghegan-Quinn, who became the first woman cabinet minister since Countess Markievicz was Minister for Labour in the first Dáil in 1919. A broad sword was used on the ranks of junior ministers. Charlie filled the vacancies with his supporters: Seán Doherty, Tommy McEllistrim, Mark Killilea, Lorcan Allen and others. Irish politics hadn't seen the likes of it since the late twenties and the early thirties.

Shortly after the new government of which he was a member had been formed, George Colley delivered a speech in his constituency in which he said that while as a minister he was constitutionally obliged to give his loyalty to the Taoiseach, no such obligation existed as far as the leader of the party was concerned. Not only was he Minister for Energy, he was also Tánaiste, a fact which of itself made his remarks all the more sensational. Nobody had any forewarning of what he was going to say and the reports of his comments in the newspapers the following day came as a shock to both Haughey and those immediately around him in the Taoiseach's office, including myself.

There was a momentary effort to blame me for lack of foreknowledge, but that didn't last very long when it was realized that what George was actually doing was challenging Haughey to sack him and to make him a political martyr in the eyes of his supporters in the parliamentary party. The situation was fraught with danger for both sides. If Haughey did nothing, he would be weakened in the eyes of his own supporters and he would be giving a signal to others that they were free to challenge his authority whenever they thought fit. On the other hand, if he sacked Colley, there was no doubt that the unthinkable would finally happen and there would be a split in what had been – and, despite everything, still was – a monolithic party. A significant number of both senior and back bench TDs, including some members of the cabinet, would walk, causing serious difficulties for government stability. Were that to happen, Charlie and the government could not depend on the parliamentary party to continue to support the government in the Oireachtas and defeat in a vote would simply be a matter of time.

Charlie sought advice immediately. There were various comings and goings from early morning and eventually I was summoned. As usual, Pádraig Ó hAnnracháin was present when I arrived. Ó hAnnracháin, a veteran civil servant who had become very close to Haughey over the years, had arrived into the Taoiseach's office within hours of Charlie being elected on 11 December and, despite the absence of a title or a clearly defined role, had immediately assumed the position of most senior civil servant in the department, effectively a chief of staff, though no such position existed. I did not know, and to this day I do not know, what others advised. I was asked a simple question: 'What should I do?' My answer was equally simple: 'Sack him now.' I could see the surprise on the faces of both men; and when I was asked if there was no other way to deal with the situation, I said that in my view there wasn't. Charlie said nothing, but Ó hAnnracháin said that there was no way the Taoiseach could sack his Tánaiste. It dawned on me pretty quickly that Ó hAnnracháin had advised against dismissing Colley and he wasn't about to have his advice gainsaid. A fairly animated discussion took place between Pádraig and myself in front of the Taoiseach, which was brought to an end only by Haughey himself saying that he would decide later. I have read, and heard, people who held senior ministerial positions at the time say that they advised that Colley be dismissed. These may be examples of a common condition – retrospective wisdom – but if that was indeed their advice, Charlie decided to ignore it. He called in George, and by all accounts they had a very amiable chat and George undertook to loyally support the Taoiseach, something he had never said he would not do. Charlie had been challenged and everybody knew that he had bottled out.

I found the whole episode upsetting, and not merely because of having to advise that a man whom I knew well, and who was a decent, honourable person, be dismissed from his ministerial office. None the less I was convinced, and still am, that this was the proper advice. But the circumstances were disturbing. My read of the situation was that George was not acting out of pique as a result of his defeat in the leadership election, but rather that he was putting down a marker for Charlie, spelling out loud and clear that what had been sauce for the goose in the past – sniping at the leadership – was now going to be sauce for the gander. Charlie was going to be given a taste of his own medicine. Would Fianna Fáil ever learn that as long as it indulged in this type of infighting the only outcome would be defeat at the polls? True, Jack Lynch had proved that it was possible to have internal opposition and to go on to electoral success. But Jack was exceptional. In terms of electoral appeal, Charlie did not possess the same quality, or at least not to the same degree.

Though my advice had been ignored, to my surprise it became known outside the Taoiseach's office, which caused no end of problems with some of George Colley's supporters. Eventually I had to go to George and outline the circumstances of what had occurred. Ever the gentleman, he said that both of us had to do what we thought was right. I continued to have very good relations with George but gradually lost contact with him as the life of Charlie's first government progressed.

8. Serving Charlie's image

I couldn't have envisaged that barely a week after the conversation in which he said we would make a great team, Charlie Haughey and I would be at loggerheads. The first I knew that there was trouble brewing was a curt phone call from Pádraig Ó hAnnracháin to say that the Taoiseach wanted to see me immediately. When I arrived in Charlie's outer office a few minutes later, his Private Secretary raised his eyes to heaven and I guessed that something was up beyond the double doors of 'the Boss's' office. (Everybody calling Haughey 'the Boss' was a new development. I don't know how it started, but in a short time it was the accepted way of referring to the Taoiseach. I actually heard Ó hAnnracháin use the expression to Haughey's face on a number of occasions.)

When I entered, Ó hAnnracháin was sitting in an occasional armchair and the Taoiseach was sitting at his desk with his head in his hands. There was total silence. Ó hAnnracháin signalled to me to remain quiet and then shook his head in what I took to be a sign of resigned frustration. He spoke to Haughey and said, 'Frank is here now, Taoiseach.' I had sat down and looked with horror as Haughey raised his head from his hands. His face was puce and the thin strands of his hair were almost erect as if frozen into place with hairspray. He glared at me and said, 'Where the fuck were you yesterday?' Knowing him as I did – or, more accurately, knowing him as I thought I did – I adopted a nonchalance I was far from feeling and said, 'Yesterday – Sunday – I was at home in the bosom of my family.' Haughey went ballistic. 'We're making some progress – the fucker knows yesterday was Sunday.' With that my reserve broke. I stood up and approached his desk. 'Don't you ever speak to me like that again,' I said, and made for the door. Haughey shouted after me to come back, but I kept going.

Minutes later Ó hAnnracháin was in my office. Apparently the problem was that no member of the Government Information Service had been present at a function in Charlie's constituency the previous day, a Sunday. The event was a political one, and the standing rule in the service was that no civil servant attended such events. This resulted in an absence of photographs in the morning papers – always a matter of considerable importance to Charlie. Ó hAnnracháin remonstrated with me in words to the effect that I could not speak to the Taoiseach in that fashion, no matter what my position. 'Pádraig, you are missing the point. He can't speak to me like that,' I said. Ó hAnnracháin looked at me as if I had two heads and left. Haughey didn't speak to me for a week. This, I was to discover, was his method of letting you know you were out of the loop: life could continue on without you and in my case any communication with the media could be made as easily through Ó hAnnracháin as through me.

The political correspondents wondered what was going on. I didn't make them any the wiser and I waited. Towards the end of the week Ó hAnnracháin began to thaw and mentioned that the Taoiseach had been inquiring about my family. I resisted all attempts to get me to break the ice, and eventually, on the following Monday, a week after the incident, my phone rang and Charlie 'wondered' if I might be free because there was something he needed to consult me about. That was the end of the matter. It was never referred to again. This was Charlie's way of apologizing without actually having to do so. Both sides knew what had happened and both sides were willing to proceed as if nothing had occurred. But the message was clear. The parameters of the relationship had changed: I knew that Ó hAnnracháin was now the chief communications link with Haughey and Haughey knew that there was a limit to what I would accept as part of a working relationship. Of course, it didn't stop him taking the same tack again from time to time, but he knew that I would not take abuse as a matter of routine.

Pádraig Ó hAnnracháin had been on the circuit for many years. He had served under de Valera and Lemass and was head of the Government Information Service under Jack Lynch between 1969 and 1973. He was a civil servant, albeit one with recognized Fianna Fáil sympathies, and when the Fine Gael–Labour coalition took office in 1973, he was 'exiled' to the Department of Education, then something of a political backwater, where, it was thought, he would be out of harm's way. Little did they know Ó hAnnracháin. He struck up a fantastic relationship with the new Minister for Education, Dick Burke, and served him faithfully in the best tradition of the civil service. Burke came across as somewhat formal and Ó hAnnracháin punctured the outer shell of stuffiness and reserve as often as he could, with the result that Burke became more approachable. He certainly got more than his fair share of positive publicity, which was due solely to Ó hAnnracháin's efforts and his unrivalled relationship with the education correspondents.

Pádraig believed that Lynch had been unfair in not recalling him to head the Government Information Service in 1977. This took no account of the fact that Jack and Fianna Fáil had hired me in the interim. However, I suspect Ó hAnnracháin's resentment against Lynch went back to their relationship during the 1969–73 government. These had been turbulent, not to say traumatic, times, and Lynch knew that from 1969 onwards, with the events in Derry and Belfast, the Irish government was losing the propaganda war. This was certainly the case with the international media. As for the home front, in 1969 television came into its own when the violence in Northern Ireland was brought into Irish living rooms. The sight of people with blood streaming down their faces after being assaulted by policemen had a huge impact on Southern viewers and doubled as a valuable recruiting tool for the IRA. Lynch had the extraordinary idea of establishing a government news agency within the GIS, not only to counter the influence of the British press in the presentation of the Northern story, but also to fight the increasing Republican propaganda. In these circumstances Ó hAnnracháin was lost: he was used to dealing with a compliant Irish media and found the British media much more difficult to cajole. He ceded control to the Department of Foreign Affairs and after the events of May 1970 was sidelined, virtually permanently. It is difficult to imagine his views when, as head of the Government Information

Service, he had to preside over the announcement of the sacking of his friends Charlie Haughey and Neil Blaney in the middle of the night and then to watch while Lynch eviscerated them politically over the following months, culminating in the ultimate humiliation of a state trial.

Ó hAnnracháin maintained a close friendship with Haughey during his wilderness years. He lived in Sutton and called to see him frequently in nearby Kinsaley. He played a dangerous game in that, as a civil servant, he acted as an unpaid adviser to Haughey through the seventies. Haughey's decision to stay within the ranks of Fianna Fáil after his sacking, and more particularly after the débâcle of the arms trial, had all the hallmarks of Ó hAnnracháin's advice. Charlie was given to bouts of hot-headedness and, although he was usually calculating and took the long view, sometimes he would rush into decisions. Ó hAnnracháin knew that if Haughey left Fianna Fáil there would be no turning back, so he advised him to swallow his pride, live with the humiliation and wait in the long grass. The events of December 1979 were the result of that strategy, and Ó hAnnracháin had no intention of staying away from the heart of the action for a moment longer than necessary. So he arrived in the Taoiseach's office almost unannounced, with no specific responsibilities or role, other than that of the closest civil servant to the new Taoiseach – a fact that he was not slow to broadcast to the officers of the department. After his arrival it was obvious to me that he was gradually positioning himself as a buffer between the Taoiseach and everybody else in the department. If you wanted to get a message to the Taoiseach, you went to Ó hAnnracháin. He became, in effect, a type of political post office and in that role was extremely valuable because he loved to talk. The odds were that if you went to see Ó hAnnracháin about one thing or another, you would learn something useful about what was currently on the Taoiseach's mind.

Shortly after Charlie became Taoiseach the British Ambassador, Sir Robin Haydon, invited me to lunch. I had been to lunch with ambassadors before. If anything of importance came up, I reported it either to the Taoiseach or to the appropriate officer in the

Department of the Taoiseach or in the Department of Foreign Affairs. I rarely, if ever, told anybody in advance of such meetings. Neither did I do so on this occasion. I already knew the Ambassador somewhat; he had served as Press Secretary at No. 10 Downing Street under Ted Heath for a short time. There was a view that by appointing this relative lightweight to the Dublin embassy to succeed assassinated Ewart-Biggs the British had made known their views about Ireland as a diplomatic posting. Unfortunately for him he landed in Ireland at a time of political turmoil and found it difficult to come to terms with all the upheavals. He was a very genial man, extremely polite and very anxious to learn. We exchanged stories about the experience of working in government press relations and about the fractious relationship that existed between Jack Lynch and Ted Heath. It was obvious that his real purpose in meeting me was to find out about Charlie Haughey. There was no doubt in my mind that he had been briefed by officials at his embassy as to what he should ask. I surmised that the Department of Foreign Affairs had conducted its own briefings about Haughey, and that this was an attempt to either confirm some of the contents of such briefings, or to weigh them against the views of somebody who had served a former Taoiseach and was now part of the new regime. He was blunt and to the point. He didn't know Haughey and didn't envisage any circumstances in which he would be able to get to know him. He wasn't anticipating any calls to the Taoiseach's office for an in-depth briefing on relations between Ireland and Britain or on developments in the North for that matter. He wanted to know what Haughey was like as a person. What motivated him? What made him tick?

I don't recall telling anybody about the lunch afterwards. There was no point. Nothing of any substance had transpired. It was just a fishing expedition on the part of the Ambassador. In response to his queries I told him about Charlie's managerial style and how it contrasted with Jack's. Anything I said was very pedestrian and non-contentious. Imagine my surprise, therefore, when two days later I received a call from Pádraig Ó hAnnracháin who was now, technically, my boss. When I went to see him he was irate and wanted to know what I had been doing, having lunch with 'Sir Spy'. It became pretty obvious in the first few seconds of this conversation that he didn't know when the lunch had taken place, or where. Somebody had spotted the Government Press Secretary having lunch with the British Ambassador, reported it to the department and Ó hAnnracháin took it upon himself to investigate or else was asked to do so. He wanted to know what had transpired and, in particular, what I had said about the Taoiseach and the government. Having given him the appropriate assurances, and noted his reference to the British Ambassador as 'Sir Spy', I forgot about the matter until a week or two later when I was passing through the lobby of the Shelbourne Hotel. I glanced into the dining room and there was Ó hAnnracháin dining with the British Ambassador. The poor man must have been rightly confused.

When Ó hAnnracháin questioned me, he said I was not permitted to meet or socialize with the British Ambassador without express permission. I was mildly surprised and asked when, if ever, this had been decided. I was somewhat shocked when Ó hAnnracháin said something to the effect that I had better remember that Jack Lynch was no longer the Taoiseach, that I couldn't do as I liked and that there were new regulations. The reference to Jack Lynch was the key to this conversation. Whenever Ó hAnnracháin was angered about something or other, he reverted to sarcastic comments about Lynch. Anybody who had been associated with Lynch in the latter part of his leadership of Fianna Fáil was the enemy. He believed that my relationship with the former Taoiseach had been too close and it was clear that he was not going to allow anything similar to develop between Charlie Haughey and myself. This was a defence mechanism arising out of insecurity and out of his knowledge of Haughey's personality. Ó hAnnracháin came from a modest background but, by virtue of having been de Valera's Private Secretary, he had a somewhat elevated notion of himself. Now that he had arrived in his rightful place at the heart of power, he considered it to be a zero-sum territory: the more access to Haughey anyone else had, the more it took away from his influence and standing. He knew Haughey trusted him more than he did most others, but he also knew that it suited Haughey to keep people wondering where they stood. If Haughey found someone else to depend on, then he might reduce his reliance on Pádraig Ó hAnnracháin.

Inevitably the establishment gravitated towards Ó hAnnracháin, not out of any sense of respect for the seniority of his position as a civil servant but solely because he was the man to know if you wished to have your views transmitted upwards. Ó hAnnracháin revelled in his new status and milked it for all it was worth. He became something of an *éminence grise* and virtually nobody, including some of Charlie's own ministers, approached the Taoiseach without first making overtures to him. Indeed, as time passed I also used Ó hAnnracháin as a conduit to Haughey – but this was in circumstances where my relationship with the Taoiseach had become fraught.

Charlie and I had agreed at the outset that there would be no change in the routine that I had operated with his predecessor. And in his mind there was no change – other than that he wanted to know everything and that Pádraig Ó hAnnracháin was now acting as a sort of buffer between Charlie and me. In other words, the expectations had changed utterly. Whereas I had operated with a fair degree of independence in Jack's time – I was able to use my own background knowledge to deal with most media queries without referring to civil servants – that was no longer acceptable. This took the spontaneity out of my dealings with journalists. I couldn't just give them an instant steer when they rang me looking for a quick comment on a story they were working on to a deadline. As a result of the teething problems of the first few weeks, I realized that my modus operandi would have to change too. And so it did. Now I ran upstairs to check everything with Charlie. I met him every morning at 9.45 a.m., immediately after he arrived in his office, and we did a brief review of the newspapers followed by a discussion of what was to be expected for the rest of the day. Ó hAnnracháin usually attended these meetings and reported on any discussions he had had with Tim Pat Coogan, editor of the *Irish Press*, or Douglas Gageby, editor of the *Irish Times*, both of whom he knew well. Apart from the most trivial of matters, when anything came up concerning him or the government, I consulted Charlie before dealing with it. When I had to deal with issues that were not directly relevant to the day-to-day operations of the Taoiseach's department, I checked with those whom he authorized to brief me.

With Charlie's arrival the somewhat relaxed atmosphere in the Department of the Taoiseach was replaced with a more businesslike approach, and if there had been any doubt about where the centre of operations was prior to his taking office, there was none afterwards. At times, during Lynch's period in office, you could be forgiven for wondering whether he was in the building. Not so with Charlie. Everybody knew when he arrived. Everybody knew he was there. And everybody knew when he left. From the outset he generated frenetic activity, often without anybody being fully aware of what its purpose was. He seemed to revel in creating tension. This didn't apply solely to the time he spent in the office: calls came from Kinsaley at all hours. And there was a very unpalatable development for civil servants when he started to hold meetings in his home on Saturday mornings. They were aghast: apart from foreign trips – for which there were generous expenses – weekends were sacrosanct. But going to Kinsaley, on a Saturday, to meet Charlie Haughey. Unthinkable.

Charlie was demanding. He could not abide incompetence or inefficiency, and treated harshly those whom he found guilty of either. He paid enormous attention to the small details of proposals and submissions and woe betide anybody who could not stand by the contents of what they had written. He was not predictable in his attitudes, which civil servants found extremely disconcerting. If there is anything civil servants dislike, it is an unpredictable minister. The relationship between ministers and civil servants is largely based on the officials knowing the limits to which they can go in making recommendations to their political masters. Some of them, at least some of the ones I knew, prided themselves on being able to draft policy suggestions that would suit their ministers' ways of thinking and save them a lot of effort in the long run. However, second-guessing the new boss's strengths and weaknesses, or his likes and dislikes, and making life easier by pandering to those, wasn't going to work with an old hand like Charlie Haughey. Instead, they were constantly on their toes, never knowing how he would receive things or what he might expect them to tackle next.

A year after the Pope's visit, various proposals for dealing with the area around the Papal Cross in the Phoenix Park were under consideration. It was felt that something should be done to ensure that it didn't become derelict and the Board of Works was asked for its recommendations. To my chagrin, one Friday afternoon at about four o'clock Charlie called me and asked me to come up to his office. There was no preamble, no forewarning about what might be on the agenda: just be there. (The two worst times to have a meeting with Charlie were Monday mornings and Friday afternoons. After having a weekend to mull over things, he was at his most unpredictable on Monday mornings, and on Fridays he would come up with a volume of work that would rule out a relaxing weekend.) The minister of state responsible for the Board of Works and some of his officials were already in the Taoiseach's office when I arrived. Charlie welcomed me with the words, 'We are looking at what we can do with the Papal Cross in the Phoenix Park. What do you think, Frank?' I refrained from indulging myself by naming a few of those I would like to see suspended from it and came out with some inconsequential remarks. I knew that whatever I said he would be prevailing on officials to prepare a proposal for his perusal the following morning. And that was exactly what happened. I saw the look of horror on the officials' faces and so did Charlie, which probably made him very satisfied. Just as we were all about to leave, he inquired which of them had been responsible for the recent refurbishment of the Taoiseach's office. This was asked in a particularly benign way and I'm sure that the relevant official expected to be praised for some aspect of the work, or indeed all of it. One of the men acknowledged that he had been responsible. Charlie said, 'There's no heat in my toilet.' I knew him well enough to recognize the tone, so I waited for the punch-line with baited breath. In his innocence, the Board of Works man went into a long and detailed technical explanation about the fact that there were six radiators along the corridor off which the toilet was located, and no radiator had been installed because the heat from the radiators in the corridor would be 'subsumed' into the bathroom. I could only cringe in anticipation of the put-down. Charlie took a single key out of his pocket, slid it down the highly polished conference table and, just as it was about to land on the lap of the official, he said, 'There's the key. Try it on your way out and I hope it freezes the balls off you.'

When suffused by a new idea, or what he considered to be an imaginative 'stroke', Charlie expected everybody around him to agree with it. When they didn't, they were given a variety of sobriquets. He was constantly looking for the Holy Grail – some-thing that would so fire the imagination of the public that there could be no question as to his role in the pantheon of Irish political heroes. He seemed to believe that he needed to reinforce in the public mind the idea that he had taken imaginative decisions while he was Minister for Finance and in other departments. Nobody, regardless of how inimical they were towards him, could deny that he had taken his duties seriously and had served the state well. But there was this constant recurring need to do something else – what I don't know, and I don't think he knew either. The entire motivation of the Department of the Taoiseach while he was in office was to achieve, even if it was only to achieve those things that would be done anyway in the course of everyday business. When I ran into Jack Lynch some months after he had retired, he started to mock the new telephone system that Charlie had had installed in the Taoiseach's office to replace the antiquated model that had been there. 'I hear ye don't have to do any work over there any more, ye just press a few buttons and it all happens,' he said. But what Jack didn't realize, or refused to recognize, was that Charlie was always on the hunt for new systems, new methods of doing things, new ideas. This did not always sit well with his detractors, both internally in Fianna Fáil and elsewhere. They portrayed his innovative style as a means of camouflaging the fact that he could not or would not solve the real difficulties facing the country and as an attempt to distract the public from coming to negative conclusions about his stewardship.

Quite quickly I saw that one of my big problems would be that Charlie appeared to be open to every suggestion for alternative ways of handling his publicity, regardless of source. Since I wasn't as close to Charlie as I had been to Jack Lynch, I wasn't in a position to take him in hand and discipline his approach to the media. There seemed to be a plethora of advisers and handlers – people like his friend and neighbour, the solicitor Pat O'Connor, supporters from his constituency, PR people, journalists from RTÉ, back benchers on the make – but no coordination or focus. Some of this retinue believed that because they were in frequent contact with him they could indicate to others his putative views on specific issues. So, ironically, a man who was wary of the press, and should therefore have wanted to run a tight ship media-wise, had people around him who shot their mouths off to the wrong people about the wrong things. From time to time it got really out of hand. On one occasion, I discovered that a 'pal' of Charlie had briefed a reporter from RTÉ about a sensitive policy matter to do with the upcoming budget, which had not been finalized by the cabinet. I heard that the two men had been seen having a drink together the previous evening. When the pal admitted to excessive enthusiasm in talking about something of which he had no knowledge, other than hearing some loose talk among a few politicians, the Taoiseach apologized and undertook to rein in some of his more unbridled supporters.

The other interesting aspect of working for Charlie, which was new to me, was his peculiar sense of his own destiny – and how it was being nurtured by this gang of advisers. A month after he became Taoiseach, he called me back from the country on a Sunday afternoon to discuss a matter of vital, though unspecified, urgency. When I arrived at Kinsaley, I was bemused to find that this matter was the shooting of a British soldier in the North – 'The first,

Frank, since I became Taoiseach.' When I inquired as to the relevance of his being Taoiseach to the shooting of a British soldier in the North, he said that he was surprised that I had not recommended that he make a statement marking this occurrence. I told him that such a thought had never crossed my mind and now that he had brought it to my attention I considered the idea even more ridiculous. When I argued with him about the precedent he was setting – if he issued a statement on this occasion, he would have to issue one every time there was an incident – he let it slip that he had been advised that it would be a good thing for him to do. When I asked him, somewhat tentatively, the source of this suggestion, I discovered that it was an RTÉ reporter, one of his would-be pals, who was working in the news room that day and wanted a story to beef up a slow news day. Such was the state of affairs that a reporter felt he could advise the Taoiseach as to what he should comment on regardless of the consequences or the precedents established. There was no arguing with Charlie that afternoon, and the best I could do was to issue a toned-down version of what had been proposed initially. When I had drafted it and presented it for clearance, he said that it should be sent to one journalist only, and named the RTÉ reporter. I subsequently confronted the person responsible for telling Charlie to make a statement. He denied it, but rang Charlie none the less to complain about my interference in 'freedom of the press'.

I now knew I had to be alert: if one or two RTÉ reporters felt able to make direct contact with the Taoiseach and sow seeds in his mind of what might be desirable or appropriate by way of public comment, then anything could happen. I soon put two and two together about his small cabal of supporters in the RTÉ news room. I knew these people from the time that Charlie was Minister for Health; they socialized with the people who were close to him and wanted to get closer. They were proffering advice that, in their misguided view, would provide Charlie with valuable radio and TV coverage. In the interests of alleged journalistic objectivity they kept their association with Haughey relatively low-key. They fed him a diet of rumour and speculation, and constantly undermined ministers and criticized dedicated civil servants' efforts to carry out their jobs.

RTÉ was a strange place at that time and was riven by internal politics, with news dominated by people with Nationalist sympathies, and current affairs the domain of the anti-Nationalist 'Stickies'. From time to time they engaged in territorial warfare, with the content and political orientation of their programmes being the ammunition. There were those who resented Wesley Boyd becoming head of news. That he was from County Fermanagh's Protestant tradition seemed to arouse the worst paranoia on the part of some of the more extreme nationalistic reporters in the news room. Apart from being sectarian, their attitude was grossly unfair: Boyd displayed an admirable even-handedness at all times, sometimes in the most pressurized circumstances. Anonymous letters to Charlie and myself about the attitudes of news managers and journalists in the RTÉ news room arrived in like confetti. One such, which detailed the allegedly unsympathetic political orientation of every key person in a senior editorial role, concluded with the words, 'Add to this more than our fair share of non nationally-minded Northerners, and non Fianna Fáil-minded Southerners among rank and file and a bit above, and we have our work cut out to hold on to the few reasonably crucial positions we still have pinned down.' (At the end it said, 'For security and protection it is essential that this paper be destroyed as soon as facts have been noted.' I keep it as a souvenir of an extraordinary era.)

The opinions in such memos were, no doubt, the stuff of bar-room discussions in the haunts of politicians and journalists, and partly explain how senior Fianna Fáilers' paranoia about RTÉ was nurtured from within the station. However, the national broadcaster would be a sore point for whoever was in power. During its period in office the coalition government believed *Hall's Pictorial Weekly*, the satirical show that depicted the venal, petty and stupid doings of fictional politicians who often closely resembled those in government, to be a Fianna Fáil-inspired attack on it and tried, unsuccessfully, to have the series stopped. The programme had a significant audience at a time when most of Ireland was a one-channel area, and after the 1977 election some senior members of Fine Gael and Labour claimed that it had contributed significantly to the negative perception of their government and its ultimate defeat. When Fianna Fáil came into office, the programme continued but didn't appear to have the same bite and was eventually taken off the air. Shortly afterwards Frank Hall, its writer and presenter, was appointed film censor. Frank Cluskey, who had been a junior minister in the coalition government, was furious and said, in words that are unrepeatable here, that the government had rewarded Hall for services rendered. What few of us knew was that Frank Hall and Pádraig Ó hAnnracháin were close friends and cooperated from time to time on various ventures. In fact, Hall provided lines to Ó hAnnracháin that were ultimately used in his ministers' speeches, though I have no proof that any ever made it into a Haughey script.

Charlie did not have many friends in the print media, but Michael Hand, the editor of the *Sunday Independent*, was one. Hand was an ebullient, larger-than-life characer who knew everyone, and Charlie was inclined to take his advice at face value and could not understand it when things then went wrong. He did manage to stifle some criticism in the *Sunday Independent*, and one of its journalists who was seen as being anti-Haughey appeared to have been sidelined for a time. This was attributed to Haughey's influence and was spoken of in journalists' watering holes around Dublin as an example of Haughey's interference with the 'freedom of the press'. But the truth of the matter was that it had nothing to do with Charlie Haughey and that Michael Hand just wanted to use an experienced member of staff in another part of the paper.

Unfortunately Haughey was a sucker for the kind of whispering advice his media coterie provided, and, while he despised those who indulged in it, he couldn't resist soaking up the gossip and throwing it about whenever he saw fit. I recall a difficult discussion when he told me, 'People tell the Taoiseach of the day things, Frank'; he went on to say that he knew what some of my staff were saying about him in Doheny & Nesbitt's, a pub around the corner from Government Buildings frequented by an eclectic mixture of politicians past their sell-by dates, journalists looking for gossip, economists of a mostly left-wing variety, poseurs and pseuds. It was pointless arguing with him about matters of this sort, which, invariably, had absolutely nothing whatever to do with the subject under discussion. It was just Charlie's way of letting you know that he was keeping his finger on the pulse of what he thought was happening. Understandably, most of these advisers (apart from those who were genuinely close friends like Pat O'Connor) were very pleased with themselves to have direct contact with, and apparently influence over, the Taoiseach. But, of course, things changed somewhat when the going got rough; they slunk back into the shadows whence they had come. Theirs was a self-serving, sycophantic modus operandi, and I think that Charlie saw through it eventually.

Apart from those people from whom he got gossip, Charlie's attitude towards the media was one of suspicion at best. He had excellent rapport with photographers: he knew what they wanted and he was prepared to go to any lengths to accommodate them. But when it came to the written word – or indeed the spoken word on RTÉ – he was a different man. And no one was in any doubt that he had an abiding hatred of the political correspondents. This was not a movable feast; it was permanent. From the day he became Taoiseach it was obvious that all sides were in for a stormy passage. The positive relationship that had developed – through no little effort on my part and that of my predecessor, Muiris MacConghail – between the Government Press Secretary's office and the political correspondents was now regarded as distinctly unhealthy. Ó hAnnracháin didn't help in this because he shared Charlie's suspicion of the media. He had run the Government Information Service in the old days, when journalists were more compliant, and certainly more dependent on the GIS for information, and its boss had a certain power. But times had changed. The media in general had become far more demanding and the pol corrs had attained a power that they had never envisaged themselves. While I had an excellent personal and professional relationship with the vast majority of them, this counted for nothing when they were in pursuit of a story. I understood this perfectly and never took it to heart.

I began to realize that the very fact that I would spend so much time talking to members of the correspondents' lobby – and would regularly be seen with them in the Dáil bar or restaurant – suggested to some, like Ó hAnnracháin, that I was somehow confused in my loyalties and my duties. It was an impossible situation, particularly so when the new Taoiseach's views were taken into account. There was little, if any, room for manoeuvre in guiding the political correspondents in their coverage. And by this I do not mean *misleading* them; I mean that in the normal working relationships between an intermediary such as myself and senior journalists a certain understanding develops that is based on trust. If that trust is broken, then the entire relationship breaks down and is very difficult to repair.

For a man who took so much trouble about everything that he did, it is surprising that Charlie didn't take a more subtle approach to the pol corrs. Despite his reputation for calculation, where they were concerned he seemed to lose all rationality. I pointed to the good relations that had been built up, but he said that it was playing with fire to become too close to the media because ultimately they would turn on you. He pointed to the demise of Jack Lynch as an example. I couldn't argue with that: in the end Jack's relationship with the political correspondents had turned sour, mainly because of the manner in which the various machinations of his opponents leading up to his departure had been reported. However, to suggest that the media were responsible for his premature resignation was farcical.

Early on I made one stab at getting Charlie and the pol corrs together and then I gave up. After Jack Lynch became Taoiseach I had continued an arrangement that had been initiated by Muiris MacConghail whereby the Taoiseach and/or senior ministers would meet the members of the lobby reasonably regularly for lunch. These occasions were strictly off the record, and if the journalists wanted to report anything that had been said they did so in such a way that it wasn't traceable to members of the government.

Both sides maintained the essential element of trust that was required to make the arrangement successful, and it worked well for everyone: the pol corrs were able to write knowledgeably about issues that might not normally be aired, and members of the government were able to discuss sensitive policy matters without being accused of by-passing the parliamentary party or the Dáil. Needless to say, Charlie was not enamoured of the system and didn't want to participate. The pol corrs became restive and kept asking me why Charlie was unwilling to meet them. The usual excuses of 'demanding schedules' and 'unexpected eventualities' had long run out by the time I finally got Charlie to agree that it would be in his, and the government's, best interests if this silly impasse was resolved. When the day arrived, I was confronted by a group of very suspicious journalists who knew well that Charlie didn't really want to meet them, and a Taoiseach who was going along with something that was complete anathema to him. Clearly he decided that an over-the-top enthusiasm would smother any further desire on the part of the pol corrs to spend time with him, and when he entered the room he spread his arms wide, as if to embrace his guests, and said, apparently sincerely, 'My favourite people.' Sadly there were no photographers on hand to record the correspondents' faces, which showed astonishment, disbelief, downright contempt and a mixture of all three. To add insult to injury Charlie refused to discuss anything of any substance and the event was a dismal failure.

When I argued about media strategy with both Charlie and Ó hAnnracháin, I was told not to worry, with the nonsensical explanation that Ó hAnnracháin would be able to talk to Tim Pat Coogan and prevail on him to keep Michael Mills in line. Nor would the *Irish Times* be a difficulty, because, again, Ó hAnnracháin had excellent relations with Douglas Gageby, who apparently had a soft spot for Charlie; and, if all came to all, its political columnist, John Healy, could be spoken to. Of course this bore no relation to reality. There was no question of Coogan or Gageby interfering with their senior journalists' work in this way. This was media relations of the 1950s, and it was a measure of Charlie's naivety and misplaced trust in Ó hAnnracháin's dated communication skills. But he was not to be gainsaid. The media were to be kept at arm's length and only carefully selected items of information were to be divulged. Anything relating to cabinet meetings was taboo and briefings with the Taoiseach were to be kept to a minimum. Ultimately it was a policy of disaster.

I decided I would have to tell the political correspondents that they could no longer rely on me for the totality of any given story and, in the absence of information from my office, that they would have to use their own resources to establish the facts. I knew that I was ceding control to others by doing this, but I had very little option and anyway it was an approach that Charlie required. As far as he was concerned, the more spade-work the journalists had to do, the greater the likelihood that they would get the wrong end of the stick. It was a novel way of managing the press and one that had a certain value to it, particularly in circumstances – and there are always such circumstances, perhaps because of timing or the sensitivities of third parties – where the government did not want to provide information to the media. The new strategy made little difference in day-to-day operations, except that the political correspondents found themselves a little further out in the cold than they had been. We all knew what the outcome of this approach would be: not only would journalists have to go elsewhere for their information – much to the satisfaction of some of the ministerial backwoodsmen, who believed that the correspondents were essentially lazy and being spoonfed by me – but a new hungry breed of reporters would emerge and produce stories that would cause increasing difficulties for the government.

As to how all these adjustments in my working life affected my relationship with the Taoiseach, the fact is that they didn't. I accepted that it was his right to lay down the parameters within which I was to operate and it remained for me only to advise him, when required, of the practical difficulties that these parameters caused. From the outset there were legions of stories about my 'difficult' relationship with Charlie Haughey. While most of these were either untrue or were quite out of proportion to their original grain of truth, it would be silly to say that all was rosy in the garden; life, and particularly political life, is not like that. But what is essential in politics is a capacity to adapt to new situations, and that is exactly what I had to do. There was little point in trying to relive the glory days of the Lynch era when Jack really didn't concern himself with the operations of the Government Information Service. Nor was there much point in trying to persuade the new Taoiseach that the tried and trusted system was the one to follow. The only thing to do was to roll with the punches.

Charlie applied his peculiar man-management style to the media. Despite stories to the contrary, outside of those in his daily working life and his immediate circle, he rarely dressed anybody down personally. Usually he let his anger be known to one or two trusted lieutenants, who then passed on the message to the unfortunate recipient. The façade could be maintained. The relationship between the two – Charlie and his subordinate – was on an even keel. There were no harsh words. Any suggestion that something was amiss could be stoutly denied, publicly and otherwise. Likewise, despite the fact that Charlie distrusted the media and was not overly willing to cooperate with them, he never displayed any personal animosity to individual journalists that I'm aware of, even when he might have been justified in doing so. He left it to Ó hAnnracháin and to me to express whatever criticism was necessary to the relevant people. I never did, of course, much to Ó hAnnracháin's annoyance, who liked us to be seen to operate in a macho style.

When he became a minister in 1961, Charlie started a practice of giving those journalists and photographers with whom he would have had most contact throughout the year a bottle or two at Christmas time. The gesture carried no obligations nor had it any import, other than the normal friendly expression of seasonal goodwill. When he became Taoiseach, Charlie asked me whether it would be appropriate for him to extend the practice to the political correspondents, whom he knew to be a prickly bunch. When I didn't demur, he included them on his Christmas list. There wasn't the slightest difficulty about this development until his second year in office, when one of the group, a relative newcomer, was accidentally overlooked. This was immediately interpreted, both by the person concerned and a number of the journalist's colleagues, as a coded message of displeasure and it became the subject of gossip around Leinster House. The situation was resolved, apparently amicably, when the journalist was belatedly given a Christmas present. Far from softening an already less than friendly attitude, the festive bottle appeared to have the opposite effect and this journalist's reporting of Charlie subsequently was marked by a particular stridency.

This puzzled Charlie. He came to the conclusion that, just like in politics, there was deep hypocrisy and cynicism underlying the operations of the media. He believed, with some justification, that there were members of the media who, with the connivance of their proprietors, indulged in egregious behaviour. For him to say so publicly, or even to indicate that he thought as much, would have been sufficient to attract the charge of paranoia. There was already a belief amongst some of them that he was paranoid anyway, and of course, to a certain degree, they were correct; but then their actions sometimes fed his paranoia and the whole thing just went around in circles.

My morning sessions with Charlie were very instructive about how he was thinking and what his priorities were. He knew that his back benchers wanted some progress towards a resolution of the Northern Irish problem, which his supporters in the party believed was possible only under him, but, even more than that, they wanted to see an improvement, no matter how slight, in the dismal economic outlook. However, far more revealing than these meetings were the weekly lunches Brian Lenihan, Ray Burke and I took to having after cabinet meetings, when we would review the latest developments in the party and the government. We also discussed means by which we could temper some of Charlie's more ambitious plans. These were invaluable because Lenihan and Burke would fill in the gaps in Charlie's anodyne accounts of what had occurred at cabinet and tell me who had said what and repeat any colourful exchanges. Of course, there were occasions when both of them apologized and said that they could not, for security reasons, tell me certain things, but I was extremely grateful for what amounted to an in-depth briefing of what was happening at cabinet. Charlie eventually copped on to what was happening, because Lenihan rather sheepishly approached me one day and said that we would have to be careful. 'I think the top man suspects me of giving you too much information,' he said. None the less the practice continued and so vivid were the descriptions, Brian's in particular, that it was as if I had a secret camera in the cabinet room.

It was obvious – not that I needed these têtes-à-têtes to establish this – that Charlie ran the cabinet with a style all his own. Years earlier, in a book on the Irish political system, Brian Farrell had asked if a Taoiseach is a chairman or a chief. In Charlie Haughey's case there was no doubt: he was a chief. Ray MacSharry, undoubtedly his star appointment, was able to stand up to Haughey, but the majority of his ministers feared him because they knew what he was capable of doing as far as their political careers were concerned. He had shown little compunction in ridding himself of men of such standing in the party as Gibbons and Molloy, so the new appointees knew that they were in cabinet on sufferance; it wouldn't take a great deal to see them replaced with ambitious back benchers. Many ministers held Charlie in something approaching awe. They knew he was intelligent, imaginative and inventive, but, even beyond that, there were some who regarded every word he uttered as akin to the Wisdom of Solomon. This may sound fanciful, but the truth is that the quality of some of the politicians at that time was not impressive. There were men at the cabinet table who did competent jobs – jobs that were largely administrative and could have been undertaken with ease by anybody in the community with a modicum of brains – but when it came to confronting the country's economic difficulties, there were few who could rise to the challenge and look beyond the immediate political horizon to future decades. Rumour had it that Charlie was less than kind to Dr Michael Woods, his Minister for Health and Social Welfare, who was jocosely referred to from time to time as the party's expert in tomatoes – the subject of his doctoral thesis.

There were others too who let themselves in for disdainful treatment and these were the ones that Charlie constantly worried about
in the management of their departments. He knew how powerful
civil servants could be in the manipulation of a minister, and it was
for this reason that he kept a close eye on what was happening in
departments other than his own. (It is telling that the following
story – no doubt, apocryphal – is told of both Charlie and Mrs
Thatcher, who was also well known for her disregard for her
ministers. Charlie was presiding at the cabinet's traditional Christmas dinner and the waiter, having ascertained his choice of starter
and entrée, inquired about the vegetables. 'They'll have the same,'
he is alleged to have said.)

Interestingly, Charlie never interfered with or inquired about
what was happening in departments run by ministers such as
O'Malley or Colley. This was not because he knew that he would
be told where to go if he did, but because he knew that these men
could run large departments and could distinguish between what
was possible and what was politically acceptable. But it was men
such as O'Malley and Colley who propagated the notion that
Charlie was operating as some sort of Sun King who felt that all
ministerial satellites orbited him and without whom none of them
could exist. And it was to O'Malley and Colley that disaffected
ministers and TDs went for consolation and reassurance.

Charlie had the bright idea of speeding up decision-making by
setting aside a room adjacent to the cabinet room to which ministers
could bring their senior civil servants if they thought something
might come up at cabinet about which they might need additional
information or guidance. The idea was that such discussions could
take place immediately, rather than when the ministers got back to
their departmental offices. In some instances it would have suited
civil servants better if their minister had arrived back at the department without a decision and further 'consultation' was required.
Charlie was having none of that, so it was agreed that when a
minister thought it might be necessary he or she gave advance
notice to the civil servants involved and they arrived and took up
residence, as it were, while the cabinet was in session. Within the

civil service this duty became known as 'serving at the court of King Charlie', a phrase that had an extra sting because he had bought in the poet Anthony Cronin as an adviser. As with all the innovations for which he was responsible, despite initial criticism, the system was adopted and continued by his successors.

Charlie's attitude to the civil service was that it was exactly that – a service. He changed the approach that had prevailed up to his time whereby ministers deferred to the expertise of their civil servants and did not 'upset' them. During the Lynch era there were civil servants whose influence was all-pervasive and who were involved in deciding on every detail of every measure. From the outset Haughey made it known that while he was prepared to listen to advice, he was the political head of government and would make the final decision about what it did or didn't do. Some civil servants did not like him establishing a barrier beyond which they had no more control; after their advice was given, listened to and evaluated, there was no further involvement between the two sides. Officials also became aware that not only had they to deal with their own minister but the likelihood was that they might get a telephone call from, or a summons to meet, the Taoiseach. Some ambitious civil servants liked this; it was an opportunity to shine outside the confines of their own bailiwick. Most of them didn't, particularly those in the Department of Finance, who saw control slipping from their grasp and into the hands of one man. This was where Pádraig Ó hUiginn, who moved into the Department of the Taoiseach after the Department of Economic Planning and Development was disbanded, began to emerge as the major influence on Charlie's economic thinking.

Neither George Colley nor Dessie O'Malley liked Charlie's way of running the government, but there was little they could do about it. Apart from MacSharry, other ministers meekly toed the line. While he knew he could not be in charge of all departments, this did not stop him trying, and he spent a considerable amount of time in consultations with his ministers, advising them and exhorting them to come up with the type of imaginative and eye-catching proposals that he himself would encourage were he in charge. In the past ministers probably met Jack Lynch once a week, at the cabinet meeting; now they were receiving calls daily, and sometimes more often than that, from the new Taoiseach asking detailed questions – and giving instructions – about matters relating to their specific remits. This was all new. In the past, the Department of the Taoiseach had seemed remote and somewhat like the equivalent of a non-executive chairman's office. It was a small place and very few people worked there, and, while its symbolic position was important, it wasn't the engine-room of new ideas or policies. The action was elsewhere, in the large departments where ministers were making decisions that had an impact on the public weal. But now the Taoiseach's office became the powerhouse of government activities and everybody knew who was in charge. Ministers who might never have graced its portals before became regular visitors, and there was a succession of meetings with some of the most senior civil servants from virtually all departments. This led to its own difficulties in that certain ministers, particularly those who had not held either cabinet posts or junior ministerial office previously, became wary of taking decisions in their own departments without first checking in with the Taoiseach's office. The result was that the system became very congested. However, it had the advantage that everybody in the Taoiseach's office knew what was going on in the rest of the government and could advise accordingly.

The man who was probably most affected by this was Gene Fitzgerald, who took over Finance when Michael O'Kennedy became Ireland European Commissioner in December 1980. Gene was a somewhat surprising appointment to Finance and was very uncomfortable in the role. Hardly an hour, let alone a day, passed without Charlie ringing him about something or other. As soon as he put the phone down from Charlie, Gene would ring me and plead: 'What do I have to do to satisfy that man?' After a particularly lengthy consultation one day he came into my office for refreshment and expressed the view that no matter what he did the Taoiseach would not be satisfied. 'How do you put up with him, Frank?' he asked.

This was a question I was asked frequently by both ministers and TDs. They did not seem to understand that when dealing with

Charlie Haughey there was a time to speak and a time to stay silent. Those who spoke too much usually ended up the worse for wear – as I found in my early days with him – and those who stayed silent became that little bit wiser. I did have enormous rows with the new Taoiseach – rows that I would never have imagined possible when Jack Lynch was Taoiseach – and the odd thing was that most of these rows were about trivial matters. But I suffered no real damage as a result, and there wasn't a day when I was working closely with Charlie Haughey that wasn't in some way exhilarating.

On one occasion – and on one occasion only – did a row end with my tendering my resignation. Yet again he had become apoplectic about the lack of coverage of an event in his own constituency and criticized me for not seeing to it that the appropriate media were present. The discussion got somewhat out of hand on both our parts and culminated in my saying that if he wasn't happy with the way I was doing my job he could get somebody else to do it. This annoyed him further and he asked, rather belligerently, if I was capable of having a normal discussion about matters that affected him deeply without having to resort to threats to resign. Of course this took no account of the manner in which he had raised the matter in the first place, but it did underscore a characteristic of Charlie as a leader: when challenged he tended to back off. This is rather at odds with the argument that he was a bully who brooked no opposition. I found that you could raise virtually anything with him and, in general, get a response. You might not like the response, or it might not be the response that you wanted, but you got a response none the less, and you were left in no doubt about his attitude. This, I believe, was part of the problem with some of his ministers. For whatever reason, probably because they were afraid of the robust way he might deconstruct or even ridicule their ideas, many of them refrained from asking him for his views. Instead they waited for him to express an opinion and inevitably by the time he got round to doing so it was negative. Thus, an elaborate system of monitoring Charlie's thinking and moods evolved, more or less organically, in which senior ministers checked and rechecked with those of us who were in constant contact with him to see if what they were going to propose or say would be acceptable. This network included Ó hAnnracháin, Brendan O'Donnell, a super-efficient operator whom Charlie had brought into his private office from the Department of Health, and to a lesser extent myself. Charlie couldn't understand this approach at all. He expected his ministers to have the courage of their convictions and if what they were proposing did not stand up to scrutiny, then so be it: go back and try again. But unfortunately the desire to please was uppermost in the minds of those who owed their preferment to him and, instead of taking on the challenge of running their respective departments, some of them spent most of their time devising ways to impress him.

Charlie expected you to stand up for yourself. In fact he preferred a situation in which there was some cut and thrust and genuine passion as distinct from the usual bland language that characterized much of what passed for debate within the confines of the civil service. I had a very interesting conversation with a senior civil servant who had once served under Charlie in the Department of Health, when we compared notes about the best way to deal with him. He told me that in frustration at its contents Charlie had once thrown a file at him; without thinking, the civil servant had reached over the desk, grabbed Charlie by the lapels and warned him, in crude but succinct language, never to do such a thing again. Charlie apologized and the civil servant believed that their subsequent excellent relationship was based on that display of courage on his part.

I never had a file thrown at me. (In fact the only physical abuse I ever suffered in my career in the public service was when a minister who disagreed with my advice kicked me in the shins. Admittedly the advice was to stop drinking in circumstances where he was already the subject of attention in a public place and where it could have led to embarrassing media coverage.) The only time I witnessed anything untoward with Charlie was when, in the face of severe criticism from the Taoiseach, a relatively senior civil servant broke down and cried, much to the embarrassment of those of us present, including Charlie himself.

Coming to an understanding of Charlie's way of doing things didn't mean that I got used to his flare-ups. Sometimes, however, they had a comic element. Ireland's first government jet was a small cramped eight-seater, and we were in it on the way to Strasbourg for a summit meeting of the European Council when Charlie beckoned me over and whispered, 'I hope you know what your job is on this trip?' I nodded as knowingly as I could, though I hadn't a clue what he was referring to. 'It's to make sure that Lenihan doesn't get pissed.' That was the same Lenihan who was sitting within feet of us. There was a conspiratorial grin on Charlie's face and all I could do was acknowledge that I had my instructions and hope that his Minister for Foreign Affairs hadn't heard him.

As events turned out, there was constant bickering at this meeting arising out of Mrs Thatcher's strident demands to reform the Common Agricultural Policy; she wanted back some of the vast sums she claimed the British had paid into the European budget. There were frequent interruptions for consultations between national delegations. One of these intervals took place close to lunchtime, but lunch wasn't on the menu for Mrs Thatcher. She wanted everybody back in the room within thirty minutes. Brian asked me to get him a drink. When I explained that only orange juice, tea or coffee were available, he said he knew a little bar near by, within the confines of the building, where we could go for a quick snifter. I tried to tell him that the Taoiseach would probably be looking for him and his absence would be difficult to explain. In his usually persuasive and engaging way, he convinced me that we would be back in ten minutes and if asked we could say that we were on the phone to Dublin about something or other of importance.

In the bar we ran into three pol corrs: Michael Mills, Chris Glennon and Dick Walsh. A discussion about what Mrs T. was up to was progressing nicely, as were the drinks, when I was drawn aside by a particularly oleaginous individual from Foreign Affairs with the ominous message that the 'Teeshock' (as he pronounced it in the faux nasal intonations affected by some members of that department, which used to drive Haughey berserk) was looking for me urgently. I made my apologies to the political correspondents and said that the minister and I had to go, promising to link up with them later in the day.

I had always known that Lenihan was possessed of sensitive antennae, but I had never seen them in operation until then. The bar was a short distance from the main staircase leading up to the concourse where the meeting room was located, but between the bar and the bottom of the staircase Lenihan disappeared. As I made to climb the stairs, I looked upwards to see Charlie glaring down. At the top he asked whether it was at all possible for me to carry out the one simple task that I had been given. When, tongue in cheek, I asked what exactly he meant, he hissed, 'You bloody well know what I mean. Where's Lenihan?' I looked behind me, as if fully expecting to see Brian there, and, on finding that he wasn't, said that he was probably on the phone to Dublin about something or other. Charlie exploded and said that I'd better find the Minister for Foreign Affairs or else. Staying as calm as I could in the circumstances – by now there were a few sniggering senior civil servants standing near by anticipating the delightful prospect of seeing Dunlop being publicly filleted by the Taoiseach – I replied that it was unnecessary for him to adopt either that attitude or that tone. If he wanted the Minister for Foreign Affairs urgently, I would arrange it, but in the meantime I would return to the hotel and catch up on matters at home. As I departed, Charlie called me back, but I ignored him and stayed out of sight for a few hours.

When I came back to the venue I was met by an agitated Pádraig Ó hAnnracháin, who wanted to know where I had been because the Taoiseach had been looking for me. He floored me by saying that the Taoiseach was so anxious about me that he had phoned my wife at the school where she was teaching. I couldn't fathom why Charlie would be ringing Sheila at work, nor did I have an opportunity to ask him, because as soon as he saw that I was back in the building he called me over and pointedly asked my view on something or other – his way of indicating that I was back in the circle. Meanwhile, of course, Brian had turned up, affecting an air of total innocence that was as maddening as it was endearing. When I told him the whole story later, including the bit about having to make sure that he didn't get pissed, his response was priceless. 'Sure, doesn't the fecker know that I never get pissed.' That was typical Brian: 'fecker' was the strongest form of opprobrium he could ever summon about anybody. I found out afterwards that Charlie's call to Sheila was along the lines of what a wonderful fellow I was and how sorry he was for taking me away from home so often. It was classic Charlie: he knew he was in the wrong and, while he would never apologize directly, he would do everything he could to indicate that he was contrite. If you were tuned into the correct channel, everything was OK. If you weren't, and there were quite a few who weren't, you were on the road to early insanity.

Some months after Charlie took over the leadership of Fianna Fáil, in a move that had been negotiated secretly between them, Séamus Brennan resigned as General Secretary. It had always been known that Séamus would eventually take the plunge into national politics and recognized that it would be inappropriate for him to do so as General Secretary of the party. The resignation was to be announced by agreement on a specific day. Matters got slightly out of hand when John Feeney of the *Evening Herald* carried a front-page story alleging that Charlie was about to sack Brennan. I was not aware that an announcement was to be made and had had no contact in the matter with John Feeney. Not for the first time, and certainly not for the last, I was furious with the Taoiseach; it was a clear example of a potential story about which I should have been informed, even though it was, strictly speaking, a party-political matter. Charlie and Séamus both denied that they had had anything to do with the leaking of the story. Of course, the presentation of Séamus Brennan's resignation as a 'sacking' did nothing to hinder his prospects within the party. Neither did it do anything to assuage the fears, real or imagined, of those who wanted to believe that Charlie was intent on removing the last vestiges of the Lynch era from the political landscape. But the fact that it appeared and the manner in which it did contributed to the further souring of relations between the Taoiseach, the wider media and elements of his own party.

As episodes like this played out, I came to expect the inevitable question, from within Fianna Fáil, the Dáil or the media, about how I, who had been so close to Jack Lynch, could bear to work with somebody like Charlie Haughey. They seemed to think that I should not show him any support and that I should refuse to serve him. It sounds far-fetched and paranoid now, some twenty-five years later, but there were forces at work in the media and elsewhere – particularly anti-Nationalists who saw Haughey as unsympathetic – whose activities, had they been successful, would have caused problems for the conduct of government business. Had Garret FitzGerald been Taoiseach, he would have been faced with an equally vicious amalgam of forces out to undermine his allegedly anti-Nationalist stance. Such were the times that the normal political opposition that every government expects, and should expect, took on a dangerous toxicity. In effect there was an underground political movement at work to destabilize Haughey in his leadership not only of Fianna Fáil but of the government itself, and this was convenient for those who resolutely refused to accept the outcome of the leadership race and was selfishly indulged by them.

In addition, it is worth noting that the politically correct types who seem to have infiltrated all sections of Irish life, including the highest reaches of politics and government, and who now claim that they were right all along when they averred that there was something amiss with Charlie's private income and that as a consequence he ought to have been hounded from office, would never have been seen dead near Fianna Fáil in the first place. Such people evince the 'proof' of Charlie Haughey's compromised position to say that this is why they were wary of Fianna Fáil in the past. But, for all kinds of cultural and social reasons, even if the party had been purer than the driven snow, they would not have gone near it with a barge pole. Fianna Fáil just didn't have the patina of bourgeois respectability associated with the class from which most commentators emerged or that they aspired to join.

As I have already mentioned, at his first press conference as party

leader Charlie had been asked by Vincent Browne about the source
of his wealth. From then on the question was permanently on the
agenda. I had to deal with the matter a countless number of times.
Foreign reporters came with the most outrageous suggestions,
picked up from pusillanimous Irish sources who used visiting journalists to propagate, or attempt to propagate, stories of a type that
could have only one result: Haughey's removal as Taoiseach and
leader of his party. Every so often magazines such as *Phoenix* and
Magill, read more by fellow journalists in search of juicy stories than
by anybody busy enough to be working at a normal job, delved
into the morass that Charlie's finances were alleged to be. Inevitably
they emerged no wiser than when they had started, but they raised
enough questions to enable those congenitally opposed to Haughey
to use his wealth, and its supposedly mysterious origins, as another
stick with which to beat him. Charlie never commented on the
stories and I never asked him to. While people might say to me
that they had 'heard' something, nobody ever asked me directly to
check out any facts, so I never had reason to bring up his finances
with him. Frankly, I thought the matter none of my business.

In time I realized that if journalists couldn't get anywhere with
the big themes of Charlie's life, they would try to make something
out of little things. It was revealing to discover that even the most
innocent gesture was capable of being read in a mischievous or
suspicious light. After a European Summit meeting in Venice in
June 1980 – one of those at which Maggie Thatcher was again
causing mayhem about the amount of money Britain had to pay to
fund the European Community and was looking for a rebate – he
asked me whether it would be appropriate for him to buy a gift for
a particularly helpful female official from the Department of Foreign
Affairs. The Irish delegation had been anxious not to appear to be
taking an anti-British stance merely for the sake of it and he wanted
to recognize the fact that this official had gone to great lengths to
ensure that the Irish point of view was tabled properly and given a
status that it might not otherwise have had in the heated atmosphere.
I told him that I thought such a gesture would be perfectly proper
and then I found myself deputed to go buy some expensive perfume,

the name of which he gave me. Subsequently, in the presence of at least half a dozen witnesses, Charlie presented the perfume to the woman from Foreign Affairs and thanked her for her hard work. I don't know how it happened but a member of the accompanying media learnt about my shopping trip on behalf of the Taoiseach. There was an unseemly outburst of interest in why the Taoiseach had had me buy perfume at a European Summit. One less than cerebral member of the press corps thought it might be a gift for Mrs Thatcher, but most were trying to find a way to ventilate the name of Terry Keane – not because they intended to publish anything, but because it was a way of undermining Charlie's authority and showing off to each other. Needless to say, I wasn't going to entertain that kind of inquiry for a moment; as far as I was concerned it was another matter that was none of my business.

I never saw Terry Keane and Charlie Haughey together. The fact is that they were extraordinarily discreet and met in the houses of mutual friends. Everybody seemed to know what was going on and nobody wanted to admit to not being up to date with the latest piece of gossip about it. So there were legions of stories – more of them apocryphal than true, I imagine. These included accounts of expensive handbags being thrown into the Royal Canal and Charlie having to dive in after them, of emotional outbursts in every dingy bar and lounge in Ireland (even the people who were dubious about the idea of an affair seemed to enjoy imagining those), and of reported sightings in the most exclusive hotels and clubs across Europe. From a media point of view the liaison was forbidden territory – not by diktat of Charlie but because nobody at the time believed that the relationship had anything to do with the day-to-day running of the country. Yes, the establishment might – and did – snigger over it as they drank their glasses of chateau-bottled wine in expensive houses on the outer fringes of the city, but they also secretly admired Haughey for his brazen and contemptuous attitude towards their or anybody else's opinion. He would be judged on his political record and nothing else.

Of course, there was always *Private Eye*. The vast majority of the Irish public had never heard of, much less read, this satirical British

magazine. Why it began an occasional column about the relationship between Charlie and Terry Keane I do not know. Who wrote
this column is still a mystery to me. At the time there was much
speculation that it was an Irish journalist using a nom de plume,
but this was discounted on the basis that no Irish journalist could
keep such an assignment secret, particularly when it became de
rigueur amongst the chattering classes to spread the latest 'revelations' around the watering holes of Dublin. I was told that it was
the work of the spouse of a well-known Irish journalist living in
the UK, but I never had any proof of that. And a worried Ray
Burke told me that his brother-in-law worked for the magazine;
he was afraid that Charlie would find out and assume he was the
source of the material for the column.

I hadn't put *Private Eye* on the Government Information Service's
shopping list, but I bought it myself. I thought I should know what
was in it in case of any unforeseen eventuality. Inevitably the
eventuality occurred: Charlie rang me late one morning and invited
me to lunch in the dining room in Leinster House. As I was about
to hang up, he added, 'And you can bring the latest *Private Eye* with
you.' I was dreading some wild instruction to try to prevent the
magazine from continuing with the column, or to find out the
identity of the author and have him, or her, silenced. As we walked
together to Leinster House, without preamble, he said, 'Give it to
me.' Then he asked, 'What page?' and proceeded to read as we
walked. His reaction astounded me. He doubled up with laughter
and said, 'Jaysus, Frank, she'll go fuckin' bananas when she reads
this', and pointed out a reference to 'the ageing Terry Keane'. This
was the only occasion he ever referred to Terry Keane in my
presence, but the whole exchange was based on the assumption
that I knew of their relationship. He never asked to see *Private Eye*
again, but I kept buying it for insurance purposes. I don't know if
Charlie ever found out about Ray Burke's brother-in-law. I certainly didn't tell him and, even if he knew, it wouldn't have made
a whit of difference in his attitude because he seemed to be getting
as much enjoyment out of the articles as everybody else in political
circles.

I suspect that Charlie relished his rakish reputation. I recall going to the west with him when Ray MacSharry had persuaded him to open a new factory that was part of an American operation. We flew in by helicopter. On arriving, I found that the wife of the Chief Executive, an immaculately coiffed, exquisitely groomed and utterly formidable lady, had corralled a group of local Fianna Fáil councillors away from the VIP area. They complained to me and I in turn approached her. I identified myself and said that the Prime Minister would be deeply offended if he thought that some of his party's elected officials in the area were being discriminated against and that he was being denied an opportunity of meeting them. Of course, the fact of the matter is that Charlie probably didn't want to see or hear from them at all, but my argument worked and the councillors were let into the VIP section – where they promptly let me down by diving into the brandy and cigars. When we were leaving, waiting in the helicopter for the rotors to start, I pointed out the Chief Executive's wife and said something to the effect that she was 'one thundering fucking bitch'. Charlie turned to me and said, with a withering look, 'Dunlop, you couldn't even begin to imagine what I could do for her.'

Charlie's real personality was impossible to fathom. Sometimes he seemed to go out of his way to adopt what appeared to be a haughty and disdainful attitude to others. When he was in opposition – and still exiled from the front bench – he invited me to the races at Leopardstown one day. He drove the Daimler. (I only got to drive it returning from those far-flung cumainn meetings around the country.) When we arrived at the racecourse it was surrounded by the shawlies – they recognized Charlie's car – selling racecards, programmes and the like, but we didn't buy anything. On his advice I put a few very precious pounds on a horse that I had never heard of. The horse won and I made what I considered to be a fortune. On the way out the car was again surrounded by the shawlies. He lowered the driver's window, stuck out an arm and opened his fist: a handful of coins fell to the ground. I have a vivid recollection of seeing the shawlies scrambling for the coins and of Charlie's laughter over their imprecations. I couldn't figure out whether he was being cruel, or kind, or both. On another occasion, when we were chatting about the ups and downs of life, Charlie said, in an entirely matter-of-fact way, 'Most people live miserable lives.' The comment struck me as being very odd, but since his tone was anything but condescending, I presumed it came out of what he had seen over years of being a TD.

Though he often displayed his devilish and arrogant sides, I knew he could also be a kindly family man, someone who was generous and sympathetic to people going through personal difficulties. But that was something he revealed rarely and never when there was any kudos to be earned from it. Once, when we were on an official visit to the Irish Countrywomen's Association college in Termonfeckin, a member of the association made a point of telling me that her husband, who had been a senior civil servant in the Department of Agriculture when Charlie was minister, had died suddenly at work and Charlie had dropped everything to come and spend the day with her and her family and couldn't do enough to help them. Whatever anybody else thought of him, she and her children regarded him with great warmth and respect. I knew myself that he was capable of the most touching gestures. When Sheila and I were due our second child, sadly it was a stillbirth. Because of the trauma involved, I had taken a few days off from work and he knew what had happened. One day when I went to see Sheila she told me that Charlie had arrived in the hospital unannounced and spent over an hour chatting with her about his own family and the trials and tribulations that Maureen and he had encountered when their children were young. On another occasion, at the invitation of Charlie and Maureen, I brought Sinéad out to Kinsaley for a visit. He was brilliant with children and he took her in his arms and marched off to show her the horses, the ducks and anything else he thought she might enjoy. They were accompanied by the family dog, a little Jack Russell, who obviously thought that she had been supplanted in Charlie's affections by this interloper. She snapped at Sinéad and nipped her in the leg. Charlie was distraught and very embarrassed, and Sinéad was presented with all sorts of goodies to comfort her, including a small china horse that became a treasured possession. Even when he appeared to be at his most unforgiving, there was often a magnanimous gesture aimed at reconciliation. A bottle of champagne provided for him to launch the naval training vessel *Asgard II* failed to smash on the boat's bow, because it had not been properly scored to enable it to break easily. I knew he would be furious. Predictably Charlie wanted to know who was responsible. When the unfortunate individual was identified, he was asked if he thought it would be easier to have the bottle broken over his head. The poor man was mortified. Yet, after the event was over and the incident forgotten by everyone else, Charlie sent him a case of champagne to make up for the embarrassment of the day.

By one route or another the episodes of Charlie losing it found their way into the hands of gossip columnists, most of whom wrote under pseudonyms. This then became a rich vein of material for those who were implacably opposed to Charlie, and the most lurid rumours began to circulate about the internal workings of the Department of the Taoiseach. At the time we laughed these stories off, but, as time passed, we began to realize that there were those who had a vested interest in portraying the operation of the Taoiseach's office in a sinister light.

I could never quite figure out the two Charlies, but I often wondered why he didn't let the softer version emerge from behind the mask. Maybe he knew that his supporters wanted him to be hard, that they thought his tough-man image added a kind of macho flintiness to their own personae. Or it may have been that he did not want to appear vulnerable because he didn't consider it manly. It may just have been that he wanted to keep the real Charlie Haughey private. But, whatever the reason, there were occasions when I thought that if he was prepared to let the mask slip just a little, it might benefit his public profile. Of course it never did.

9. The right men in the right jobs

The eighteen months between January 1980 and June 1981 were trying and difficult and got more so as time passed. Part of the difficulty was practical: for nearly a year we were working in what was effectively a building site. Early in 1980 Charlie had decided to have the Taoiseach's office gutted and refurbished. Nothing had been done to it, or the building in which it was housed, for many years, and parts were pretty run-down. Charlie believed that no matter who the Taoiseach was, his or her office should be a showcase for the nation. This was an admirable undertaking but not very enjoyable to live through. The result justified the discomfort, and it was just a foretaste of what Charlie would ultimately do in turning the UCD School of Engineering in Merrion Street into a fitting seat of government. I could never understand why, but newspapers had an avid interest in the style and furnishings of ministers' quarters, so the work on Charlie's office was the subject of countless stories. The older generation remembered an amazing controversy from the mid 1960s when Jack Lynch complained that the wash-hand basin in his office was chipped. John Healy, then writing under the pseudonym 'Back bencher' in the *Irish Times*, excoriated Lynch and contrasted his chipped wash-hand basin with the lack of facilities in parts of the west of Ireland from where Healy himself came.

As part of the renovations Charlie ordered a state-of-the-art telecommunications system. The old system was antiquated and had been there since de Valera's time. The value of the new phones was that they were instantaneous: you knew immediately if someone was available and you did not have to go through Private Secretaries or intermediaries. But the system had one drawback: the more sophisticated phones in the offices of Charlie and his senior staff in Merrion Street and Leinster House, and in certain offices in

the Department of Finance, had an override facility. This was meant
to be a convenient feature that would allow colleagues to have
three-way conversations. The function was activated by pressing a
button on the phone, and it came into play when two parties were
on a call to each other and a third tried to phone one of them.
Instead of getting an engaged tone, he or she would be linked
straight into the existing conversation and could interrupt it. However, they could also simply listen to the conversation already taking
place unbeknownst to the people talking. When they were first
installed nobody was made aware of this facility, and I doubt if
anybody knew that it was part of the technology; I certainly never
used it. But inevitably this was added to the list of scandals in 1982
when Charlie was accused of installing them deliberately to provide
a means of eavesdropping on ministerial and senior advisers' conversations. Only a select number of phones had the override button
and it worked only on these phones, but the story was spun that
any of the extensions in Leinster House could be accessed by using
it. The belief that the phones were installed for sinister reasons is
unadulterated nonsense. Charlie was nothing if not efficient, and
the phones were commissioned solely for ease of contact and
effective communications between key people. Some people actually had them installed in their homes, but because the range was
short and I lived fifteen miles from Dublin I avoided that. I had
more than enough telephone availability with the normal line and
the scrambler line Justice had insisted on.

Sadly, Charlie did not proceed with Jack Lynch's proposal to
create a permanent residence for the Taoiseach. From the beginning
of his political life, even though he was a TD for Cork, Jack had
lived in the same house in Garville Avenue in Rathgar in Dublin.
It would be unheard of now, and was unusual even then, for a
country TD, albeit a minister or Taoiseach, to have his or her
permanent address in Dublin. Jack didn't go back to Cork every
weekend, and he depended on Gerry O'Mahony, who operated as
a type of constituency agent, to keep him abreast of what was
happening locally. It did not seem to do him any harm electorally:
in the 1977 general election he received over 20,000 first preference

votes, the highest number ever recorded up to then. From time to time after he became Taoiseach I heard him complaining that Ireland had no official Taoiseach's residence and that the absence of such a facility caused serious logistical problems when foreign heads of government came on official visits. Most political parties seemed to appreciate the problem. When the Papal Nuncio decided that he was leaving his residence in the Phoenix Park (a building that was owned by the state but that had been allowed to deteriorate) and moving to a custom-built Nunciature in Cabra, Jack announced – after consultation with whom it is not clear, but most people suspected Máirín – that the state would build an official Taoiseach residence on the site. The cost was projected to be in the region of £1 million and there was political uproar. In fairness to Jack, no one could accuse him of living it up and he knew better than to be seen to do so. (I recall that after the explosion on the *Betelgeuse* oil tanker at Whiddy Island in January 1979, he decided to visit the scene and to talk with representatives of the company and with the local population. I tried in vain to get him to hire a helicopter to make the journey down and back. He refused on the grounds that it would be too 'flash'. The trip took the best part of twenty-four hours, most of it travelling.) Notwithstanding the fuss, Jack was determined and an international architectural competition was to be held to select an appropriate design. At a time when there were constraints on the exchequer finances, there was an onslaught of criticism about the insensitivity of the timing and the cost. Matters rested and political life went on, eventually resulting in Jack announcing his retirement. One of the first decisions Charlie Haughey took as Taoiseach was to cancel the plans for an official residence. He did so with the inimitable words: 'I couldn't live in a smaller house than the one I currently occupy.'

Comments like this added to the notion that Kinsaley was little short of a Versailles and to the vision of Charlie as an aspirant Sun King. I was a regular visitor there from the mid seventies, and, although it was a grand and elegant mansion, Abbeville was also homely and welcoming. There was ample evidence of wealth, but, apart from a pair of large oil paintings of Charlie and Maureen in the hallway, on either side of the entrance to the dining room, it was of a fairly subdued variety. On the walls of the drawing room there were original Malton prints of Dublin, and the house was full of the work of talented young painters, many of them unhung. There were no servants. Any hospitality provided was served either by Charlie himself or by Maureen. Her warmth and down-to-earth approach added enormously to the easy atmosphere. It seemed to operate like any normal traditional Irish household, with Maureen doing the shopping locally and coming back with all the news from everyone she had met. The young Haugheys and their friends came and went, and their stories were listened to attentively and appreciatively.

Charlie seemed a different man in Abbeville – more relaxed and at ease in himself – and, apart from crisis situations, it always struck me that he was far less tense when dealing with matters from home than when he was in his offices in either Leinster House or Government Buildings. When official business was concluded, guests were invited to the 'pub' at the back of the house. Charlie had bought the old mahogany bank-counter of the Ulster Bank in College Green when the building was being refurbished and used it to make a very attractive counter for his own bar, which was fitted out exactly like a comfortable bar in any town in Ireland. Pals of Charlie, like Pat O'Connor, would arrive at the house unannounced and make their way into the bar if he was tied up.

Stories began to circulate to the effect that Jack was commenting privately, and unfavourably, on developments, political and other-wise, that had taken place since his departure. I had very little contact with him after he resigned. The realities of political life prevailed, and he went his way and I went mine. He had decided to take a back-seat in politics and had accepted a number of directorships in companies such as Irish Distillers, the Jefferson Smurfit Corporation and Galway Crystal. Although he had a private office in Leinster House, he wasn't much in evidence around the House or its immediate environs, apart from situations in which his presence was necessary, such as a three-line whip. I was somewhat disconcerted, then, when Charlie asked me to approach Jack and persuade him to stop making comments about how Charlie was running things. Two things struck me about this. First, if Jack was indeed making less than diplomatic remarks about his successor, why didn't Charlie pick up the phone himself, or arrange to meet him, and deal with the matter in a man-to-man fashion? Second, why would Charlie be worried about what Jack was saying, and more particularly why would he want me to approach him? I suspected where this was coming from, and my suspicions were proved correct when, some hours after I had been asked to carry out this unusual task, Pádraig Ó hAnnracháin rang me to find out if I had spoken to 'that bastard Lynch' yet. I told Ó hAnnracháin what to do with himself and arranged to meet Jack some days later.

I knew there was only one way of handling this and I told Jack up front how I had come to request the meeting and exactly what Ó hAnnracháin had said, expletives not deleted. He saw through the ruse immediately. 'Your loyalty is being tested,' he said. When I told him that I knew that to be the case, and after I had apologized to him for the intrusion, we concocted a message that I could bring back to Charlie that could bear whatever meaning he chose to give it. Jack then asked me some pertinent questions that indicated that he was being kept very well informed about what was going on internally in the government. He asked if I was enjoying the experience of working with Charlie. However pleasurable it was to talk with him again – and that was the very last time I met him privately – it was a little uncomfortable to have been put in the invidious position of having to ask him to shut up about his successor.

In January 1980 Charlie had proceeded with a number of personnel changes. Martin O'Donoghue's Department of Economic Planning and Development was abolished, much to the delight of the Department of Finance. He siphoned off some of its brighter staff and the remainder were scattered to the four winds of the wider civil service. The three most senior officials who joined the Taoiseach's staff were Pádraig Ó hUiginn, Noel Whelan, who had been

Secretary of the defunct department, and Paddy Teahon. Both
Ó hUiginn and Teahon went on to become Secretaries of the
Department of the Taoiseach, and Whelan was subsequently
appointed to the European Court of Auditors. Ó hUiginn was to
play a significant and vital role in Haughey's administrations from
then on. Charlie held him in very high regard, and he is the only
civil servant that I ever heard Charlie actually praise; he once told
me that he considered Ó hUiginn 'the best civil servant that I have
ever come across'. I don't know what he said to the man himself –
those who had any knowledge of Charlie knew that he wasn't
given to over-praising people – but his admiration was only ever
thinly veiled.

Dan O'Sullivan who had been Secretary of the Department of
the Taoiseach during the Lynch period, was still there but he was
ageing and when the time came for him to retire I think he did so
with relief. The hyperactivity introduced by Charlie was not his
style. Dermot Nally, who had come to the Taoiseach's office from
the Department of Local Government in 1972 on the recommenda-
tion of Bobby Molloy, was expected to succeed him. Nally had
developed a wide brief that included the economy and Northern
Ireland. He worked closely with the Department of Foreign Affairs
and had a very sound relationship with his counterparts in the UK
that was invaluable at times when the politicians got themselves
into almost irretrievable situations and looked to their advisers for
a way out. Dermot Nally was the quintessential civil servant.
He was widely read and always gave objective, informed advice,
regardless of the personality or the politics of the Taoiseach of the
day. When Liam Cosgrave was Taoiseach, he relied heavily on
Nally for counsel. So did Lynch. This was why Haughey's relationship with him was less dependent. He thought that Nally had been
too close to Lynch and had been responsible, for example, for
advising him to appoint Seán Donlon as Ambassador to Washington, something that Haughey seemed determined to rectify.
Charlie's initial prejudice against Nally was reinforced by Pádraig
Ó hAnnracháin, who seemed to resent the close relationship Nally
had had with Jack Lynch. Ó hAnnracháin transmitted this resent-

ment to the new Taoiseach and it took some time, almost a year in fact, before Charlie realized that however well he had got on with Lynch, or indeed Cosgrave, Nally was giving him the same dispassionate advice as he would have given to his predecessors. In due course the relationship warmed, but never to the degree that it had with either Lynch or Cosgrave.

Unfortunately for Nally, the relationship was still frosty when Dan O'Sullivan retired. Although Nally seemed like the automatic choice to replace him, and his department colleagues thought the announcement to be a foregone conclusion, it wasn't. Charlie decided, again, I believe, on Ó hAnnracháin's advice, to split the job, an unheard of precedent. Noel Whelan became Secretary of the Department of the Taoiseach and Dermot Nally was appointed Secretary to the Government. This was an attempt to curb Nally's influence on departmental policy and to confine him to the more mundane tasks associated with being Secretary to the Cabinet. On the day these appointments were announced, there was one additional announcement that was less prominent but just as important: that of Pádraig Ó hAnnracháin as Deputy Secretary of the Department of the Taoiseach. The Department of the Taoiseach had never had such an official previously, and, given that the Taoiseach had just announced two Secretaries in the one department, people wondered why a Deputy Secretary was needed. The truth was that Charlie was repaying his debts to Ó hAnnracháin, which those with a nose for such deals regarded as cynical on both their parts.

The irony of all of this was that within a very short time Charlie appeared to be disillusioned with the changes he had made. Noel Whelan was given to writing considered memoranda about the ideal way of doing something in the long term instead of coming up with instant solutions. There was constant interaction between Ó hAnnracháin and Whelan, with the former advising the latter as to how best to present matters to Charlie for favourable approval. I knew of all of this because Ó hAnnracháin never stopped talking about it. I also knew that those who depended on this method for advancement were destined for a hard fall. More and more Charlie began to place his confidence in Pádraig Ó hUiginn, who had become an Assistant Secretary, and Dermot Nally. Nally accompanied him to all EC heads of government meetings and to meetings with Mrs Thatcher; and keen-eyed journalists noticed that at press conferences after these events it was always to Dermot Nally that he turned for advice.

It is absolutely essential that there be a good relationship between the political head of a government department and his or her Private Secretary. In a curious way that relationship colours the entire ambience of the department, and if there is any uneasiness, wariness or discomfort, it is transmitted into the overall bloodstream. When Charlie took over from Jack Lynch in December 1979, Brian McCarthy, who had been Jack's Private Secretary, was still in situ. This was quite normal and whether a Private Secretary continued in the post under a new political master was a matter of mutual agreement between them. Brian suited Lynch's personality: he was genial, efficient, non-threatening and deeply committed to the job. A short time after Charlie arrived Brian was promoted to another section of the department and he was succeeded by Seán Ó Riordain. It was pretty obvious from very early on that the relationship between Charlie and his new Private Secretary wasn't an easy one. There was no overt hostility; there were no complaints about the quality of the work; there was no unpleasantness; but there was a perceptible wariness in both of them. At times the atmosphere was bristling with uncomfortable and irritating static. Seán was determined to do a good job and was particularly masterful when it came to detail, but the level of trust that is sine qua non for a successful professional relationship seemed to be missing. It was a chemistry thing and it was inevitable that there would be a parting of the ways. A minister might not get on with, or even talk to, the Secretary General of his Department – and that had been the case from time to time – but it would be unsustainable to have the Taoiseach and his Private Secretary not gelling.

Seán Ó Riordain was succeeded by the Assistant Private Secretary, Seán Aylward, the person who should have been appointed when Brian McCarthy was promoted but was then considered too young and inexperienced by the powers that be in the department. Aylward was Charlie's type of person. Not only could he take instruction, but he also had an innate ability to second-guess the Taoiseach, an invaluable quality in a Private Secretary. An additional quality was that he didn't suffer fools gladly – something that endeared him to Haughey. The Private Secretary is the gate-keeper and controls access. It was very difficult for anybody whom Aylward didn't believe Haughey needed to see to get past him.

At the time before Dermot Nally became a confidant of Charlie, I accompanied Charlie to a meeting between him and the German Chancellor Helmut Schmidt, which had been arranged at Charlie's request. Normally before such a meeting briefing papers are circu-lated to all those travelling with the Taoiseach. In this case there were no such papers, and the travelling party was kept to a mini-mum. In fact nobody, other than the Taoiseach himself, knew the purpose of the meeting. When we arrived in Bonn, Charlie called me aside and said that he wanted me to act as note-taker for the meeting. I knew that this would cause Dermot a degree of angst, and it was left to me to tell him that he was not attending the meeting, which the two leaders had restricted to one official for each side. Dermot took the news well, although he did wonder why the Taoiseach would be breaking with the normal practice. I merely told him that these were the Taoiseach's wishes, and, though I had no authority to give such an undertaking, that I would keep him informed about what occurred.

The meeting between the two men was fascinating. Its real purpose was that Charlie wanted to know if Schmidt would lend Ireland money on the back of the oil and natural gas that were being discovered off our coast. Schmidt chain-smoked throughout, and both seemed very cautious about saying exactly what they had in mind. Every now and again the Chancellor's note-taker and myself would be instructed to lay down our pens and not write, but in my case, whatever about my German colleague, I remembered as much as I could for the five or ten minutes that elapsed before we began discreetly to take notes again. When the meeting concluded Charlie gave me instructions that I was not to tell any of the accompanying officials about the content of the meeting and when I had prepared a note of it I was to give the original to him and not keep a copy. There was consternation amongst the travelling party when I told them what Charlie had requested me to do – the biggest embarrassment for a senior civil servant is to find yourself outside the loop of information, particularly if your counterpart in another administration is aware of the details of a policy proposal or of a meeting between principals about which you are in the dark. All manner of conspiracy theories were mooted, and they imagined that something unusual had been discussed that would cause them difficulties with their counterparts in Europe. Various ploys were used to get me to break the silence that the Taoiseach had imposed on me, but I refused.

When I had written my note of the meeting, I put it into an envelope marked 'Private and Confidential' and handed it to Seán Aylward. He opened it, marked it as having been received from me at a certain time on a specific date and put it amongst the normal papers for the Taoiseach's attention. That was standard procedure: Private Secretaries opened all correspondence on behalf of their ministers. But World War Three broke out. Charlie was furious. I had not done as he asked. Others had now seen my note, and the secrecy that he had demanded had been breached. I remonstrated with him, pointing out that his Private Secretary was just that – private. His instructions to Seán Aylward would be obeyed implicitly, and Seán was not about to go noising abroad the contents of a private note. But nothing I said would placate Charlie, and we never repaired the difficulties that arose from that incident. Obviously nothing came of the proposal to have Germany bankroll Ireland on the back of its oil and gas reserves, and I heard nothing of the matter again. I only wonder what happened to my note. It may well have been destroyed or, *mirabile dictu*, it may appear among Charlie's own collected papers in due course.

When critics try to pin the accusation on Charlie Haughey that during his various periods in office there might have been some attempt, however tentative, to interfere with the normal workings of the civil service, their main example is usually the attempt to move Seán Donlon from his post as Ambassador to Washington to the less prestigious one of Ambassador to the United Nations in the summer of 1980. While nobody disputed the right of the government, or that of the Taoiseach in consultation with his ministers, to make changes that he and they deemed appropriate in furtherance of government policy, it appeared that the motivation for proposing the change was other than Ireland's best interests.

In truth, it was hard to understand the decision to move Donlon, and it ran contrary to the way in which Charlie usually worked. Yes, as with ministers and taoisigh before him and since, there were personality clashes and people were changed around, but the norm was for him to accept the bona fides of those he found in a department and to trust them. The only explanation for the Donlon affair was that there were outside influences at work. While I have no evidence to this effect, none the less I know from comments made to me at the time by Pádraig Ó hAnnracháin that there was distinct dissatisfaction on the part of extreme Irish Nationalist opinion in America, and on the part of Neil Blaney at home, with the Lynch policy – continued by Charlie – of deliberately undermining their claim that money they collected was for the 'relief of distress' of Catholics in the North of Ireland. After the affair had died down Ó hAnnracháin told me about a conversation in which Blaney told him how disillusioned he was with Charlie. 'He can't even change an ambassador now,' he told his old friend Ó hAnnracháin. So Donlon's supporters surmised correctly when they alleged that the decision had been taken at the behest of Blaney and the Nationalist lobby in America, who wanted an ambassador who was more sympathetic to a Republican interpretation of events in Northern Ireland and to the activities of IRA-supporting organizations. As a result of this accusation, a potent combination of top-level Irish-American political influence and media pressure followed and resulted in a volte-face. Donlon would remain in Washington.

Charlie did not discuss any move against Donlon with me. The first I heard of it was when the political correspondents brought it up. When I asked Charlie about it, he merely shrugged and didn't reply. I spoke to Brian Lenihan, the Minister for Foreign Affairs, and it was then that I realized that there was indeed a plan afoot to move Donlon. In effect I was completely out of the loop on this issue, but, none the less, as Government Press Secretary, I was expected to make the issue go away or to keep it out of the media. When the speculation was at its height, I received a phone call at home from Seán Donlon, late at night, which began with the words: 'Frank, what are you trying to do to me?' Seán had been told that the matter had come up with the political correspondents and he genuinely believed, or gave the appearance of believing, that I was part of some conspiracy to get him removed from Washington. I wasn't, and at the time I found the whole episode embarrassing and dispiriting. I had known Donlon from the time Jack Lynch was leader of the opposition, had welcomed his appointment to Washington and was sorry to see that his back was to the wall.

There is no doubt that the episode – both the allegation that the Taoiseach was somehow under the thumb of hard-line Nationalists, and the reversal of the decision when it came under attack – severely and adversely affected the reputation of a number of senior politicians, particularly Charlie himself and Brian Lenihan, and led to an undermining of the authority of the Taoiseach and the government. Having decided to move Donlon, Charlie dithered when the controversy blew up and lost the advantage of being the decision-maker. It was an interesting contrast with how Jack Lynch and Gerry Collins had approached the sacking of Ned Garvey. They decided that they were going to remove him and did so, fully conscious of the brouhaha that would ensue and fully prepared to ride out the storm.

As with all such crises in public life, the issue receded into the background, but not without leaving scars. However, neither Charlie nor Donlon appeared capable of bearing a grudge. I do not recall any incident subsequently when either man showed dislike of the other; both were too professional for that. Some time afterwards we were in New York for the Taoiseach's address to the United Nations, and Donlon, as Ambassador to the United States, was with us. As we went up in the lift in our hotel in Manhattan,

Charlie made a jocose remark to the effect that he hoped he was in the penthouse suite. It was a joke and taken as such by everybody present, but one mischief-making member of the official party, in an attempt to embarrass Donlon, pointedly asked why the Taoiseach had indeed not been given the penthouse suite. Donlon, with a completely straight face, said that it was on the advice of the FBI, which was concerned that there might be snipers at work on adjacent buildings. Other than the merest touch of a smile on the famous basilisk countenance, Charlie gave no indication that he even heard the exchange. There was no further reference to the top floor. When I questioned Donlon about it later, he grinned and said, 'Did you like that?'

Amongst the American politicians who had protested so vigorously against Donlon's removal, Haughey remained a source of suspicion. While on a visit to Washington he was to address a major dinner at which Senator Daniel Patrick Moynihan was also speaking. It was known in advance – at least I knew – that Moynihan had something of a WASPish disdain for the Taoiseach. Even though he was one of 'The Four Horsemen' – the influential group of US politicians that actively canvassed the American administration on the Northern Irish problem – he could scarcely hide his contempt and tried to belittle Haughey in front of his own home audience. It went down very badly, and Haughey, despite some scepticism about him in the upper reaches of the American administration – a scepticism that was not actively discouraged by some of Ireland's diplomatic representatives – gained a few brownie points by virtue of being a missed target of the blue-blooded senator's renowned biting wit.

In the early days, there was always a frisson of antagonism between Haughey and the officials of the Department of Foreign Affairs. For the most part he regarded them as gin-swilling arrivistes with affected manners of speech and behaviour in whom he had very little confidence. When asked innocently by a gauche employee what the Taoiseach thought of a particular diplomat, after only a second's hesitation Charlie replied, 'Some unfortunate village is obviously missing its resident idiot.' Likewise, though they were careful to camouflage their true feelings, there were plenty of clues that the DFA officials and those in the circles in which they moved weren't too taken with Charlie either. I recall a peculiar encounter between Charlie and the American Ambassador, William Shannon, the month after Charlie became Taoiseach, which seemed to bear out the idea that not only did he mistrust the self-importance of diplomats, but some of them could barely cope with a man they regarded as no more than a boorish arriviste himself.

Within hours of Ronald Reagan's swearing in as President of the United States in January 1980, the Iranian authorities announced that they would release American hostages they had been holding. The Irish government agreed that the plane taking the men home could land in Shannon to refuel. I cannot recall who first suggested that the Taoiseach should go to greet the Americans, but the appropriate arrangements were quickly made. A number of people from the Taoiseach's office, including Ó hAnnracháin and myself, and from the Department of Foreign Affairs flew to Shannon for the occasion. It was no more than a photo opportunity, really, because the Americans were strictly forbidden to speak to the media other than to express the normal courtesies and to say how glad they were to be going home. There were the usual comments from the opposition as to the appropriateness of the Taoiseach's actions, and he was accused of turning the event to his own political advantage. The criticism didn't seem to worry him unduly – in his view it was merely a courtesy matter and something that any Taoiseach would do – but for those of us who had an eye to the activities of others it was a foretaste of things to come. It suggested that no matter what Charlie did, it was going to be subjected to intense scrutiny.

After the Taoiseach greeted the ex-hostages and the photographs were taken, we went to a lunch Aer Rianta had laid on. Accompanying us were William Shannon, his wife and family. Shannon had been appointed in Jack Lynch's time, and the two men had got on well. Shannon was a former syndicated columnist who had written a number of books about Ireland and was reasonably well liked in those circles that ambassadors and their colleagues usually frequent. Charlie didn't like him, however – I never understood why – and the feeling was mutual. So, while everybody else chatted amiably over the meal, not a single word was exchanged between Charlie and Shannon.

Even after relations between Charlie and Foreign Affairs had improved, a certain scepticism lingered amongst the mandarins. Many years later, long after my time working in the public service, an Irish diplomat gave the game away totally when he made indiscreet comments about Charlie while hosting an official function. At the time Fianna Fáil was in opposition and one of its front bench spokesmen was present at the event. The Foreign Affairs man momentarily let the diplomatic façade slip and made an ungracious and unusually candid remark about Charlie's private life. For a diplomat on a mission abroad to criticize a former Taoiseach and, as it turned out, a man who was to become Taoiseach again simply wasn't done. The Fianna Fáil TD took exception and left the dinner. He subsequently complained to the Department of Foreign Affairs, and, as is the way with all such matters, it wound its way into the national newspapers. An attempt was made to portray the TD in a sort of peevish light, but there was no denying that the remark had been made. The impact of such remarks at home and abroad cannot be calculated, but there can be little doubt that they were bad for Charlie Haughey's image as Taoiseach or as potential Taoiseach.

Though he didn't have the usual junketeering mentality that you find amongst many politicians, Charlie loved foreign travel and particularly those events that brought him on to the world stage. Not that all these always went as planned. I remember being in the White House for St Patrick's Day when Charlie presented Ronald Reagan with an ancient map of Tipperary showing Ballyporeen, the village from which his ancestors allegedly hailed. Reagan was at his B-movie best and made a short speech, the prompt notes for which were printed on his shirt cuff. When the ubiquitous Irish tenor sang 'Danny Boy', the American TV cameras, on cue, turned on Reagan, who took an immaculately starched white handkerchief from his breast pocket and dabbed his eyes. The image was shown on all the network news broadcasts that evening. After we came home Charlie, through Fianna Fáil channels, requested a copy of the footage from RTÉ, for use by the party in preparing party political broadcasts – a standard procedure at the time – and we discovered that the RTÉ crew that had been travelling with us had somehow managed not to film the event at all. Charlie lost his rag completely.

During his ministerial career Charlie had probably covered a wide swath of the globe, but he had an affinity for European cities, particularly Paris. Whenever we found ourselves there, he liked to take private time to visit restaurants and bistros that the official delegation would never aspire to, simply on the basis of cost. There was very little likelihood of an Irish delegation, no matter how senior, staying in or dining at the George V, where he was well known. But he was extremely discreet. He was always aware of the accompanying news crews and never gave them the slightest opportunity to report anything other than the fact that he represented his country abroad with dignity and aplomb. In recent times his preference for Parisian style has been publicized. On one occasion, when we had been to see President Valéry Giscard d'Estaing, he insisted that Hugh McCann, the Irish Ambassador, Brian Lenihan, Pádraig Ó hAnnracháin and I accompany him to an exclusive tailoring establishment. He was greeted with the type of deference that only the French can muster for their political masters. Charlie loved teasing people from Foreign Affairs – whether it was to puncture inflated egos or to ensure that they realized that he was in charge, I don't know – so when the manager asked him who we were, he replied, with an offhand wave and a glint in his eye, that we were his personal security detail. This brought hoots of laughter from Lenihan, Ó hAnnracháin and myself, but it was obvious that the Ambassador was not too amused.

Apart from any clash of personal styles that might have caused antagonism between Charlie and the Department of Foreign Affairs, he did not trust its officials because he suspected that they were too close to Whitehall. In time he and department officials established some sort of working relationship, and he developed a good rapport with individual members of its staff, and a very high regard for one of its more famous officers, Noel Dorr. But at the beginning, particularly when it came to Northern Ireland, he wasn't willing to take material he received from Iveagh House at face value. Dr Martin Mansergh's appointment to the Department of the Taoiseach was a public indication that he wanted his own advice about the North. Mansergh was a colleague of Pádraig Ó hAnnracháin's daughter Orla in the Department of Foreign Affairs, and when Ó hAnnracháin met him at a family party he was impressed by this bright young man who, notwithstanding his credentials – an Anglo-Irish background, a British public-school education and an Oxford degree – displayed Nationalist sympathies. Charlie was determined to show that he was going to move things along, in spite of the views of the sceptics – not only amongst his political opponents and in media circles, but also in his own party, where some regarded his activities in the late 1960s as an insurmountable impediment to his achieving anything on the North. When Charlie expressed dissatisfaction with the advice he was receiving from the Department of Foreign Affairs, Ó hAnnracháin mentioned Mansergh and the young man was summoned to a meeting. Mansergh was the antithesis of everything one expected of somebody working closely with a Fianna Fáil Taoiseach, particularly Charlie Haughey, but Charlie was nothing if not cosmopolitan in his tastes, and he gave Mansergh his head. As time went on, he began to rely on him more and more for draft material on a number of issues. Mansergh was a one-man powerhouse of policy ideas and produced prodigious amounts of material for consideration not only by the Taoiseach but by other ministers also.

Little did Ó hAnnracháin or anybody else in the department realize when he was appointed what a central and seminal role Mansergh would play for nearly two decades in attempting to resolve the Northern problem. He went on to serve Albert Reynolds and Bertie Ahern, and when John Bruton became Taoiseach in 1994, he invited Mansergh to remain on as an adviser on the North. Mansergh opted to stay with Fianna Fáil. The interesting thing about the Bruton invitation is that one of the Taoiseach's key advisers then was the former Irish Ambassador to Washington, Seán Donlon. It was Mansergh's work in developing contacts with the Northern political parties, and with the many Nationalist and Unionist organizations, that laid the foundations for an increased and better appreciation on the part of policy-makers in Dublin of what would be required if any movement were to take place. His weren't the first or the only valuable links between North and South, but they were the first personal contacts between Northern parties and an officer of the Taoiseach's department.

Back when Mansergh was appointed, members of the Department of Foreign Affairs were astounded. The word was that the Taoiseach had plucked from their midst a low-ranking officer with no track record and made him his adviser on Northern Ireland. Clearly, they concluded, the new Taoiseach was an even worse judge of people than they had suspected. As he did so many times, Charlie was to prove them all wrong.

Shortly after Charlie arrived there was some discussion in the Department of the Taoiseach about the political allegiances of some of those heading up the more high-profile semi-state commercial organizations. This was nothing new. The appointment of the chief executives of these organizations was still a function of the cabinet. At the very least, cabinet approval was necessary before any such appointment could be ratified. Despite the fact that the tradition of providing the same service to the government of the day, regardless of its political colour or make-up, was a principle underlying and governing the relationship between government and the public services, none the less all politicians, bar none, have their preferences and sometimes the action of a chief executive under one administration is used against him or her by another. Therefore such discussions took place after every change of government. I recall a dinner party shortly after Fianna Fáil came into office in 1977, at which at least three cabinet ministers were present, when this was one of the main topics of conversation. The name of a member of the board of Bord na gCon came up, and this led to a broader discussion about the way the coalition had filled every available vacancy on state boards with its own people before it left office and the difficulties that this caused for the new government in trying to get its own people appointed. The problem seemed to be one of how to explain to Fianna Fáil supporters that there were no vacancies, rather than any view about the qualifications or otherwise of the incumbents.

As far as I can recall, the talk about these appointments in the Department of the Taoiseach did not go so far as to suggest changes in existing arrangements. However, it was another area where Charlie's coterie of advisers appeared determined to make mischief. For instance, at that time, before the purchase of a government jet, when the Taoiseach and members of the government had no option but to fly with Aer Lingus, one of its CEO's more mundane functions was to be present, if possible, in the VIP lounge for both the departure and the arrival of the Taoiseach. This came to be accepted as a matter of protocol and normally these were very pleasant occasions involving no more than the standard courtesies attached to those who hold high political office. David Kennedy, the Aer Lingus boss when Charlie came into office, was a close friend of Jack Lynch. Without any evidence whatsoever some of Charlie's pals claimed that Kennedy was not as attentive when Charlie was passing through the airport as he had been when Jack was flying. But I never heard of or witnessed any comment or action by David Kennedy that led me to believe that he was not treating Charlie with the same courtesy as he had Jack. Similarly, nothing Charlie ever said or did suggested to me that he was anything other than satisfied with David Kennedy's performance and service.

This was one of many instances of one or two people around Charlie appropriating for themselves the right to decide whether an individual was behaving as deferentially as they supposed he or she ought. I could never understand why Charlie did not nip this kind of behaviour in the bud. Perhaps, a bit like modern popstars who have teams of people to make ridiculous demands on their behalf, so they can then impress everyone with what simple, unspoilt creatures they are, it suited him to have a retinue of loyalists to create a fuss. Their efforts would then allow Charlie to act as if the deference he received was a spontaneous response to his greatness, and to graciously acknowledge it. If that was his strategy, it backfired, merely exposing his Achilles heel: a craving for recognition. It inevitably led to unnecessary trouble and conflict, the result of which was that his reputation was adversely affected.

I recall one encounter between Charlie and Kennedy that started seriously but ended on a comic note. A former Trappist monk hijacked an Aer Lingus plane. The plane landed in a tiny airfield in northern France, where the hijacker revealed his demand: that the Pope make public the Third Secret of Fatima. All those on the list for immediate contact in the event of a major emergency were telephoned, including the Taoiseach and some of his ministers, and a meeting was arranged between the Garda, the army and senior officials from Aer Lingus and Aer Rianta. When everyone arrived at the airport, an Aer Lingus executive provided a detailed briefing, by the end of which it was clear that it would take some time before a final outcome, either good or bad, was reached in the delicate negotiations between the hijacker and the French police.

It was agreed that everybody would reconvene in an hour, and, since Kinsaley was only ten minutes from the airport, Charlie decided to return there, inviting the Aer Lingus and Aer Rianta officials to accompany him to await developments. On arrival, instead of inviting everybody into the house, Charlie, after a conspiratorial wink at me, led the party around to the back of the house to a lake. He picked up a stick, leant forward and began to agitate the surface of the water. He invited them to look at the oil floating on its surface. Then he turned to David Kennedy and said, 'Look at what your planes are doing to my lake. They're killing the swans.' Kennedy, normally a suave and polished performer who, one suspected, wasn't surprised by anything, was clearly taken aback and said something soothing to the effect that he would look into the matter. But that wasn't going to satisfy Charlie. He had obviously given the matter some attention and began to recount the number of planes that flew overhead each day and the estimated volume of pollution that occurred as a result. Whatever expectations the officials had had – presumably something in the nature of a welcome Saturday afternoon drink – were dashed, and there was a mass exodus back to the airport to see if anything had developed with the potential national emergency. 'That will give them something to do for a day or two', was Charlie's only remark as he and I repaired to his bar.

10. Meeting the Iron Lady

After all that has happened with regard to the North it may sound trite now, but I remember Charlie giving an instruction that when official state dinners and receptions were being held senior Unionist politicians were to be invited, including Ian Paisley. The first such invitations were dispatched and a response was not long coming from the Paisley headquarters on the Ravenhill Road. The actual invitation card was returned and written across it in bold black ink were the immortal words 'No Surrender'.

But at a very early stage after he became Taoiseach Charlie realized that he could achieve nothing on the North unless he could convince Margaret Thatcher that Ireland and Britain would have to engage in some meaningful way before a solution could be brought about. Charlie knew he was not well regarded by either the British establishment or Mrs Thatcher, and he could also see that she had never really focused on the Northern problem. Thatcher and the establishment's reported antipathy to Charlie may have added to his standing amongst his more Nationalist supporters, but in a curious way it also added impetus to his determination to be the first Taoiseach to achieve some softening in the impasse between the two countries. Normally the Taoiseach and Prime Minister would meet in the margins of European summits. These were little more than courtesy calls, however. Apart from the humiliating meeting between Thatcher and Jack Lynch after Lord Mountbatten's funeral, nothing of substance had occurred since she had become Prime Minister.

When it was announced that there would be a meeting between Charles Haughey and Margaret Thatcher in Downing Street in May 1980, it was as if there had never been a meeting of this kind previously. Nobody said so, but it was clearly anticipated that there would be some sort of dust-up that would end any hope of progress while they were both in office.

After all the preparations had been made and the appropriate briefing papers read, Charlie was anxious to know which media were travelling to London. When I told him that the event would receive blanket coverage, particularly on television, that there would be an army of Irish journalists present, and that he would be expected to hold a press conference at the Irish Embassy after the meeting, which would be carried live on radio and TV, he appeared unusually satisfied and didn't make any particular requests about limiting interviews. Interviews were the bane of Charlie's existence, and he either couldn't or wouldn't understand that one interview with one reporter would not satisfy the press corps' requirements for individual treatment. It got more complicated when you had to explain why he was expected to do six or seven different interviews for six or seven different RTÉ programmes. 'Don't they all work for the same bloody organization?' was his usual reply.

In his office in Leinster House he appeared quite relaxed on the eve of the meeting and showed me the box, wrapped in green paper, in which he had placed an Irish Georgian silver teapot to present to Mrs Thatcher as a surprise gift. 'She likes silver, or so they tell me,' he said. A messenger arrived with another package and Charlie showed me the silver tea strainer that he had had engraved with the words of St Francis, used by Mrs Thatcher when she entered Downing Street as Prime Minister for the first time: 'Where there is disharmony, let there be peace.' He was very pleased with himself and said, 'That will knock her back a bit.'

The following morning, however, Charlie's mood had changed. Geraldine Kennedy, then on the political staff of the *Irish Times*, had a story to the effect that the Taoiseach was to present Mrs Thatcher with a special gift at his first meeting with her and that the *Irish Times* could exclusively reveal that it was an Irish Georgian silver teapot. The element of surprise was gone, and, as far as Charlie was concerned, the whole thing had lost its impact. I have never discovered how, or where, Geraldine Kennedy got the story.

Interestingly, it did not include the fact that the Taoiseach was also presenting the Prime Minister with a tea strainer with an inscription. Her source obviously didn't know about it or had overlooked it. No doubt the relevant official in No. 10 Downing Street with responsibility for such matters read the *Irish Times* and the appropriate cutting was presented to Mrs Thatcher in advance of the meeting.

On the morning of the meeting Pádraig Ó hAnnracháin was seen delicately carrying the box containing the teapot through the corridors of the Irish Embassy in Grosvenor Place; he placed it on his lap in the back of the limousine following the Taoiseach's car and carefully lifted it out on arrival at No. 10. One of the British journalists shouted, 'Is that the teapot?' Unusually, Ó hAnnracháin refrained from replying. After the official photographs were taken and the usual diplomatic pleasantries had been exchanged, officials indicated that the parties should move to the meeting room. At this, Ó hAnnracháin stepped forward with the box and handed it to Charlie, who in turn presented it to Mrs Thatcher as a memento of their first meeting. She accepted graciously and was about to pass it to an official when Ó hAnnracháin took a pair of nail scissors out of his top pocket, stepped forward and snipped the tricolour ribbon around the box. The wrapping fell away and Mrs T. was obliged to look at the gift. As for the meeting, well, the two prime ministers agreed that there would be regular meetings between them to discuss Northern Ireland, so that was progress.

At home, however, when it came to Northern policy, Charlie had an incipient problem in the person of Síle de Valera, granddaughter of the founder of Fianna Fáil and something of a thorn in Jack Lynch's side in his latter days as Taoiseach. She had been outspokenly critical of Lynch's approach to the North, and after a speech in September 1979 he had told her not to speak on the subject again. The symbolism of the granddaughter of the founder of the party criticizing its current leader over his handling of the Northern situation was not lost on anyone. The speech was seen to have been a vehicle for the more cerebral elements of the anti-Lynch faction to destabilize the consensus approach that had been adopted to the Northern problem and to undermine his leadership. The speech was generally regarded as having been written for de Valera. Pádraig Ó hAnnracháin, a former Private Secretary to her grandfather, clearly had a hand in it. I know that Charlie Haughey had nothing to do with either the script's preparation or the choice of Síle de Valera to deliver it, but those who wanted to see Charlie's influence on anything that might be injurious to Lynch saw it there. The event was ultimately overshadowed by the over-flights controversy and Charlie Haughey's own speech praising Pádraic Pearse's philosophy two months later. After Jack Lynch resigned and Charlie had taken over, de Valera had sought, and been granted, permission to speak publicly on any issue that interested her. She, presumably, thought that with Lynch gone the party had a leader who was a stronger shade of green; he, presumably, thought that, as one of the young deputies who had helped him on his way, she was totally onside. He was wrong and we never knew what she might come out with next, or why.

The Northern situation reached crisis point in October 1980 when a number of Republican prisoners announced that they were going on hunger strike in order to achieve political status. Thatcher refused to accede to the prisoners' demands. This provided fertile ground for the more fervid Republicans in Fianna Fáil who wanted to criticize Haughey for developing any relationship with Thatcher but had not had a ready excuse up to then. Charlie knew that he was walking on very thin ice and he wanted to keep both sides happy – the Republicans in his own party and Thatcher in London – so that he could pursue his ambition of reaching some sort of rapprochement. To add to the difficulties there was a by-election in a border constituency, Donegal, and secret preparations were under way for a second meeting with Thatcher. The last thing he needed was a high-profile Fianna Fáiler inflaming passions with unnecessary rhetoric. When Síle de Valera stood up at a by-election rally in Letterkenny and launched an attack on Thatcher for her callous treatment of the hunger strikers, the implied criticism of a Taoiseach who would have anything to do with Thatcher – a

Taoiseach sitting feet away from her on the same platform – was unmissable. Shortly after she began to speak, Charlie realized that she was about to cause trouble and he beckoned me over. He asked if there was anything we could do to stop her and when I said nothing other than taking the microphone from her, he swore. I went to the front of the platform and, in the manner of a prompter in a Shakespearean drama, tried to get her to desist. (Afterwards Charlie said that I looked like a 'dancing dervish' in front of the stage.) She was having none of it. Besides, the crowd was lapping it up. When she concluded, she left the platform before Charlie spoke.

There was consternation amongst the ministers present. When the rally ended, Charlie asked that we all meet in fifteen minutes. The venue was provided by Bernard McGlinchey, a senator who had stayed with Fianna Fáil when Neil Blaney had broken away to form Independent Fianna Fáil in 1970. The Taoiseach, the Minister for Foreign Affairs, a selection of party supporters and myself (though technically, as a civil servant, I shouldn't have been present, but then I was often in places I should not have been) gathered in McGlinchey's office in the Golden Grill Restaurant to assess what had happened. It was a Saturday evening, and both Charlie and I knew that the timing had been perfect for the following morning's papers. What intrigued me was that to guarantee coverage the speech would have to have been submitted to the Sundays in embargoed form by mid afternoon at the latest. Yet, contrary to the normal procedure with a controversial speech of this type, we had heard nothing about it and had not been contacted for a reaction. Meanwhile Síle de Valera could not be found and was not contactable by telephone. Suspicions began to grow about her motivation. Speculation reached fever pitch when it was discovered that she had been seen driving away from the rally in the company of Charlie McCreevy.

McCreevy's initial enthusiasm for Charlie had faded and he was deeply disillusioned with his leadership. Those who wanted to dismiss him attributed his turnabout to disappointment at not being made a junior minister. I knew this to be totally untrue. McCreevy had built up a successful accountancy practice in Naas with offices elsewhere in the country. He was not noticeably interested in ministerial office. Nor had he the remotest interest in Northern Ireland or in any relationship that Charlie might be thinking of having with Mrs Thatcher. What he was interested in was causing trouble for Haughey with a view to making him do what he had promised to do: namely, get the economy back on an even keel and bring some order to the public finances. He had come to realize that if he wanted to reach Charlie he had to do so where it hurt most. He knew that realistically he could not achieve much of a change in economic policy, at least not in the immediate run-up to the general election. But he could use the Northern issue as a bargaining chip: he would shut up about the North if Charlie would promise to change his tack on the economy. So he deliberately teamed up with de Valera to deliver a blow to Charlie's political solar plexus.

In retrospect his actions didn't appear to have had any great coherence. Very few realized what a formidable opponent McCreevy would become, and on that fateful night in Letterkenny if anybody had suggested that he would become a long-serving Minister for Finance in future Fianna Fáil governments and an EU commissioner, they would have been laughed out of court. Back then he was something of a loner and regarded as a maverick; he did not command any great support amongst the back benchers, who were looking to the next election and were not interested in becoming involved in a bruising battle with the leader over policy issues. All they wanted was for the Taoiseach to make things right again so that their seats would be guaranteed.

I recall that Donegal by-election having its comic moments too. On the Sunday morning after the rally at which Síle de Valera had made her speech, few of Fianna Fáil's elected representatives put in an appearance at the regulation after-Mass meeting. So Charlie dispatched messengers to the various hotels and guest houses to collect the under-performing – and under-the-weather – TDs, senators and county councillors. (From that time on he banned alcohol during by-elections, an embargo that was honoured more in the breach than in the observance.) For their penance Charlie, against all local advice, decided that they would spend the afternoon canvassing housing estates in Letterkenny. Everybody knew the golden rule of by-election politics: you don't canvass on a Sunday afternoon. You find out where the local football or hurling team is playing and you put in an appearance there. But Charlie was adamant. The teams set off, and Brian Lenihan and I accompanied Charlie, with Brian operating as something of an advance man, knocking on doors and inquiring of those who answered if they would like to meet the Taoiseach. One woman expressed great eagerness to meet him, and Brian proudly introduced Charlie, who was graciousness personified. The woman wasn't the slightest bit overawed, and she stood there in her apron demanding to know what Charlie was going to do about the exchequer borrowing requirement. About this time Garret FitzGerald had been speaking publicly and repeatedly about the EBR, and, while the vast majority of the public had little or no understanding of what he was talking about, it sounded important and impressive. Charlie inquired what she thought he should do about it. She was not deterred by that tack and persisted in her view that something — what specifically remained a mystery — had to be done. Charlie said that the only man who could do anything about something as complicated as the EBR was Dr Garret FitzGerald. 'Don't be daft, man. Garret doesn't know what he's talking about!' The poor woman was nearly flattened in her hallway when the Taoiseach of the country and his minister collapsed in paroxysms of laughter. Just before the canvassing was finished, we came across a parked car with steamed-up windows. From its rhythmic movement there was no doubt about what was going on inside. Nothing would do Charlie but to tap on the driver's window; and when it was lowered a fraction, he asked, in a voice laced with innocence, 'I'm not disturbing anything, am I?' The expletives rang out over the hills of Letterkenny. 'Another first preference,' he said.

Charlie was justifiably worried that Síle de Valera's comments would be interpreted by the British as evidence of his real attitude to Thatcher and in particular to her handling of the hunger strike.

He was furious that McCreevy didn't seem to appreciate the sensitivities involved. It took some time for matters to cool down, and extensive efforts were made both in Dublin and in London to reassure the British government, and Thatcher in particular, that such statements by Fianna Fáil back benchers did not represent official Irish policy or attitudes to current events. Preparations continued for a summit at Dublin Castle in early December, and Charlie took a personal interest in all the arrangements. He didn't want to leave anything to chance, particularly since Thatcher had decided that she would stay in Dublin overnight. For security reasons it was agreed that she would sleep in Dublin Castle. The symbolism, yet again, was lost on nobody. The date of the meeting was 8 December, the feast of the Immaculate Conception. After subsequent events did not go to plan, a Fianna Fáil wit subsequently referred to the occasion as Charlie's Immaculate Deception.

There was huge media interest in the meeting and intense speculation, not denied by official sources on either side, that something significant was about to occur. Senior members of Fianna Fáil believed that Charlie was about to pull off the political achievement of a lifetime by starting a process that would result in the ultimate resolution of the problem of the North. Some of them, including some senior ministers whose involvement was minimal, were not behind the door in giving optimistic private briefings to the media. There was an air of expectation that history was about to be made in the fortress that had been the headquarters of British rule in Ireland.

Margaret Thatcher and her high-powered delegation, which included the Foreign Secretary, Lord Carrington, the Chancellor of the Exchequer, Sir Geoffrey Howe, and the Secretary of State for Northern Ireland, Humphrey Atkins, arrived at the castle by helicopter and never left its precincts. I was present as a member of the Irish delegation, but I did not attend any of the meetings with Thatcher. Instead, together with her Press Secretary, Bernard Ingham, I dealt with the hundreds of reporters, photographers and camera crews. We both knew that the prime ministers' statements after the meeting would be very important, and over lunch we discussed the text of a draft statement. After the meeting both sides said it had gone well and expressed themselves satisfied with the outcome. Bernard Ingham and I issued a joint communiqué, based on a briefing from the senior civil servants present at the meeting, that referred to an agreement to conduct 'joint studies' on a variety of matters including 'possible new institutional structures' – a phrase that would be the cause of much angst later.

Charlie, as was his wont, said that there had been an 'historic breakthrough' and that 'the totality of the relationship' between Ireland and Britain was up for review. He was in high good humour after the Thatcher entourage had taken off from the castle yard and invited his immediate party for a celebratory drink. As we passed through the throne room, Pádraig Ó hAnnracháin jocosely remarked that as a result of the day's events the Taoiseach could now sit on the throne once graced by Queen Victoria. 'Sure after today aren't you the King of Ireland?' he remarked, to much amusement. Charlie promptly skipped up the steps and sat there regally. Out of the corner of my eye I noticed a British Embassy official watching the proceedings. When he saw that I had spotted him, he said, 'Don't worry, Frank, I won't be including this in my notes.' It made me wonder what he actually would be including, since he seemed to have attached himself to the Irish party for most of the time immediately after the conclusion of the summit.

The afterglow from the summit was a pleasant break from the constant dreary sniping about Charlie I had to deal with in the press. The following Sunday, however, the *Sunday Tribune* carried an interview with Brian Lenihan in which he told Geraldine Kennedy (who had moved from the *Irish Times*) that 'joint studies' would cover everything, including constitutional matters. All hell broke loose. The Northern Unionists had already expressed serious concern as to what these joint studies entailed, and, despite repeated assurances from their own government that the constitutional status of Northern Ireland was a matter for the British government and the Northern Irish people alone, they now had confirmation from a senior member of the Republic's government that constitutional matters would be on the table. Garret FitzGerald threw petrol on the fire by accusing the Taoiseach and the government of attempting to resolve the Northern problem over the heads of the Protestant majority. The suspicion that there was something of real substance afoot was given further credence when the hunger strike in the North was called off. This would not have happened, so the argument went, unless the Provisional IRA had been convinced that real progress was being made. Haughey was furious with Lenihan, and the two had a very nasty row. Lenihan, with some justification, argued that constitutional matters had not been excluded and pointed to the fact that there had already been media speculation to that effect – speculation that had neither been denied nor corrected by either the Taoiseach's own department or by the Department of Foreign Affairs. The arguments and the counter-arguments rumbled on into the New Year until other issues, mainly economic, took over.

Mrs Thatcher never forgave what she considered to be the overselling of the Dublin Summit, and she made her views known to the Taoiseach at a subsequent encounter at the margins of a European summit meeting at Maastricht in Holland. While Charlie and the Irish delegation knew that Lenihan's comments had caused a diplomatic frisson, no one expected that they would lead to any huge difficulties in what was regarded as a relatively routine event. Normally each of the politicians would be accompanied by an official – Dermot Nally on this occasion – and the encounter would last about thirty minutes. However, before the meeting, the British made it clear that the PM wanted to see Charlie alone, and he took off, thinking nothing of it. To our surprise he reappeared after five minutes. From the dark look on his face it was clear that something was amiss. As we crowded around him, somebody said, 'How did it go, Boss?' He answered in a lugubrious voice: 'She's very upset.' Then, giving Lenihan a baleful look, he added, 'And it's all your bloody fault, Lenihan.' Apparently Thatcher, in no mood for small talk, had given Charlie a dressing-down about what his foreign minister had said and then peremptorily dismissed him.

Overshadowing everything Charlie did during his entire first period as Taoiseach was the dire state of the national finances. Even before he had taken over from Jack Lynch, Charlie had spoken incessantly in private about the disastrous fiscal prognosis. He was scathing about the effects of the Fianna Fáil manifesto and blamed Martin O'Donoghue for its excessive pump-priming policies. As soon as he became Taoiseach, Charlie took advice – reputedly from banker Brendan Menton (senior) – and decided that the only way out of the situation was to confront it head on. He was angry that he had to do this but felt that the public, having come through the damaging postal strike, gone on tax marches and seen unemployment rising, had an appetite for the truth. People needed reassurance that things would be brought under control. So in early January 1980 Charlie arranged to address the nation on television. There was much speculation about what he was going to say, and there were lurid rumours in certain watering-holes around Dublin that there was going to be some kind of *coup d'état*. When the first draft of the script became available to a small circle of advisers, it was obvious that Charlie was not going to hold anything back. I, amongst others, was thrilled to see some positive confrontation of the problems facing the country instead of more of the old canards – 'a small open economy', 'if Europe sneezes Ireland gets a cold', and so on.

It sounds tame now, but then it was almost revolutionary for a Taoiseach to go on television and say, as Charlie did that night, that the finances of the country were in deep trouble, that the state was overspending, and that we would have to tighten our belts. (His critics say he was hypocritical to ask the rest of the country to tighten its belt back then while his apparently opulent lifestyle was being financed by rich businessmen. In my view his personal circumstances were completely irrelevant. They undermined neither the accuracy of his diagnosis on the economy nor the wisdom of his prescription for it.) Newspaper coverage of the broadcast was extremely positive, if tempered with the usual rider that the problem had been created by the politicians in the first instance. The financial markets reacted well. Since the back benchers were happy, the impression that the public welcomed it too (notwithstanding the fact that the remedies outlined by the Taoiseach were unpalatable and reinforced some voters' cynicism about politicians' promises) seemed accurate; they would have been the first to know if it had backfired. It is difficult now, nearly twenty-five years on, to convey the sense of relief that was palpable throughout the country when Charlie announced that he was going to put the country back on an even keel and that hard decisions would have to be made. The glory days were over, and the public mood for politicians buying off their problems with goodies that could not be paid for had been exhausted. The whole exercise augured very well for the country's future and for Charlie's political standing. It seemed that he now had the opportunity not only to endear himself to the public but also to copper-fasten his reputation as a prescient politician and write himself into the history books for the right reasons. However, when the crunch came he bottled out.

While basking in the populist approval that followed the broadcast, the back benchers began their usual campaign for the maintenance of 'vital' services in their own constituencies. The Not-In-My-Back-Yard syndrome applies not only to communities opposing unglamorous developments, but also to TDs when a hospital is closing or a decision to build some local facility is reversed. And so it began. There seemed to be a requirement for a hospital at every crossroads in Ireland. Every nun in charge of a secondary school seemed to think that while others could wait, she was the only one entitled to either an extension to her existing school hall or, preferably, a new gymnasium. As we travelled around the country, we were met by delegation after delegation who would preface their remarks with heartfelt, no doubt, expressions of congratulations to the Taoiseach for his courage in grasping the nettle of the public finances and then proceed, without any embarrassment or recognition of the contradiction, to make a passionate appeal for investment of one kind or another, mostly on the basis that the particular area had been neglected by successive governments and they were sure that Charlie Haughey would be the man to break the mould in that regard. These weren't any ordinary Joes, but TDs and senators who were looking to their own electoral backs. This of course is one of the downsides of the proportional representation system: the competition between TDs within a party is so intense that objectivity goes out the window and they try to get advantage by making direct appeals to the leader, citing previous personal support.

Sadly, Charlie now displayed an uncharacteristic political weakness: he just couldn't say no. This was not in the script. His ability to get things done was legendary, and, while he had shown himself capable of divining the populist mood and acting accordingly, there was nothing in his political CV to indicate that once having set his mind on a particular course of action he would not persist in the knowledge that it was the correct thing to do. A big consideration was that a general election was scheduled for June 1982 at the latest. That left him with little time to play with. Jack Lynch's prophetic comment about the danger of having such a substantial majority was in Haughey's mind. He knew, as did all his back benchers, that it would be impossible to repeat the success of 1977. The most he could hope for would be a good working majority, preferably six or seven. This caused TDs to worry about their seats and led to renewed indiscipline and unrest. He opted to allay their unease by doing the very thing for which he had condemned Martin O'Donoghue: using the public finances to satisfy the egos of Fianna Fáil TDs, the careers of some of whom were already doomed regardless of what he did. He knew that he should have refused to accede to his back benchers' demands. However, he also knew that by refusing them he would be making enemies. And since almost half the party had already registered their votes against him in the leadership contest, he could ill-afford to cause any further difficulties for himself.

Meanwhile Fine Gael, which had been demoralized and in some disarray after the 1977 election defeat, had been given a new impetus with the arrival of Garret FitzGerald in the leader's office. Garret was hard at work on the Fine Gael organization, which had been in need of drastic reform. He appointed a new General Secretary, Peter Prendergast, who was intelligent, articulate and highly competent when it came to organizational matters, and the party headquarters relocated to Upper Mount Street, almost directly opposite Fianna Fáil's HQ. The move demonstrated a new attitude: Fine Gael meant business under FitzGerald. It was determined to become a modern, streamlined, well-organized machine.

Fine Gael strategists were determined that the public would soon be seeing the choice between Fine Gael and Fianna Fáil as a choice between Garret and Charlie, a choice between a saint and a devil – a simplistic model that perfectly suited a common misconception about the way politicians relate to each other. Sometimes people who have never been close to politics have no idea of how politicians actually behave when in one another's company. In the main such people are surprised to find that members of opposing parties talk civilly to one another, and in some cases actually enjoy one another's company more than that of members of their own party. It is quite rare that the public's – or indeed the media's – perception of naked hostility between senior members of opposing political parties actually lives up to its billing. However, if there is the slightest hint of animosity between high-profile opponents, particularly party leaders, it is exploited relentlessly in the interests of portraying politics in terms of some sort of battle royal between the forces of good and evil.

I never heard Charlie Haughey say anything derogatory about Garret in private. Whatever animus there was between them was political, and both men kept it that way, except when Garret made his unforgivable remark about Charlie's 'flawed pedigree'. In essence they were civil enough to one another outside the Dáil on those occasions when they actually met. In the immediate aftermath of Charlie's election as Taoiseach much was made – mostly by the media – of the fact that the two had been at college together and knew one another. The line was that they were Dubliners (even though Charlie was born in Mayo) of the same generation, the new, educated, political elite who were ambitious for their respective parties. There were contrasts, of course: Garret, the garrulous, absent-minded professor who had been a brilliant Minister for Foreign Affairs in the Cosgrave government; and Charlie, the go-getter – wealthy, colourful, controversial. While this was useful colour material it belied the reality. The truth is that knowing each other in college meant virtually nothing in the days when the student population at University College Dublin was so small that it was almost inevitable that everybody knew everybody else. The two were from completely different backgrounds. Garret's was solidly south Dublin middle class. His father, Desmond, had been a minister in the first post-Treaty government of the state in 1922 and moved in the type of circles that Charlie could only aspire to as a teenager and young man. His political philosophy was liberal and Christian democratic. He was educated by the Jesuits at Belvedere, so it was virtually axiomatic that he would end up at UCD. On the other hand, Charlie's family could not even be described as well off. His father, from Swatragh, in Derry, was a former Free State army officer. The family moved a number of times before finally settling on the northside of Dublin – a world apart as far as southsiders were concerned. His father was an ill man and died relatively young. Charlie was educated by the Christian Brothers and he was obviously motivated enough to win a scholarship to UCD, where, by all accounts, he integrated well into the college's cosy atmosphere. Apart from the coincidence of being in the same university at the same time, Garret and Charlie had nothing in common.

Jack Lynch and Garret had had an almost unhealthy regard for one another politically, and there were few problems between them during Jack's two and a half years as Taoiseach up to December 1979. It wasn't that Jack Lynch was of Cork merchant prince stock; on the contrary, his father had been a tailor (something that, in a remark that spoke volumes about the bitterness in Fianna Fáil, Neil Blaney used against him during the arms crisis debates when he alleged that Jack's father had made uniforms for British soldiers). But Jack and Garret were like-minded people who moved in the same circles, met one another at the same diplomatic dinners and observed the same unwritten rules of behaviour while others, mostly their own back benchers, indulged in the raw savagery of jungle politics. In contrast, there was no natural empathy between Charlie and Garret. It is normal for the Taoiseach of the day to brief the leader of the main opposition party, and indeed the leaders of other political parties in the Dáil, on various matters but most especially on security issues, although the general public and the supporters of the respective parties are not aware of the existence or the frequency of these meetings. Jack and Garret largely agreed on Northern Ireland policy, and Garret was given regular briefings on the developing situation by his old department, Foreign Affairs. I am not aware that either Garret or the leaders of the other parties were briefed by Charlie during his various terms of office.

This lack of rapport between the two leaders suited Fine Gael strategists down to the ground. At that time the party's handlers, under the direction of Peter Prendergast, had a raw political ambition (this has since withered somewhat). So, with the obvious approval of FitzGerald and the group of businessmen who seemed to control the party machine, they started a very clever propaganda campaign that sought to undermine Charlie's credibility. The subliminal message was simple. Garret was good; Charlie was bad. Garret was honest; Charlie wasn't. Garret could be trusted; Charlie couldn't. Garret was the darling of the media; Charlie was despised by them. Every effort was made to portray FitzGerald as somebody who was on the inside track, a man who, as a former Minister for Foreign Affairs, had contacts all over Europe, who could pick up the phone to presidents and prime ministers and who was held in the highest of regard in the corridors of Brussels and elsewhere. Charlie, allegedly, was viewed with baleful suspicion by the British and unknown to other European leaders. Most of all, Garret was depicted as a brilliant economist, a man who had to be replaced by five computers when he left Aer Lingus, someone who could argue with authority with regard to what should or should not be done about the public finances. That Garret was a statistician and not an economist didn't seem to matter. Neither was it relevant that Garret was arguably more at home with airline and railway timetables than with the actual running of the economy on a day-to-day basis.

And so every action of the government, every political development, was presented in terms of this 'good guy–bad guy' dichotomy, and the footsoldiers in Fianna Fáil and Fine Gael lapped it up. Garret turned up everywhere commenting on everything – and with an eagerness that created the impression that he knew what he was talking about. The media loved him – mainly because he was available and guaranteed them good copy. Admittedly the dotty professor image was the subject of some sniggering, but generally Garret was regarded as something of a breath of fresh air, not only as an alternative to Charlie but in the context of Fine Gael itself, which had had a fusty old-fashioned image. Garret caused consternation amongst Fianna Fáil's rank and file, which were adept at sniffing the air and interpreting the signals. The party members got the unpalatable message that Garret seemed to be more popular than their own leader. I thought there was the gravest danger of a damaging paranoia developing that would inevitably cloud the wider political agenda. And I was right. Despite the efforts of Haughey and his advisers, he could not win in such a climate.

Strange as it may seem, Haughey adopted a disinterested demeanour. Public affection was not something he craved. He wasn't worried about being loved, but about being elected. Being loved was simply a means to power. He was only interested in the political fallout of Garret's popularity. I do recall Charlie – very uncharacteristically – acknowledging that he and his government faced something of a problem when Garret announced that if elected he was going to pay every stay-at-home wife £9.50. 'I should have thought of that', was his reaction, even though he went on to say that it was a daft suggestion and correctly predicted that the housewives of Ireland would be whistling for their money. The only other occasion I recall Charlie raising anything about Garret – apart from the usual second-guessing that goes on in everyday politics about what the opposition might say next – was when he showed me an old press clipping he kept in his desk reporting Garret's opposition to a Labour Party wealth tax proposal. Garret had outlined the disastrous consequences that would follow the introduction of a wealth tax, including the risk that ladies would have to secrete their jewels 'under the mattress'. Charlie wanted me to use the article to embarrass Garret, particularly after he had got into bed with the Labour Party to form an alternative government in 1982. I never made any concerted effort to use the material other than to raise it casually when I was entertaining the political correspondents to dinner. The lack of interest shown was such that I knew I need not proceed any further.

It is difficult to put this into words, but it always struck me that Garret adopted a somewhat condescending attitude to Charlie. He certainly did not trust him. It seemed to him that the arms crisis had implications for the totality of what Charlie said and did subsequently in both his political and private life. I have no doubt whatever that this jaundiced view was influenced by the actions of Jack Lynch. The very fact that a Taoiseach would have the bottle to sack his Minister for Finance, particularly such a strong character within his party as Charlie, impressed Garret. Such ruthless action just wasn't in Garret's nature, and when he came to make a few changes in one of his own governments some years later he made a mess of it (Labour's Barry Desmond refused to move from Health to Social Welfare and Garret had to change his plans, ending up appointing Gemma Hussey instead, arguably a highly unlikely candidate to become Minister for Social Welfare). It seemed that, in Garret's view, Jack had been betrayed by his colleagues and when informed he acted with decisiveness. While there were some difficult questions as to the extent of Jack's and the cabinet's knowledge about what Charlie and others were allegedly up to, a general absolution was given simply on the basis that Jack was decent and honourable.

Arising from the arms crisis was the old chestnut about Charlie's so-called ambiguity on the Northern question, and it was clear that Fine Gael had a strategy of highlighting that as often as possible. In the absence of anything more damaging, there were frequent Dáil references by Fine Gael back benchers to the old canard that Charlie, by his alleged actions in 1969–70, was responsible for the establishment of the Provisional IRA. This was grist to the mill of those who wanted to damage him by associating him with that organization's brutal campaign. But it also served another purpose: to impress on the British that there was little prospect of progress towards a resolution to the Northern problem while Charlie was Taoiseach. To say that this Fine Gael strategy was treasonous might be over the top, but it was certainly politically selfish, self-interested and irresponsible. It dissipated somewhat after Charlie's opening gambit with Mrs Thatcher, and particularly after the Dublin Castle meeting in December 1980. Unfortunately the British began to believe that there might be some substance to the accusation when the atmosphere between the two administrations subsequently soured.

A subtle, if barely articulated, thread in the Fine Gael and media campaigns against Charlie Haughey was that he had notions above his station, that his apparent love of the arts and his interest in horses – something associated in previous times with the Ascendancy and Castle Catholics (who tended to support Fine Gael after independence) – were just manifestations of a vulgar and pathetic desperation to join a class supposedly more elevated than the one into which he had been born and to which most of his supporters belonged. There is no doubt that Charlie was streets ahead of his contemporaries as far as intelligence and political cunning were concerned, and it is likely that he was smart enough to know there were gaps in his knowledge that he wanted to fill for both personal and social reasons. So he may have cultivated sophisticated tastes and tried to learn about the arts. But only elitists, who regard some minds as inherently less worthy than others, would see that as a personality defect. When I knew him, Charlie had a deep and genuine appreciation of the arts in general, without any particular insight into what was good or what was bad. I recall a delegation of Church of Ireland hierarchy, led by the Archbishop of Dublin, Dr Donald Caird, coming to see him at his office and admiring a painting of a church that Charlie had asked the Board of Works to procure for his office from the dungeons of the National Gallery. (This was standard procedure: the gallery wasn't big enough to exhibit its whole collection, so both the board and the gallery liked to display work in ministers' offices.) The painting was of St Doulagh's, a church on the Malahide Road a few hundred yards from the gates of Charlie's house. Charlie gave the bishops a talk on its history and the provenance of the painting. Apparently one or two of the bishops present were heard to say afterwards that they hadn't expected 'that chap Haughey' to be so well informed.

Like many an enthusiastic amateur, Charlie knew what he liked. He was greatly enamoured with those who could create beautiful artefacts from wood or stone or could replicate both scenery and animals, particularly the horse, in paint. It is true that the general run of TDs or senators did not – and does not – have these interests. In fact some of them would scoff at the notion that they should appreciate some of the finer things in life on the basis that any such inclination on their part might be a disincentive to voters' support. Yet these were the very type of people who supported Charlie. They were enthralled at his apparent ease in areas that made them feel uncomfortable or embarrassingly out of their depth.

A part of this aspiration towards greater things was Charlie's desire to produce something other than the usual banal political cut and thrust in his important political speeches. Charlie's penchant for the literary allusion didn't start when he became Taoiseach. When he was Minister for Finance he used various authors and journalists (including a young Englishman called Bruce Arnold) in the drafting of speech material. Charlie was deeply conscious of Irish art and culture, and he rarely spoke without some reference to one or both. When he became Taoiseach he asked the poet Anthony Cronin, who had long been an influential associate, to write the occasional script of a cultural nature. Cronin also kept Charlie informed of what was happening in the arts and literary world. This was about the time that it became fashionable to talk about Charlie's Napoleonic notions. He never wore a watch or carried money, and wherever he was, there was always a fine gold fountain pen close by. Behind his desk in his office in Kinsaley hung a large poster with the slogan 'Think Big'. After Cronin's appointment there were jokes amongst journalists in the Dáil bar about Charlie's appointment of a poet laureate.

Working closely with Haughey, it was easy to see how he could be viewed as using his less culturally appreciative supporters as a means of furthering his own personal and political ambitions. He was inclined, at times, to become impatient with those who either could not or would not persuade themselves of the value of some of his ideas. A practical example was his long-term campaign to remove UCD's School of Engineering from its prestigious location in a beautiful, if shabby, Merrion Street building, so that he could make it the new home of the Department of the Taoiseach. On becoming Taoiseach, Charlie had been appalled to discover that the steps of the old Government Buildings (also on Merrion Street, and now the entrance to the Office of the Attorney General) had to be wiped down with a mop minutes before the French Prime Minister arrived for an official visit. Even the tearing apart of the inside of the building after he arrived did nothing for what was supposed to be the premier ministerial office in the country. So he set his sights on the UCD building. There was huge resistance to the notion that the university should cede such a prime location in order to satisfy the grandiose ambitions of this latter-day Napoleon. But in the end he got his way. I was no longer working in the public service when the buildings were completed, but, as far as I am aware, none of the project's opponents – including a Labour Party Tánaiste – demonstrated any inhibitions or unease about fitting into the elegant new surroundings when they entered government.

In the eighteen-month period between his election as Taoiseach in December 1979 and the general election of June 1981 the targeting of Haughey by Fine Gael was something of a slow-burner.

After the election it was rumoured in political circles that when Charlie became Taoiseach Peter Prendergast had commissioned a psychological assessment that portrayed him as weak and indecisive and having an ingrained inability to say no. If such an assessment was carried out around the time of Charlie's famous broadcast on the dire state of the economy, nobody knew about it, or said anything about it, then. On the contrary, Fine Gael and Labour seemed terrified that he would actually do as he had said and bring discipline to the public finances, improve the economy and enhance Fianna Fáil's chances of being re-elected.

Within Fianna Fáil, TDs condemned or secretly applauded the Fine Gael strategy of demonizing its leader, depending on their vote in the leadership election. Though there is no proof, given the nature and content of some of the stories that Fine Gael had about Charlie, it's hard not to conclude that his enemies in the party colluded with Fine Gael by leaking information of a private and political nature. Presumably the thinking was that defeat for Charlie in the polls would lead to another leadership election, the selection of a more acceptable and politically palatable leader, and a return to more consensual politics where there would be less bare-knuckle street-fighting and a more gentlemanly approach to matters generally.

While everybody knew that a general election had to be held before June 1982, it was obvious from Charlie's and other senior ministers' attitudes that it would take place long before that; they clearly felt that the longer they held on, the harder they would find it to be re-elected. Unfortunately Charlie had not taken advantage of the goodwill his television address on the state of the economy had generated. Whatever his intentions, good or otherwise, he had done the opposite of what he said was necessary if the country were to be restored to economic health, and thereby lost the confidence and respect of those who were prepared to give him the benefit of the doubt as the right man for the job. Deep down I believe that Charlie always regretted that he lost his nerve when it came to the hard decisions. He had been Minister for Finance and he knew that the economy wasn't something that you could treat whimsically.

But that's what he had done, so going to the polls was going to be a big gamble.

In the Taoiseach's office we discussed the desirability of holding the election in the immediate aftermath of the Dublin Castle Summit in December 1980. Private opinion polls taken by Fianna Fáil HQ showed a healthy rating for Fianna Fáil and for the Taoiseach personally. This was attributed to a feel-good factor arising from the positive meeting with Mrs Thatcher. However, experienced ministers knew that in any campaign practical issues such as the economy would ultimately dominate the agenda. From my chats with Brian Lenihan and Ray Burke it was obvious that both were against an election being held until there was clear evidence that Fianna Fáil could win – in so far as such evidence was obtainable. Despite the opinion polls, neither of them believed that it was possible in the early part of 1981. They advised caution. This was unnecessary, because when it came to elections no one was more cautious than Charlie Haughey himself. It was par for the course that whenever we were travelling or were thrown together for a few minutes between engagements, Charlie would start speculating about the electoral impact of particular decisions or ask me what I thought such and such a TD's prospects might be or what I thought of the performance of a particular minister. In early 1981 these conversations took on a new urgency. He was not in favour of a post-budget election but did nothing to discourage rumours amongst his ministers that he might announce an election date in late January. Once budget day had come and gone, speculation started that he would announce the general election at the end of his Ard Fheis speech in February. There was absolutely no basis for this. The general tenor of the script was upbeat, but there was no hint that an election was imminent. After the tragic events at the Stardust Nightclub, when forty-eight young people died after a fire broke out at a St Valentine's weekend disco, the Ard Fheis was postponed to another date.

Shortly afterwards the political landscape was dominated by events that would be difficult and politically damaging for Charlie and Fianna Fáil: the 1981 hunger strikes. These tested his and the party's resilience to the limit. One of the hunger strikers, Bobby Sands, was elected to Westminster in April, and the pressure mounted on the government to support the men's demands. Charlie knew that he was trapped in a vice, caught between sympathizing with the protesting prisoners in the H-Blocks and keeping faith with the process that he had agreed with Mrs Thatcher. When it became clear that he was not going to bow to the pressure to support the hunger strikers' demands, it was announced that a number of them would stand in the general election whenever it was announced.

The inevitable diplomatic communications between the Dublin and London governments as a result of the crisis were intensified by the prospect of a general election in the Republic. Both sides knew that, notwithstanding the public's aversion to the IRA's violent campaign, the emotive sight of young men going on hunger strike and dying could cause enormous political damage and give an unwelcome boost to the recruiting activities of the Provos. And both sides were anxious to see if some resolution could be found to minimize the damage that everybody knew would be caused by hunger strikers standing for election to the Dáil, particularly in the border constituencies.

Meanwhile, the Pope decided to send a personal representative, Monsignor John Magee, to the H-Blocks to intervene with the hunger strikers. Magee, from Newry, was one of the Pope's Private Secretaries and was being tipped as a possible future Archbishop of Armagh. Ó hAnnracháin knew Cardinal Tomás Ó Fiaich, and when it was announced that Magee was on his way to the North, he rang the cardinal and asked if he could arrange for Magee to come to Dublin to speak to the Taoiseach either before or after his meetings in the H-Blocks. Ó Fiaich rang back some hours later and, according to Ó hAnnracháin, said, 'I don't know what the feck he's at, and I don't think he knows either.' He said that there was little he could do because Magee was abiding strictly by his instructions from the Pope to talk only to the prisoners. Under no circumstances would he talk with either the British or the Irish governments in case that would prejudice his mission, which was to persuade the strikers to give up the protest and to avoid unnecessary deaths. Magee flew back to Rome and the hunger strikers vowed to continue the fast.

Incidentally, it is worth noting here that the relationship between politicians and the Catholic hierarchy was always an interesting aspect of working in Irish politics. Members of the hierarchy don't lose their political preferences when they become bishops and, just as some in the political arena could not hide their distaste for Charlie, so some bishops appeared to be uncomfortable with him. At the funeral of Peter Birch, the Bishop of Ossory, in May 1981, apart from Tomás Ó Fiaich the only one who had any time for Charlie was the Bishop of Down and Connor, Cahal Daly. Dermot Ryan, the Archbishop of Dublin, appeared remote, and his personality didn't seem to allow for even the most casual of conversations with the Taoiseach, despite the fact that they were in the same small room in the presbytery at St Mary's Cathedral in Kilkenny and that there were only four other people present. Therefore on that occasion I found myself in the disconcerting position of receiving the exclusive attention of an archbishop.

It was odd that the two who had a good relationship with Charlie – Ó Fiaich and Daly – could not have been more different, and even odder that, if anything, Charlie was somewhat friendlier with Daly than Ó Fiaich. Daly was not particularly noted for his Nationalist inclinations, whereas there was no doubting where Ó Fiaich's affiliations lay. Ó Fiaich was an amiable, hail-fellow-well-met, one-of-the-lads sort who, although he was an academic, could put everybody at ease with his genial wit; Daly was austere, a former Professor of Philosophy at Queen's University Belfast and an intellectual to his fingertips, with a demeanour that didn't attract conviviality. Ultimately the characteristic both Ó Fiaich and Daly shared was a huge social and intellectual confidence that allowed them to mix it with this 'black sheep' without fearing that they would be tainted by association.

Charlie announced the election for June 1981 in circumstances that he knew were less than propitious: there had been vicious arguments in the Dáil about the formulation of the budget in

January and the opposition accused the government of doctoring the figures. But the opinion polls held fast, and Charlie and the government took heart from results that, if they were maintained, would give Fianna Fáil a very good chance of forming a majority government. He believed that he could win out by the strength of his arguments on both the economy and the North. On the latter he could argue that, while nothing of substance had been achieved, the very fact that Mrs Thatcher had come to Dublin and was prepared to become involved in joint studies on issues of importance was evidence of his ability to move matters further than anyone else had since the Sunningdale Agreement in 1973. As for the economy, clearly he was on less secure ground.

Charlie asked me to accompany him on the election trail. Since I was a civil servant, strictly speaking I was not supposed to have any involvement in political matters. Everybody knew that that was something of a joke, but none the less I checked it with the Secretary of the Department of the Taoiseach. He told me to maintain as low a profile as I possibly could. The idea of keeping a low profile during the course of a general election campaign, particularly one in which the Taoiseach was stalked by screaming supporters of the hunger strikers, was also a joke. But strangely enough the presence of the protesters gave me an excuse to be with the Taoiseach at all times – during an election campaign held in such circumstances the media would wish to discuss issues beyond the Taoiseach's stewardship of the country or his party's policies for the future. And it was this argument that was used subsequently when questions were asked about my involvement in the election.

Though I hardly needed a lesson on how fractured Fianna Fáil had become, it was still an eye-opener to accompany Charlie on the campaign. Having travelled the country with Jack Lynch, where you wouldn't hear a whisper of criticism of the leader, I found it revealing to visit the same constituencies in Charlie Haughey's company and to be able to distinguish, sometimes from body language alone, the levels of antipathy he generated. This was particularly true in my own hometown of Kilkenny, the bailiwick of Jim Gibbons. The atmosphere on our arrival was poisonous.

The local senator, Mick Lanigan, was regarded by the Gibbons faction as pro-Haughey and therefore somewhat suspect, and the Carlow–Kilkenny constituency was split as far as support for the two men went. The media were on high alert and watching closely for any sign of overt hostility between Haughey and Gibbons or conflict amongst their loyalists. In the end nothing untoward occurred, but there was a sense of impending doom. Neither man misbehaved. Gibbons observed the niceties by welcoming Charlie to 'my constituency' and the two didn't speak to one another for the remainder of the visit. The Gibbons people were armed with walkie-talkies and were able to alert those gathered ahead of the advancing party. Everywhere we went there were plenty of Gibbons supporters in evidence, and, as we marched along, Charlie, *sotto voce*, said to me, 'I suppose you know all these Gibbonites, Frank', in a tone that almost implied that I had had something to do with the organization of the reception committee.

A sense that something disastrous could happen at any moment characterized the Taoiseach's tour of the country. Even little things got blown out of all proportion. We were staying in Hayes Hotel in Thurles and an advance man had booked the accommodation for the Taoiseach and his party. Neither Charlie nor anyone else had made any special requests other than that, where possible, there ought to be showers in the rooms to enable us to clean up quickly after a day on the road. It turned out that there was no shower in the room allocated to Charlie in this hotel, and he asked me to see if I could arrange to have his room changed. I got on to the advance man and he sorted it out with the hotel management. The following day I got a call from a gossip columnist asking if it was true that the Taoiseach had berated the hotel manager about the quality of the accommodation and had caused severe embarrassment to the local Fianna Fáil organization because of his behaviour. It took me some time to convince this reporter that the story as he had heard it was false. None the less the alleged incident went down in local political folklore as symptomatic of the tyrannical behaviour of the upstart from Dublin. Incidents like these made me despair of anybody ever taking an objective view of Charlie, and it was even more frustrating to realize that senior members of the constituency organization were behind the warped story. But it all added to the accumulation of truth and myth about Charlie from which you cherry-picked according to your prejudices.

The activities of the hunger strikers' supporters on the election campaign were deeply unsettling for all parties. Fianna Fáil candidates were seriously intimidated by the Provisional IRA and the Taoiseach was constantly harassed. On one occasion I received a telephone call from a senior Sinn Féin figure, who, when I refused to agree to pass on a message of an unprintable variety to the Taoiseach, was able to tell me where I lived, to describe my car and to name the school where Sheila was working. The implications were very clear and I passed the information to the gardaí. When the campaign took us to Dun Laoghaire, a protester threw a paint-filled plastic bag into the air over our heads with the obvious intention of splattering the Taoiseach. His security detail pushed him out of the way and most of the paint landed on me. A good suit was ruined, to say nothing of my dignity. In typical tongue-in-cheek fashion Charlie informed me that of course it was one of the duties of a Press Secretary to interpose his body between a would-be assassin and the Taoiseach. He also told me to go to Monaghans' Tailors on Stephen's Green, order a new suit for myself and put it on his tab there. For one reason or another, I didn't take him up on his kind offer.

The result of the election was that eight independents and small party deputies held the balance of power. Since two of them were hunger strike abstentionists, in reality there were six votes to play for. Charlie came up with the bright idea of offering one of the independents, John O'Connell, the job of Ceann Comhairle. O'Connell was something of a maverick. He came from humble beginnings, but, after leaving the RAF, began a highly successful publishing business and later got involved in property deals with some Arab princes. I had met O'Connell first in 1973 shortly after starting my MA studies. Brian Farrell encouraged his students to go out and get practical experience of electoral politics in action

instead of confining ourselves to the library, so I became involved
with John O'Connell's campaign to win a seat for the Labour Party.
Brian Farrell had had the right idea because working for Johnny
was certainly an education, and for the first time I understood how
spending money translated into winning votes at election time.
He spent liberally and commissioned all the latest methods of
ascertaining what the public wanted. Having found it out, he
promised to give it to them. Though he was a member of Labour,
he had adopted an independent stance on many issues, and at
election time he always ran a highly individualistic campaign. On
this occasion, Charlie knew that he was open to offers and invited
him to Kinsaley for a chat. Charlie had tipped me off that there
might be a significant announcement and that I should go to
Kinsaley late on a Saturday morning. A group of photographers
were waiting at the gates of Abbeville, which was hardly unusual,
given the election result. When I arrived at the house I found
Charlie and Maureen doubled up with laughter. They brought me
to the window of the dining room to show me the man who was
to become the next Ceann Comhairle of the Dáil running up their
backfield in order to avoid being photographed. As it happened, it
also suited Fine Gael and Labour for John O'Connell to take the
speaker's chair. Fine Gael proposed him for the post and he was
elected. Only one independent, Neil Blaney, supported Charlie in
the vote for Taoiseach, so there were 79 votes for and 83 against
him. Garret got 81 votes to Charlie's 78. Garret became Taoiseach
and Fianna Fáil went into opposition.

Charlie predicted that the new coalition would not last long.
Even he could not have envisaged that in less than nine months he
would be back in the Taoiseach's office.

12. A new political master

I was now in an unusual situation: Fianna Fáil was out of government and I didn't know what the future held. All I knew for certain was that as a member of the civil service I would be asked to serve in some capacity. For the first time I saw how senior civil servants carried on the business of the state in a clinical fashion, almost oblivious to the fate of their political masters. There was an air of expectancy about what Garret FitzGerald would be like as Taoiseach and lots of banter during the tea breaks as to who would end up where when he took up office. Pádraig Ó hAnnracháin was the most despondent of us all, probably because he thought that these were his final days in the Taoiseach's office. He was near retirement age, and if the new government lasted the normal term of four to five years he was unlikely to serve at the epicentre of power again. When the previous coalition had come into office in 1973, he had been sent to the Department of Education and had had a very good working relationship with his minister there, Dick Burke. This time his prospects looked less inviting and he didn't relish being sent to a new department where he would have to develop a whole new set of relationships. On top of this, Ó hAnnracháin had not been slow to exercise the power attached to his status as a Deputy Secretary in the Department of the Taoiseach, and he was smart enough to know that there were people waiting for him in the long grass.

I was due a holiday so, rather than just wait around to see what would happen, Sheila, Sinéad and I took off to Enniscrone in County Sligo for some well-earned rest and relaxation. The weather was foul: it never stopped raining for a whole month. A few weeks after we arrived I was contacted by the gardaí and told to make an urgent telephone call to the Taoiseach's office. Brian McCarthy, the head of personnel, told me that there had been a discussion at the new cabinet that morning about where I should serve, given that the Taoiseach would be appointing his own Press Secretary. The options were Foreign Affairs under Peter Barry or Education under John Boland. I knew neither of these new ministers but from my knowledge of the Department of Foreign Affairs I didn't believe that I would fit in there, so I opted for Education. I was told to present myself to the Secretary of the Department, Liam Ó Laidhin, the following Monday morning for the assignment of new duties.

Ó Laidhin told me that the new minister wanted somebody solely in charge of media relations, and he asked me to set up and run a press office in the department, which had never had a dedicated media section. Unfortunately I knew very little about education, although, from listening to John Wilson who had become Minister for Education in 1977, I knew that it was something of a minefield. Still, I welcomed the opportunity.

The irony of the new situation was that once again I got a job Pádraig Ó hAnnracháin wanted. Back in 1977 I got the government press job, even though Ó hAnnracháin had done it for the previous Fianna Fáil government. Now I was taking over press relations in Education, although, when he had worked for Dick Burke, Ó hAnnracháin's duties had included handling media queries and he had continued to advise Burke's successor, John Wilson.

Subsequently John Boland told me that out of courtesy he had had a meeting with Ó hAnnracháin soon after he arrived in the department, and that he could appreciate how, because of his amiable personality, Ó hAnnracháin could become close to a serving minister. But it was Ó hAnnracháin's bad luck that Boland was not inclined to bring a former close associate of his *bête noire*, Burke, into his inner circle. Ó hAnnracháin was to spend a difficult period under the new administration in which he was given virtually no duties and spent most of his time reading. The prospect of managing the incipient tension between us, as well as getting to grips with a new department, a new minister and a new role, was daunting.

I don't know what Liam Ó Laidhin expected from his newly acquired, almost supernumerary official from the Department of the Taoiseach, but when I arrived at the headquarters of the

Department of Education in Marlborough House he could not have been more helpful. (Ó Laidhin – 'Lane' in English – was generally known by the Irish version of his name. An idiosyncrasy of Education was that, where possible, everybody used their Irish name. Notwithstanding the Scottish origins of my surname, this was not possible in my case and so, despite the efforts of a few diehards to call me Prionsias Dunshleibhe – which translates as Francis Delaney – I continued to be known as plain Frank Dunlop.) Ó Laidhin provided me with a spacious office at the top of the department, which I later found out had been the housekeeper's quarters when the building was the Duke of Marlborough's town-house. The office contained a bedroom and a separate bathroom. Later, when I got to know Boland, he used to pop in to see me unannounced – mainly, I suspected, to avoid officials in his private office – and on each occasion said that my office should be turned into private quarters for the use of the minister of the day. As Minister for the Public Service some years later, John got himself into trouble when he had an en suite shower installed in his private office in Kildare Street. That would have been nothing compared to the furore that would have ensued had he turned rooms in a departmental building into a private apartment.

John Boland was from Clondalkin in County Dublin. He had entered politics early, having been encouraged in his political ambitions by Liam Cosgrave, and, when he was elected at twenty-one, became the youngest senator in the history of the state. He had also served as chairman of Dublin County Council. Despite his youth – he was just thirty-four when he became Minister for Education, his first appointment to ministerial office – and the apparent changes in the deeply conservative orientation of Fine Gael, he remained a committed member of the old regime as far as Fine Gael's political philosophy was concerned. So he was a little surprised to have been offered a cabinet post in the first instance and even more surprised when he was sent to Education. Education involved a delicate choreography between the department, the church and the powerful teaching unions, and diplomacy and tact were not attributes John would have claimed for himself or ones anybody who knew him would have credited him with. His surprise was shared by colleagues in Fine Gael, who would not have regarded him as a FitzGerald man – which he most definitely wasn't – and by people in Fianna Fáil, who would never have expected to see him appointed to any ministry. I often wondered then, and since, whether his friend Seán Barrett, the Fine Gael Chief Whip, had anything to do with pleading his case when Garret came to look at the talent available to him for appointment.

He had never appeared on my radar when I was the Government Press Secretary and I had never met him or spoken with him. Naturally, as soon as I knew that I was going to work with him in Education, I did as much discreet research as I could, which included talking to those members of Fine Gael in the Dáil and the senate that I knew well enough to ask. I also spoke to Boland's Fianna Fáil constituency colleague Ray Burke. I don't think I am being unkind to John's memory when I say that he did not have a great many friends in politics, particularly in his own party. But right across the political divide, everyone agreed that he was a formidable and highly intelligent operator who had a tendency to get his own way despite the best efforts of his opponents. My reaction was 'What's new?' A minister with a reputation for brusqueness and a touch of arrogance wasn't going to cause me undue concern.

I met the new minister within hours of arriving at the Department in Marlborough Street. He was very gracious and said that he hoped we would work well together. We had a lengthy discussion about what he wanted to do and the issues to which he wanted to devote particular attention. I baulked when I heard some of the policy areas into which he intended dipping his toe. However, he seemed determined to get the teacher representative bodies, as the unions were officially referred to, onside, and we battened down the hatches for what promised to be a stormy passage in government.

While I was trying to find my feet I was told that the new Taoiseach wanted to see me in Government Buildings. I had no idea what it was about. When I arrived, I was shown into the office where I had had so many meetings with both Jack Lynch and Charlie Haughey, and it was a little strange to be sitting there in front of a different Taoiseach. Garret was accompanied by a senior department official. Garret said he had been informed that prior to his taking over as Taoiseach I had said that he had a black book containing the names of civil servants in the department that he wished to sack. I was flabbergasted and looked over at the man who sat impassively at the corner of the Taoiseach's desk not making eye contact with me. Garret explained that this was a very serious charge and that he had to investigate the matter fully in the interests of the reputations of the civil servants in the department who might feel that he was less than enamoured of them because they had served his predecessor loyally. I completely agreed with that. The relationship between politicians and senior civil servants is based on trust and to suggest that a man of Garret's seniority and authority held grudges or was in any way vindictive would have been as outrageous as it was wrong. After I pinched myself and realized that this wasn't a dream, that the Taoiseach of the country was indeed asking me if I had been involved in dangerous rumour-mongering, I said that I had never heard such rubbish in my life. I described the jocose remarks that had been exchanged during tea breaks before he had taken up office. I couldn't imagine what the man was thinking in reporting such harmless banter to the new Taoiseach, but I guessed that it was an overzealous display of loyalty. After I had put matters into context, Garret said that there was an obvious conflict between the two of us, and that he would look into it further. He indicated that the meeting was at an end and the official intimated that there were matters that he wished to discuss with the Taoiseach. I was furious with my former departmental colleague, and would gladly have broken his neck at that particular moment, but I had no option but to leave. To my surprise, and his, Garret said that he wanted to discuss other matters with me and he dismissed him from the room.

Garret then said that he accepted my explanation. I expressed relief and told him that, notwithstanding the fact that I had been appointed to the civil service by Jack Lynch, I believed I had a duty to serve the government of the day and that I would do so in whatever capacity I could. Garret and I then had a brief conversation about the Department of Education, and there the matter rested. I had no reason to suspect that he might entertain anything other than normal views about me, and I knew from Michael Mills, with whom he was friendly, that Garret respected the job I did with Jack Lynch and Charlie Haughey from 1974 onwards.

However, the affair rankled with me. I had come through some bruising experiences since I had first become involved with Fianna Fáil, and I thought I had developed the thick skin needed for participation in the rough and tumble of politics, but I had never experienced anything like this before. Charlie Haughey was in opposition and I felt at liberty to tell him what had happened with the man, who had also worked for him. He said very little and I eventually forgot about the matter. When the coalition government fell six months later, I was reappointed as Government Press Secretary and returned to the Department of the Taoiseach. In the interests of the smooth running of affairs I never referred to the incident again. However, one morning I was summoned to the Taoiseach's office and Charlie handed me a copy of a statement that he wanted issued later that day. It was the announcement of the man's appointment to a prestigious posting. There was a broad smile on Charlie's face, signalling his awareness that I would not be sorry to see the official go.

When I told John Boland about the encounter with Garret, he roared with laughter. He said that the whole affair was typical of Garret: the country was in an economic mess, there were a myriad other problems, and here was the Taoiseach adjudicating over a personnel squabble that would normally have been solved by other means. While I agreed that it was unusual for the Taoiseach to become involved in a matter of this nature, I none the less pointed out that the Taoiseach was entitled to expect the undivided loyalty of his civil servants. If there was even a hint that he had come into office with a predisposition about the commitment, or otherwise, of particular civil servants, then a serious precedent would have been created – one that might have very serious consequences. Boland later agreed that I had a valid point.

★

My relationship with John Boland had got off to a rocky start. I had been in the department for a few days when his Private Secretary, Paddy Heffernan, rang me early one morning to say that the minister wanted to see me. When I arrived in the private office Heffernan winked and whispered, 'Be prepared.' I had no idea what I should be prepared for and I didn't have time to ask. When I was ushered into the minister's office, Boland had a copy of the previous day's *Evening Press* spread open on his desk and, before I got the chance to exchange any pleasantries, he pointed to the paper and said, 'Did you know about this?' He indicated a photograph of somebody carrying a placard. I said no, I didn't know anything about it and what was more nobody had made any contact with my office about the matter. 'Don't you think that as Press Officer for this department it is your job to know everything about what appears in the newspapers about the department and about me?' he asked. Shades of Charlie Haughey, I thought. I said that of course he was right to expect that as far as possible the person in charge of the press office – me – ought to know as much about what was going to appear in the media as about what had actually appeared. In this case the story was about a protesting parent who had decided to take advantage of the fact that his neighbour was now the Minister for Education and begun a twenty-four hour vigil at Boland's front gate. The photograph had appeared in the later editions of the previous day's *Evening Press* and neither Boland nor I had seen it. The minister knew nothing about it until he arrived home very late in the evening to find a man parading up and down outside his house carrying a placard. That the man was there didn't seem to bother him; it came with the territory. The lack of forewarning was the issue. I said yes, I should have known and I regretted that the minister had found out about the protest, and the media story, in the manner in which he did. Boland looked at me for what seemed to be a long time without saying anything. When he realized that I was not going to try to defend the indefensible, he broke into a broad smile, held out his hand and said, 'That's exactly what I had hoped you would say and I now know how you got on so well with Haughey.' From that day onwards our relationship went from strength to strength. Over the months that followed I was struck by Boland's apparent fascination with my relationship with Charlie. From time to time he would ask, in an uncharacteristically tentative way, about various incidents in the recent past. I soon saw that was as much a test of my loyalty and ability to maintain confidentiality as a wish to extract political information.

Many in Fianna Fáil just couldn't understand how I managed to get on so well with a minister from another party. There was an unspoken suspicion that I might be taking the objectivity and political neutrality required of civil servants a little bit too far. What they failed to understand was that politics never entered into it. It became obvious that some of Boland's cabinet colleagues also looked askance at the strong professional relationship that was developing between us and regarded me as something of a Trojan horse in their midst. Boland revelled in teasing them – particularly when relations between the government and the media weren't as good as they might have been – with the suggestion that I should be called in to give them advice. This was not something that the new Government Press Secretary wanted to hear, and it wouldn't have been something that I would have wanted to hear either, had I known about it at the time.

Having left behind the intrigues of Fianna Fáil politics, I now found myself immersed in similar – albeit less bitter – intrigues in Fine Gael, a party with which I had little, if any, affinity. While I knew the vast majority of the new ministers to speak to casually, they were political strangers. I had no relationship with the party organization and I didn't know Fine Gael officials around the country. When I accompanied John Boland to official functions and he met members of his own party, even socially, I felt like an alien. In fairness, Boland always introduced me, though not always in terms of endearment. Sometimes it was along the lines that I was 'the Fianna Fáil so-and-so I'm forced to work with'. When I tackled him about it, he laughed and said he thought I had a thicker skin. It was on occasions such as these that I realized Boland couldn't give a fig what people thought of him; and when I said as much to him, he replied that you can't expect to be loved by everybody all the time. Little did he realize how prophetic that was.

There were definite factions in the cabinet made up of the old and the new Fine Gael. The old Fine Gael was represented in the main by the unlikely combination of Paddy Cooney, Peter Barry and John Boland. New Fine Gael was epitomized by Garret himself and newly appointed ministers such as Jim Mitchell, Michael Noonan and Alan Dukes. Despite his relative youth John Bruton didn't appear to be in the new Fine Gael camp; but then Liam Cosgrave had made him a Parliamentary Secretary in the Department of Education in 1973 at the age of twenty-four and, given his family background – wealthy Meath farming stock – he was believed to be more rooted in the older traditions of the party. Boland was even younger than Bruton and there was no question but that he was in the more conservative wing of the cabinet. He sometimes displayed attitudes that could be described only as to the right of Genghis Khan. He was extremely driven, and the civil servants in the Department of Education, and subsequently those in the departments of the Public Service and Environment, had their carefully regulated work-lives subjected to some fairly drastic upheavals. Again, this was all familiar territory for me.

Education had a sort of predictable modus operandi that had been worked out over decades. This meant that, whether he or she liked it or not, no Minister for Education could avoid entering into some type of partnership, amicable or otherwise, with the main unions, with whom departmental officials had nurtured delicate relationships over many years. The department even had predictable seasons. For instance, towards the early autumn there would be the annual controversy about the free school transport service, when accusations would fly about the heartlessness of bureaucrats who discriminated against families who were only yards short of qualifying to use it. In spring, when the sap was rising, there was inevitably a new row in time for the teacher conferences at Easter. The minister and his officials travelled around the country at speed to deliver speeches and to be subjected to criticism about the lack of funding for whatever project happened to be the flavour of the year with the particular teachers' union.

John Boland set out to be controversial and to generate publicity. He had the ability to arouse controversy merely by questioning whether there was a better, more efficient way of doing things. Being close to him when he was proposing drastic changes in accepted systems did nothing for one's popularity. I was amazed to discover that there were those in both the civil service and in Fianna Fáil who thought that I was the originator of some of Boland's proposals. Also, Boland sometimes led cabinet colleagues to believe that I was the progenitor of his controversial speeches and that I was responsible for the ensuing publicity, which most of them would have given their eye-teeth for. Some of them thought that Boland simply craved publicity, but the wiser ones knew that he was trying to see how far he could go on policy issues before he was reined in by the Taoiseach. Though it had been an adjustment for me to go from serving in the powerhouse of the Taoiseach's office, where it was sometimes difficult to catch one's breath with all that was going on, it turned out that working with Boland in the Department of Education did not lack excitement.

Working for a non-Fianna Fáil government also gave me an insight into a completely different approach to prioritizing issues. The coalition made much of things that would have been regarded as trivial under a Fianna Fáil administration. Its ministers seemed to think that they needed to be involved in the minutiae of things. I put this down to inexperience: some of the ministers had never been in cabinet before and Garret's natural disposition towards detail led to this particular ambience – much to the frustration of the few who had served previously. While I had no direct role in policy formulation, it was impossible to avoid the conclusion that there was a distinct lack of political common sense. Issues chosen for attention seemed Dublin-centred and the rest of the country was hardly considered. (This would become obvious to the public during the 1981 Christmas recess, when heavy snowfalls hit the east coast, particularly Dublin and Wicklow. With Boland and the

Taoiseach both out of the country on holiday, the Tánaiste, Michael O'Leary, decided to close all the schools in the country – despite the fact that there was little or no snow thirty miles beyond Dublin. The government was ridiculed and Boland was incensed because on the phone to Dublin he had strongly advised against the measure.) The government seemed to be run like a university debating society and cabinet meetings lasted for ever. This drove Boland mad. He frequently expressed his irritation at how long it took to arrive at a decision on the simplest of matters. I reminded him that the revered judge Declan Costello, who was Attorney General in the Cosgrave–Corish coalition, used to leave the cabinet room – allegedly for a smoke – in frustration at what appeared to him to be pointless and inane discussion of issues of little or no relevance to the real needs of the country. After all, he had been the author of the seminal document on social reform, *A Just Society*. This did nothing to assuage Boland's own frustration. He believed that the endless cycle of inter-departmental consultation, and the circulation of cabinet memoranda in advance of any decision being taken, were time-wasting exercises that hampered any real attempt to change policy.

It is difficult sometimes to work out why a government decides on a policy that looks bound to fail, and also why it persists with it in the face of the most unrelenting criticism and opposition. When John Boland got into a serious contretemps with one of the most important and influential unions in the education system – the Irish National Teachers' Organization (INTO) – it was a classic example of this. During the summer the country's primary schools were sent a circular indicating the department's intention to raise the school entry age to four and a half years from September 1982. Boland's – or as he would have it – the government's contention was that children were starting their formal education too young. The result was that when they came to leave school – either after the Intermediate Certificate, generally at fourteen or fifteen, or two years later, after the Leaving Certificate – they were too young to make the type of choices that would govern the rest of their lives.

As well as that, there was an increasing demand on primary school places and there was no reason, other than tradition, why a child had to go to school at the age of four. More controversially, although he was shrewd enough not to say this in public, Boland also believed, on the basis of anecdotal evidence from teachers, that some parents used their local primary school as a child-minding service by sending their children to school younger than was necessary, which was causing serious logistical problems. I was not yet fully tuned in to how the department functioned, nor to its relationship with the teacher unions, but I knew enough to realize that a fundamental change in the day-to-day operation of the national school system should have been discussed with the relevant trade union in advance. This hadn't happened. Boland later told me he believed that if he entered into consultation on the matter with the teachers' unions, the proposal would wither on the vine.

At first there was little reaction. This was not surprising: the managers, the teachers and their union representatives were on their summer break. But when I ran into the INTO General Secretary, Gerry Quigley, on O'Connell Street shortly after the circular had been sent out, he was apoplectic and left me in no doubt that the proposed measure would be vigorously opposed. Gerry Quigley was an amiable and highly competent Northerner. He had steel in his backbone and years of experience in dealing not only with politicians of all hues, but also with the mandarins in the Department of Education. Even from my relatively short time working with the education correspondents, Christina Murphy of the *Irish Times*, John Walshe of the *Irish Independent* and Pat Holmes of the *Irish Press*, I knew that the INTO under Quigley would be no walkover. But when I told Boland about my conversation with Quigley, he simply said that the measure was government policy and would be proceeded with.

This business of a proposal being 'government policy' was one of those things that fascinated me in my time working for various administrations. Describing something as 'government policy' seemed to confer on it a status that implied that it was *ex cathedra* and could not be changed. The facility with which ministers', and indeed civil servants', actions became, retrospectively, 'government policy' was intriguing. I figured out the rule: when a government decides on a particular course of action, that becomes government policy; when the same government reverses the decision, that too is government policy. What happens in the interim is most interesting: attitudes are adopted that have all the appearance of immutability, and there are robust exchanges questioning opponents' motivations, until, in time, everyone loses sight of the original proposal. And that was exactly what happened in this case.

While I could understand why the INTO would be incensed at the lack of consultation, I failed to appreciate the deep-seated suspicion with which the union regarded anything proposed by the new government, and John Boland in particular. The official line was that the union opposed the measure because it would deprive parents of their right to send their children to school at four, and children of their fundamental right to begin formal education. The unofficial reality was more complicated. The INTO was rooted in the parish network throughout the country and generally parish priests were the schools' managers. Likewise, Fianna Fáil based its organization on parish life and its cumainn were parish-based. Many INTO members also belonged to Fianna Fáil, and a number of TDs and senators were primary school teachers who had substitutes in place while they were in the Dáil. The INTO was not slow in making its views known to those TDs, and they in turn passed on the message to the party as a whole. At the beginning, though, Fianna Fáil stayed relatively quiet on the matter, mainly because it regarded the proposal as a desirable measure that it would never get away with introducing.

In contrast to the cosiness that characterized the relationship between the INTO and Fianna Fáil, built up over the previous sixteen years of the party's dominance in government, there was frostiness in the new government's dealings with the union. Boland refused to enter into the chummy intrigues that had been par for the course between a Minister for Education and the teachers' unions, particularly the INTO. Given his conservative views, he was not regarded as a friend of organized labour, and the unions scrutinized anything emanating from the Department of Education under his leadership more closely than might normally be the case. He, in turn, was suspicious of the INTO, and particularly of Gerry Quigley's colleague Joe O'Toole, a member of the INTO executive. O'Toole lived in Boland's constituency and he believed that O'Toole was, at the very least, a closet Fianna Fáil supporter, if not someone who was politically ambitious in his own right. O'Toole was teaching in a north County Dublin school and in reality he was nothing other than what he professed to be: namely an ordinary, if active, member of his union. But Boland was of the view that O'Toole was some sort of deus ex machina and that his objections to the raising of the school entry age were politically motivated.

It became obvious very quickly that there was going to be serious and wide-ranging opposition to the introduction of the measure. Boland and the government were faced with the combined wrath of the INTO and an increasingly vociferous group of parents. It seemed as if every mother in the country believed that the government, and John Boland in particular, was out to deprive her children of a primary school education. Government TDs began to feel the pressure in their constituencies, and it wasn't long before they made their views known both to Boland and to the government Chief Whip. Boland knew that he would come under political pressure as a result of his proposal, but he never thought the pressure would cause the government as a whole to become as nervous as it did.

When Fianna Fáil saw that there was a groundswell of opposition to the measure from the teachers, and when its TDs faced questions from local parents' representatives and parish priests, the party mounted a rearguard campaign against the government. And it was then that I got caught in the crossfire. Boland was determined to continue with the measure, but he could see that his own back benchers were getting worried. He instructed me to prepare a briefing document, in the form of a series of questions and answers, that covered all aspects of the proposal and its implications for parents, for children and for teachers. After this was distributed to all government TDs, it inevitably fell into the hands of the INTO, the media and Fianna Fáil. Equally inevitably, it became known that I was its author. The document was attacked as both misleading and disingenuous, and Fianna Fáil attacked the minister and the government for getting a civil servant to do their 'dirty work'. Privately Fianna Fáilers told me that I had overstepped the mark and that my dedication to my job, my minister and government policy was a little overenthusiastic. One former minister, with whom I had been very friendly when he was in office, said that he hoped I had no further ambitions to return to Merrion Street in any capacity when (not 'if') Fianna Fáil returned to government.

Fianna Fáil's attitude didn't worry me unduly. While I found the approach both crude and offensive, it never occurred to me that the government might change any time in the near future – that was if Boland's worries about Garret's ability to lose sight of the wood for the trees didn't prove well grounded. Apart from that, I knew that at the end of the day politicians opted for those with whom they could work comfortably and who did the work for them. In the past I had found that no matter how dense some politicians might be, they had a tendency to gravitate towards those who could steer a course that kept them out of trouble and that, hopefully, resulted in the achievement of something concrete and positive for their image. However, it saddened me to see senior and reasonably intelligent members of Fianna Fáil being so vindictive when they knew the truth of the matter was that if they were ministers themselves, as some of them had been, they would expect the same dedication from the civil service.

It also upset me to discover that Pádraig Ó hAnnracháin was not shy about letting people in Fianna Fáil know how closely I was working with John Boland. Given that Ó hAnnracháin was extremely proud of his fruitful relationship with Dick Burke, his mischief-making surprised me. He took me aside one morning and advised me that I should tone down my commitment to the proposal; he knew, he said, that it was going to be defeated by the INTO and that I ought not to be too publicly, or politically, associated with it. When I said that I had no option but to carry out, within reason, the wishes of the minister and the government, he said I could always find ways of opting out. I resented the implication and told him so. Our relationship became very strained and never really recovered, something that was to overshadow our future work together back in the Department of the Taoiseach.

The controversy got so heated that it became a big story on Gay Byrne's radio programme. In a campaign carefully orchestrated by the INTO, mother after mother rang Gay to complain about the proposed measure. The show invited the minister to participate. I believed it presented an ideal opportunity for him to make his case in public, but Boland refused to go on and asked – ordered – me to do so. At that time it was unheard of for civil servants either to give interviews or to speak in public on policy matters. I was very reluctant to comply with the minister's request, not only because I knew that the issue was highly emotive and anything I said would do little, if anything, to alleviate the situation, but also for self-interested reasons: it was clear by now that if I appeared in public explaining or defending a government measure, some in Fianna Fáil would characterize my actions as those of a renegade. It would be a very perilous step in career terms. Boland had a quirky sense of humour and he took great delight in the dilemma in which he had placed me. I couldn't come up with any cogent reason as to why I should refuse to do the programme, other than it not being the 'done thing'. I consulted with Liam Ó Laidhin and he advised me to do as the minister wished; he would make the appropriate note in my file so no one could say afterwards that I had gone on a solo run. Eventually I agreed and, having been told by the people producing the programme that the item would probably last no more than ten to fifteen minutes, I prepared accordingly.

The producer had never mentioned a phone-in, so imagine my surprise when I spent nearly an hour answering some very pertinent questions from the mothers of children around the country – children they had confidently expected to be dispatching to local primary schools at the beginning of the following school year, but were now going to be on their hands for an extra year. One woman said that she had ten children and she wanted me to tell her how she was going to schedule the education of her children. I tried as best I could to explain the *raison d'être* for the measure, and to assure the mothers that there would be places for their children in their local schools at the appropriate time. Gay had a field day. His phone lines were jammed with irate women dying to get at the no-longer-faceless bureaucrat from the department, and it was obvious that public anxiety was not going to be assuaged by the reassurances and explanations of an official spokesman.

Other than my brief stint as an RTÉ reporter in the North, I had never been on the other side of the broadcasting fence. When it was over, I felt like a wet rag and wasn't at all reassured by Byrne's compliments as to how well I had done. He could well say that when he had had a lively hour out of it. Gay's no doubt well-intentioned remarks were little consolation in the teeth of the virulent criticism to which I was subjected from the minute the programme ended. In my short reporting career I had got complaints, mainly from politicians in Northern Ireland, about stories I had done. But that was nothing compared to the avalanche of criticism that I received on this occasion. My former colleagues in Fianna Fáil were incensed. The INTO claimed that I had misrepresented the real implications of the proposed measure and, more suspiciously, that I had done so at the express wish of the minister. The newspapers saw only a news story about a former Fianna Fáil Government Press Secretary publicly defending a coalition government policy. I couldn't win. I comforted myself with the thought that people would hardly be criticizing me if I had made a mess of things. Boland had delayed going into a cabinet meeting so that he could listen in to the programme in his car outside Leinster House: he was delighted with the broadcast. When I returned to my office, Liam Ó Laidhin said that I had done the department proud. I couldn't explain to him that politicians had long memories and that in the event of a change of government I would most likely be put into the political equivalent of purdah. For all his guile and agility in dealing with the complexities of the educational system, Ó Laidhin was typical of many senior civil servants, who had no conception of the savagery of politics and the depths to which certain politicians would go in seeking to repay someone for what they saw as an act of political disloyalty.

In the end, it was all to no avail. Unfortunately for Boland, and for me, the government succumbed to all the pressure and the proposal to raise the school entry age was scrapped. Boland was livid and was scathing in his comments to me about the lack of support from Garret FitzGerald. Undoubtedly the matter did sour relations, such as they were, between the government and the trade unions, and there are still those in Fine Gael with long-enough memories who blame John Boland for the deterioration in the relationship between the party and the teachers' unions.

While there was never a dull day working for John Boland, in all honesty it was not easy either. He was disliked by some of his civil servants, more because of his manner than because of anything that he set out to do. It is also true that when he had a few drinks on him he could become difficult and even more argumentative than usual. Many discovered, to their dismay, that regardless of circumstances he was able to recall the detail of every conversation. He had a tendency to question everything and had an almost insatiable capacity for information, no matter how complicated or detailed it was. Although they were completely different personalities, Boland sometimes reminded me of Charlie Haughey, particularly in his ability to assimilate a brief quickly and accurately. In his case, though, you could almost hear the whirring of the computer in his mind, whereas with Charlie you never quite knew what was going on behind the sphinx-like visage.

When I think back on it, I am amazed to realize that Boland was Minister for Education for little more than six months. In that period he made more of a mark, however controversial, than had many of his predecessors or successors. His lasting achievement there was the establishment of the Curriculum and Examinations Board. This was something about which there had been a considerable amount of political guff prior to his arrival in the department, but he began the practical process that ultimately got it up and running. Given his toughness, and his penchant for debunking some of the accepted wisdom that surrounded Irish education, Boland would surely have caused political mayhem if he had remained much longer in the department. For instance, from conversations I had with him I found out that he was deeply suspicious of the religious orders' role in running schools. While he recognized their contribution to educating many, himself included, none the less he felt that a more secular approach might be better in the long run. I have no doubt that had he had longer in the department he would have caused huge controversy on the matter, though whether he would have been allowed to proceed with any major changes in that relationship while Garret FitzGerald was Taoiseach is doubtful.

Boland and Fitzgerald never settled into an easy, or even a mutually respectful, relationship – certainly not on John's part. He told me himself how much he resented the fact that before he was appointed to cabinet Garret had questioned him about allegations of corruption in the planning process that had arisen while he had been a member of Dublin County Council. These had been the subject of a Garda investigation and cropped up occasionally in the media. He thought Peter Prendergast was behind the questioning, but, as far as I could make out, Prendergast had nothing to do with it and it was merely Garret being cautious. Boland, however, never forgave or forgot, and Prendergast joined his long list of *bêtes noires*. Nothing could convince him that as Government Press Secretary Peter's only interest was in successfully presenting the government, and particularly the Taoiseach, and the policies they were pursuing. John believed that Garret allowed Peter far too much say in forming policy as distinct from its presentation. Since many of the party's old guard believed that too, he wasn't alone in that view, but in Boland's case the attitude was inexcusable: he wasn't much older than Prendergast and should have appreciated efficient and modern ways of communicating political ideas and programmes. It was something of a shock to find that his conservatism ran so deep.

While Boland recognized Garret's electoral value, he did not believe that he was the best person to lead Fine Gael and was doubtful about the worth of his modernizing endeavours. At the time his views and comments were regarded as almost treasonous, and close friends in the cabinet repeatedly warned him to curb his tongue and await developments. I also believed that it was inevitable that Garret would hear of Boland's disaffection and, while sacking was unlikely, there was always the possibility that he would lose the Taoiseach's support at cabinet. Since some of the changes he wanted to introduce into the educational system were pretty drastic, and would come up against huge opposition, they would be entirely doomed if he did not have the Taoiseach's goodwill. I spoke to him about this on a number of occasions. Initially he told me that I was out of order, but eventually he relented and undertook to keep a check on any misgivings he might have about either policy matters or the government's method of conducting its business. In the long run, of course, Boland was right. Were he alive today, I have no doubt that he would argue that Garret travelled too far too quickly with a party that had its roots in conservative Ireland.

On top of that, as time went on every week he came back from cabinet meetings increasingly frustrated at the inability, as he saw it, of the government and Garret, its chairman, to distinguish between what was actually achievable and what was merely notional. Occasionally late at night he would regale me, and one or two others from within Fine Gael, with less than complimentary accounts of Garret's and other ministers' demeanour and performance at cabinet. He believed that Garret was susceptible to flattery and that the extremes of devotion to the party displayed by some of its more ambitious new recruits had resulted in their being appointed to the cabinet and to junior ministries. (For him, the ultimate proof of this was when he saw Gemma Hussey appointed to the Department of Education when Fine Gael returned to government after the election in late 1982.) A favourite story was how, on one infamous occasion, a minister suggested a measure to resolve a problem that was taking up a lot of time. Garret, according to Boland's exasperated account, said, 'That's all very well in practice, but will it work in theory?' Thereafter, and whenever a civil servant made an inapt suggestion, Boland and I would look at one another and repeat Garret's phrase. It was my first experience of an intelligent politician becoming disillusioned with the actual exercise of power, and it went some way towards explaining the modus operandi adopted by John Boland in his subsequent ministerial career.

When the government fell over the budget in January 1982, the hardest thing for me was that I could have nothing to do with the ensuing general election. I had to watch the campaign from the sidelines. I knew that if Fianna Fáil was returned to office I would not automatically be invited back to my old post as Government Press Secretary. Quite the contrary. In the circumstances, there was nothing I could do except wait.

While the election was fought – as, ultimately, every election is – on the economy, behind the scenes Boland's enemies within Fine Gael tried to argue that the school entry age issue had offended a number of important audiences. Amazingly my defence of the proposed measure on behalf of both the minister and the government was now used in certain Fine Gael circles as an example of how NOT to go about presenting or defending government policy.

For Fine Gael TDs to blame Boland for a loss of support in the election was disingenuous and an attempt to divert attention away from the reason it was being held: political incompetence. The government had fallen because in extending VAT to clothing, it never thought to exempt children's clothing and footwear – a faux pas compounded by Garret apocryphally saying that the proposal could not be amended because women with small feet might avoid paying VAT by buying children's shoes. (That is certainly how his words were spun, though his own record is that he said children with big feet who had to buy adults' shoes might be subject to the tax.) It was a classic example of what Boland had always feared: a minister – John Bruton – getting carried away by an idea that worked in theory, but that turned out to be disastrous in political practice.

The result of the election was that neither Fianna Fáil nor the Fine Gael–Labour coalition could form a government without the help of independents, including three Sinn Féin–The Workers

Party deputies. Word began to seep out that a heave against Charlie Haughey was in train in Fianna Fáil. My heart sank. My impression, from what Brian Lenihan was telling me, was that the 'usual suspects', as he described them, had sniffed the wind and, having correctly divined that there was a very strong possibility that Charlie would become Taoiseach again, begun the process of trying to prevent this, even though they had no real game-plan as to how to proceed, or what would happen in the event of their plotting being successful. From a distance it appeared that the object of the exercise was to get rid of Charlie, not to figure out what was best for Fianna Fáil. Their antics had all the hallmarks of a school-boy plot, doomed to failure from the start. Dessie O'Malley put his name forward to be the party's nominee for Taoiseach, but withdrew it before a vote when he realized that he couldn't possibly win.

Despite the stirrings against his leadership, Haughey set about the task of obtaining the independents' support with a fervour and commitment that surprised even his own supporters within Fianna Fáil. Much was made at the time, and since, of the pact he made with Tony Gregory, a young independent socialist who was cynical about the 'establishment' parties and represented one of the most deprived areas of Dublin's inner city. Haughey did not know Gregory but others in the party did, or at least knew of him, and Charlie collected as much detail about him and what he stood for as he could. He wouldn't trust anybody else to deal with him and went alone to Gregory's nondescript offices to hear what Gregory would demand in return for his vote. Haughey took great pains to respond to each condition clearly and cogently. The answer was either yes or no. Having rightly seen that a deal with Sinn Féin– The Workers Party was a non-starter, Garret belatedly recognized that Gregory was going to be an important factor in the formation of a new government. But what he offered was far too little and far too late. When the Dáil met, and Gregory insisted on reading out in full the agreement he had reached with the leader of Fianna Fáil, the deal was depicted as further evidence of Charlie's almost manic determination to get into power at any cost. This attitude failed to take into account that both party leaders had sought a deal with

Gregory. It was a perfectly legitimate deal between two politicians whose interests happened to coincide.

When it became clear that Charlie was going to form a government, I knew that it would be only a matter of days before I would know my fate. Within minutes of Charlie's election as Taoiseach, Pádraig Ó hAnnracháin left the Department of Education and took up his old position in the Taoiseach's office. Days passed. There was no call. Eventually, after two weeks and much media speculation as to who would become the new Government Press Secretary, I got a call from Ó hAnnracháin to say that the Taoiseach wanted to see me and that I should present myself in Leinster House the following morning at 10.30. I duly did so, only to be told by the Taoiseach's Private Secretary, Seán Aylward, that the Taoiseach had made no mention of my impending arrival when he had gone through his appointments the previous evening. I thought this very odd and I walked over to Ó hAnnracháin's office in Government Buildings, assuming that there had been some mistake, but Ó hAnnracháin said that he had made the call and arranged the meeting on the instructions of the Taoiseach.

I trudged back to Leinster House to find that the Taoiseach had arrived in his office, but was about to depart again for a cabinet meeting. Seán Aylward suggested that I stick my head in the door and catch him before he left. I was quite thrown by the events – or non-events – of the morning thus far, so it was with great reluctance that I followed his advice. Charlie was completely surprised to see me. He asked about my family and we exchanged the usual pleasantries that pass between people who haven't seen one another for some time. Eventually, when I realized that Charlie was anxious to go, I said that I understood that he wanted to see me and that I had come as a result of the invitation he had issued via Ó hAnnracháin. He denied all knowledge of having issued any such invitation, but then said, 'I suppose we'll have to make a decision about you soon.'

The following day I got a call from Ó hAnnracháin to say that the Taoiseach had inquired where I was, as if Charlie expected to see me in his office for the usual review of that day's papers. He said I should come to Government Buildings ASAP. I arrived later that day and that was how I resumed the job of Government Press Secretary. In retrospect I think that if I had arrived uninvited immediately after Charlie had been elected Taoiseach in the Dáil, nobody, least of all him, would have batted an eyelid.

13. GUBU

From the very start of Charlie's second term as Taoiseach the atmosphere was febrile. Having been publicly exposed, the fault-lines in Fianna Fáil seemed ready to crack open at the slightest provocation. As it turned out, in 1982 the provocations were more than slight.

As I settled back into the job of Government Press Secretary, I discovered that, as Charlie saw it, his biggest problem was with the media. In addition to those outlets that had always been doubtful about him, he had gained more critics as a result of his failure to act on his TV broadcast of two years previously when he'd promised to manage the economy properly. Despite this, and although he had decided that the way to handle journalists was to keep them in the dark, he still expected positive coverage. Charlie rarely spoke to me personally about how he viewed my performance in the job as Press Secretary. But my antennae were sharp enough to pick up the signals, however faint: he was thinking that perhaps his media problems lay with his publicity staff – chiefly myself – and that he thought that maybe I was relying too much on tried and tested methods that might well have worked during a previous adminis-tration but were slightly out of tune with the requirements of the new dispensation. Most of what I picked up was transmitted through Pádraig Ó hAnnracháin, who, I guessed, was influencing his judgement. It was all quite ironic, because I thought precisely the same thing about his and Ó hAnnracháin's take on media relations as they thought about mine: it belonged to an era that was over. In simple terms, I thought their approach to the media, and the political correspondents in particular, was too crude; they thought mine was too cosy. Charlie sometimes praised my good relations with the political correspondents – but then implied that the lobby would be willing to accept anything that I told it, if only

I could do it in the right way. Every time we had one of these conversations, where he would explain – patiently, as if to a trainee – that my task was to charm the media into giving him the space and time to get around to managing the country as he had promised, I had to point out that he and other senior members of Fianna Fáil were living in a time warp if they thought journalists took politicians or their mouthpieces at their word any more. On such occasions he would rail at how Jack Lynch had managed to con both the media and the electorate – with my connivance – with his hang-dog charm, and that if it hadn't been for Lynch's fiscal ineptitude, and Martin O'Donoghue's economics, he would not have half the problems that he had now.

To solve his notional problem Charlie believed that the Government Information Service needed more staff – smarter staff was the implication – and he proceeded with hiring people. While I was a bit annoyed, I was cute enough to know that it wouldn't take very long for the political realities to kick in and that, whatever eye-catching or novel appointments were made, the fundamental nature of the job in the GIS would remain the same. There was – and is – a very fine line between providing information on behalf of the government of the day and providing propaganda, and politicians, notwithstanding their assertions to the contrary, prefer propaganda. Though I was not consulted about the proposed appointments, that was not to say that I didn't value some of the new blood. I certainly welcomed one recruit: Ted Smyth from the press section of the Department of Foreign Affairs, with whom I had worked closely in the past. He had done Trojan work while he was in the Irish Consulate in New York. I don't think Ted was prepared for what he found in the Department of the Taoiseach – in particular a boss who would spurn valuable opportunities to get his message across, not only with the home media but with the foreign press, which was Ted's *métier*. Ken Ryan from the *Irish Independent* was recruited as new deputy head of the GIS. Charlie thought that it would be a good idea to have a reporter from that stable working for him so that some of the hostility from it might be dissipated by one of its own, as it were. It was precisely such

woolly and misguided thinking about the nature of the contemporary media that had got him into the mess he was in: modern
journalists didn't work on that kind of nod-and-wink basis. Ken
was a political enthusiast and, I suspect, had been a closet Fianna
Fáil supporter while working in Middle Abbey Street. However,
he had no experience of the internal workings of government and
wasn't clued in to the Machiavellian nature of even the closest
political relationships. He was inclined to take politicians at face
value, with the result that he was subtly bullied into trying to sell
the unsaleable to his former colleagues.

When Charlie mentioned that he was 'thinking' of appointing
Noel Gilmore, Chief Executive of the National Dairy Council, to
head the GIS, my first reaction was that this was a move to
undermine my authority as Government Press Secretary. He spoke
of Noel's talents in such a way that it was impossible to gainsay his
intentions. This version of consultation, which was really just telling
me what he was about to do, provided Charlie – if he ever needed
it – with the convenience of being able to say subsequently that he
had asked my advice about the appointment. I remember his
enthusiasm about the prospect of Gilmore joining the service and
being left with the impression that Charlie believed all would be
well as soon as Gilmore arrived. The reality of course was somewhat
different, and it wasn't very long before Charlie was asking me why
I had recommended Noel Gilmore. Noel had done a thoroughly
good job of raising the NDC's profile, and, from what I had
gathered before he arrived, he was a highly organized and focused
individual who got things done in a determined but genial fashion.
However, he just couldn't get over the levels of inefficiency and
bad management he discovered when he arrived at the heart of
government, and he found the intricacies of the political mind
hard to comprehend. He had had little, if any, knowledge of the
day-to-day working of politics, particularly at government level,
and none at all of the deep scepticism in which even the most
senior of those charged with running the country were held.

All of this frantic change was classic Charlie. He was doing what
had served him well as a young politician: when he perceived that

there was a difficulty in a specific area – in this instance, media coverage of the government – his style was to identify the apparent source of the problem and throw resources at it. He seemed to believe that the principle of *force majeure* would apply: a combination of Smyth, Ryan, Gilmore and Dunlop would surely stem the flow of negative media coverage and, more importantly, prevent journalists either writing about or investigating anything that members of the government believed should be outside their ambit. But Charlie was on a hiding to nothing because he just didn't get the nature of his problem with the media. Remember that Charlie had come of age politically at a time when the media, by and large, deferred to politicians, took what they said at face value and reported it faithfully. Smart young TDs like Charlie, who recognized what journalists needed, were rewarded with what their colleagues regarded as an easy ride in the press. Twenty-odd years later he was playing by the same rules. He didn't seem to understand that there was a new breed of journalists about – people who couldn't be awed or browbeaten by the supposed might of a government 'machine'. Having beefed up the GIS, Charlie expected things to improve. But he starved his new appointees of the ammunition they needed to do the job – information and availability – and inevitably everything got worse.

Before Charlie appointed his cabinet in 1982, George Colley again sought the power of veto over his appointments in Justice and Defence. This time Charlie said no and, still smarting from the abortive heave in which Colley had been involved, refused to appoint him as Tánaiste. George retired to the back benches. Sadly George died prematurely in London eighteen months later while undergoing routine angioplasty to relieve his acute angina. As a mark of respect Fianna Fáil TDs and officials gathered at Dublin Airport when his body was flown home for burial. Charlie always had an amateurish interest in medicine and he told a group of his front benchers waiting on the tarmac that George had died as a result of 'bad medicine'. A journalist overheard the remark and subsequently the rumour spread that Charlie had attributed

George's death to some sort of 'bad karma' or unnatural influences.

Had Charlie given George the veto over Justice he might have saved himself a lot of trouble. His new minister in that department was Seán Doherty, an ex-garda, who had been an avid Haughey man ever since his election in 1977. His appointment was to lead to an unrelenting campaign by Fine Gael deputies, primed by the party's General Secretary, Peter Prendergast, to undermine Haughey on the basis of the alleged low calibre of some of his ministerial appointees. Admittedly, the critics weren't working on fallow ground. There were reasons for saying that Charlie had made appointments on the basis of support for him rather than on outstanding ability, and Doherty's promotion was one of them.

I had my own experience with Doherty early on during the new government's term. He and Ray Burke arrived in my office one morning a few minutes before a cabinet meeting. Since my office was virtually opposite the cabinet room, it was not unusual for ministers to pop in for a chat, so I thought little of their visit until Doherty handed me a large government-issue envelope that obviously contained a file. He asked me to copy the contents personally and, having done so, to place the copy in another envelope and give it to Ray Burke. The instructions were specific: nobody else was to make the copy and I was not to show it to anybody. Furthermore, I wasn't to read the material I was copying. Naturally, after they entered the cabinet meeting, the first thing I did was to start reading. It was a Department of Justice file containing a copy of the early seventies Garda investigation into allegations of malpractice by Ray Burke when he was a member of Dublin County Council. From time to time Ray himself had boasted that he had been interviewed by the Fraud Squad some twenty times. I made the copy on a machine in the office of the Chief Whip's Private Secretary, which was down the corridor from mine. When the cabinet meeting was over, I returned the original file to Doherty and gave the copy to Ray Burke. The matter was never mentioned again. It was the only occasion on which I was ever asked to perform such a task. At the time I was quite concerned about it but subsequently decided it was something best forgotten.

Although the whips' office was close to mine, I didn't take much notice of the young Chief Whip, Bertie Ahern. He was a quiet, unassuming operator who said very little but who kept in close touch with Charlie. I found him very personable, intensely interested in what he was doing and totally committed to the smooth running of his own constituency. Because his use of language was occasionally infelicitous, people tended to not pay sufficient attention to what he was saying, and it was only in retrospect that they wondered whether they had missed something. In the torrid months that were to follow, Bertie – almost uniquely – managed to stay on good terms with both pro- and anti-Haughey TDs. I would go so far as to say that those who had any dealings with him throughout those tumultuous events would maintain, notwithstanding that he was acting on behalf of the man that some 25 per cent of the parliamentary party wanted to get rid of, that he was on their side. I cannot recall a single occasion when I heard either faction expressing any negative opinion about his handling of affairs. In 1994, when I had long since left public service but still had strong Fianna Fáil links, I was reminded of this Teflon quality when Bertie's name was being put before his colleagues as a candidate for leadership of the party. I was deputed to do some lobbying on his behalf, and one of those on my list was Brian Cowen. Brian was happy to hear me out, but he seemed non-committal. When I pressed for a reaction, he came back with the most extraordinary response: 'But Frank, I don't know this man.' This was about someone with whom he had sat at cabinet. Whatever the truth of Charlie Haughey's famous judgement that Ahern was the most devious and the most cunning deputy in Fianna Fáil, he is undoubtedly the most gifted political operator of his or any other generation.

The business with Ray Burke and Seán Doherty was an unsettling start to what would be a troubled period. An accumulation of incidents convulsed the government and the media. Charlie described the most dramatic of these incidents – the discovery of a murderer in the apartment of the Attorney General – as 'grotesque, unbelievable, bizarre and unprecedented'. His eternal enemy,

Conor Cruise O'Brien, used these words against him and coined the acronym GUBU to describe this spell of Charlie's government. From my point of view, the events took over my job. In an ideal world, I would have continued to disseminate information on policy matters, regardless of the political controversies raging at any particular time. In the real world there was no room for such a precious approach, mainly because there was considerable unease, in Fianna Fáil circles as well as elsewhere, about the 'off-stage' activities of some members of Charlie's government. The nature of the events, and of the speculation that accompanied them, meant that there was little to do but roll with the punches. And by God, there were punches.

In April the government came under extreme pressure over its attitude to the Falklands War. Fianna Fáil's visceral anti-British instincts took over and the government adopted a position that was contrary to the Department of Foreign Affairs' advice: which was that, as a neutral country, we should stay out of things. But the government made it obvious that it was reluctant to join the other European Community countries in imposing sanctions on Argentina when it invaded the Falkland Islands, a British territory. This did considerable damage to Charlie's reputation and attracted the wrath of the British establishment and virulent anti-Irish journalism in the more jingoistic British newspapers. As Government Press Secretary I found it incredibly wearing constantly having to stress to reporters the distinction between solidarity with the European Community and acting in the best interests of the age-old policy of neutrality. The Department of Foreign Affairs was also at its wits' end, and things were not helped by the frostiness that still characterized the relationship between Charlie and its mandarins.

This impasse between the Taoiseach and Foreign Affairs was slightly ameliorated in the immediate aftermath of the sinking of the Argentinian battleship *General Belgrano* in early May. Charlie showed a restraint Foreign Affairs had not anticipated and did not launch the attack on Mrs Thatcher and the Brits that its officials were dreading. In the event it was Paddy Power, the Minister for Defence, who let the mask slip. At a party function in his own constituency he laid into the British government and gave vent to his Republican outlook. His comments were reported on radio early the following morning. Immediately my phone rang at home. Charlie told me to have Paddy Power in Government Buildings at ten o'clock and then ranted about the incompetence of those around him. On occasions such as this – and there were many of them – I had learnt to stay quiet, so I refrained from pointing out that Paddy Power and all his ministers were selected by him alone, and therefore, if he wasn't happy about how they performed in office, he could blame no one but himself. In the circumstances I thought it wise to meet Power before he encountered this maelstrom; on his arrival I explained that the Taoiseach was pretty annoyed at his remarks and there would have to be a retraction. Paddy's reaction was blunt, and brave: 'Fuck him.' None the less it was made known publicly, both through me and through Foreign Affairs, that the minister's remarks did not reflect the government's attitude. Still, the next day the government announced that it was abandoning sanctions against Argentina. So the delicate pas de deux between the Taoiseach and Maggie Thatcher, with the Department of Foreign Affairs acting as a long-suffering choreographer, continued. Matters were helped somewhat by Noel Dorr, who was Ireland's representative at the United Nations and who put the Irish case with the utmost sophistication and delicacy. He was one of those Foreign Affairs officers whom Charlie came to regard with great respect.

I was on holiday at the end of July when murder after murder after murder – four in all – convulsed the country. A 29-year-old nurse, Bridie Gargan, was beaten with a lump hammer by a man who was attempting to steal her car while she lay sun-bathing beside it in the Phoenix Park; a young farmer, Donal Dunne, from Edenderry, was killed by a shotgun blast; Robert Belton died as a result of injuries sustained in a raid on his sub-post office in north Dublin; and Patricia Furlong was strangled in the Dublin mountains after she had been at a summer festival in the village of Glencullen. Bridie Gargan's murder was particularly strange and savage. An ambulance driver had seen the nurse's car being driven out of the Phoenix Park, noted the sticker for St James's Hospital on its windscreen, saw the slumped figure in the back seat and the blood on the window, and concluded that a doctor was driving someone who had had an accident to the hospital. He indicated that the car should follow him, put on his siren and escorted it to the hospital. When the driver, the young nurse's attacker, realized that he might be about to be rumbled, he blithely drove off the grounds of the hospital again, abandoning the car and the dying woman in a nearby laneway.

Public relief when the gardaí made an arrest in the cases of the murders of Bridie Gargan and Donal Dunne (it emerged that the cases were linked because Nurse Gargan's attacker had subsequently shot Dunne dead when he went to buy a gun from him) turned to utter astonishment when their suspect, Malcolm Macarthur, was arrested in the home of the Attorney General, Patrick Connolly, on Friday, 13 August. It turned out that Macarthur, who came from a wealthy Meath background, was an old friend of Connolly and had turned up at the Attorney General's Dalkey apartment over a week earlier saying that he was in Ireland for a few days to sort out some financial affairs. When Connolly offered him a bed, he gratefully accepted. Paddy Connolly had been something of a surprise appointment as Attorney General and I don't believe I ever met him or exchanged a word with him. Now, out of the blue, like something out of a crime thriller, he was indirectly caught up in the most horrific crime in the land.

I was still on holidays, so Ken Ryan handled the press queries. Though I was back home in Meath, I got no calls there because journalists knew I was away. The only person I spoke to was Pádraig Ó hAnnracháin, who rang to tell me what was going on. We both realized the gravity of the situation but were hampered by the fact that Charlie was on his island, Inishvickillane: the telephone line to the mainland was poor and it was hard to get hold of him. We agreed to allow the situation to sit until he arrived back in Dublin. This is an indication of the modus operandi of the time: first, that neither of us was prepared to do anything without prior approval from Charlie; but also that we were not storming the island to get hold of him so we would know what to do. But it was before the era of 24-hour news and satellite communication, and the idea of letting a night go by without speaking to the key player in a major political story was not so shocking.

Charlie's Private Secretary, Seán Aylward, kept trying Inishvickillane and he managed to get hold of him and tell him what had happened. Aylward told Charlie that Connolly intended to leave the country the next day on a flight to London; from there he was going on a pre-arranged holiday in the United States. Charlie eventually managed to speak to Connolly and tried to dissuade him from travelling. That he insisted on going ahead with his plans was probably a measure of his political inexperience and naivety. But Charlie should have known better and it's still hard to understand why he didn't just forbid him from continuing. I suspect it was his way of showing a man whom he had appointed, and who was in quite a state of shock, that he believed in his assurances and still trusted him. Any objective adviser could have told them both that it was a dreadful mistake for Connolly to leave the country in the circumstances. Apart from showing appalling insensitivity to the families of the murder victims, it looked as if the Attorney General – *Haughey's* Attorney General – was leaving the country in circumstances where he could be a material witness in a serious investigation.

The international media descended on Dublin and, as usual when a large group of journalists gather in one place, the rumours became more wild and lurid as the hours and the days passed. There was no sense of looking at the matter dispassionately and saying: 'This has nothing to do with the government, with politics, with the cabinet or with the Taoiseach.' Those who believed in conspiracy theories had a field day. Ultimately any neutral assessment of the affair would show that, apart from the discovery of the suspect in the apartment of the Attorney General, any connections with the government were tangential. But at the time, though nobody would say it publicly, many journalists and politicians – some within Fianna Fáil – were prepared to believe that the Attorney General's departure on a pre-arranged holiday was some sort of set-up and that, notwithstanding his complete and total innocence in the affair, this was yet another example of there being one law for those in power and another for everyone else.

Charlie contacted Connolly in New York on Sunday and ordered him back to Dublin. After the reception he had received at JFK, where he had been subjected to a media frenzy that made the Irish reporters look like correspondents for the *Irish Messenger of the Sacred Heart*, he realized the import of his actions in leaving Ireland as well as the devastating effect it had had on the government's reputation and, by extension, the Taoiseach's. Connolly flew back to London on Concorde; the government made arrangements for him to be collected by an Air Corps plane and flown to Casement Aerodrome in Baldonnel; from there he would be driven straight to Kinsaley. In the meantime, I got a message from Charlie's private office to be in Kinsaley on the Monday evening in time for Connolly's arrival.

When I turned up I found Charlie pacing the floor, not because he was anxious about the meeting with Connolly (though he told me he had no option but to ask for his resignation), nor because he was furious with the political Fates who had landed him in this sorry situation, but because he was alone and had had no food all day. Maureen Haughey was on holiday in Spain with Pat O'Connor's wife and there was nobody to prepare a meal for him. When I began to laugh he eventually saw the incongruity of the situation, calmed down and made arrangements to go to O'Connor's to get something to eat as soon as he had concluded his meeting with Connolly.

When Connolly arrived, Charlie asked me to go into an adjacent room and Connolly was never aware that I was there. As he passed through the hallway with Charlie, I was watching from an ante-room and I could see that the man looked shattered. No doubt that had as much to do with the fact that he had flown the Atlantic twice in the space of as many days as with the trauma of the occasion. A short time later he left Kinsaley, a deeply saddened and disillusioned man. The meeting had been tense and tetchy and seemed to have a scarring effect on Charlie also; when he recounted to me what had occurred between them he did so in a weary and almost despairing fashion. He hadn't expected that the Attorney General would strongly resist resignation. Undoubtedly it was a scapegoating exercise, but it was one of those extraordinary incidents in which politics and rational argument come face to face and politics wins.

Now that the meeting was over, we had a dilemma: how to get the Taoiseach down the Malahide Road to Pat O'Connor's home, Mabestown House, without having to run the gauntlet of the photographers and reporters who had gathered at his gates earlier in anticipation of Connolly's arrival, and who were now awaiting a statement about what had taken place and whether or not the Attorney General had resigned. The problem was that he had no car. When he arrived home he had sent away his driver: he hadn't anticipated that he would need to be driven anywhere for the rest of the evening. But I had my car, a battered – and hopefully inconspicuous – Fiat Mirafiori. The brief statement I had typed on Charlie's secretary's typewriter was being distributed to the press just as we arrived at the exit to the Malahide Road. I was checking for on-coming traffic before driving out on to the road when a photographer from the *Irish Independent* spotted Charlie in the front passenger seat of my car. He raised the alarm with his colleagues and they came after us.

The concept of 'hot pursuit' took on a new meaning as I sped down the road with the leader of the country beside me and a posse of determined photographers behind me. A Hollywood movie could not have bettered it. But Charlie gave no indication that he was wound up by the events of the evening or the previous three days. Apart from getting slightly agitated when I didn't obey him and drove straight out on to the Malahide Road without stopping, he remained cool throughout. There was no sense from him that this was a matter of great political import. It was yet another of these awkward situations that arose and had to be dealt with. All in a day's work.

As we approached the entrance to Pat O'Connor's house, Charlie instructed me to stop. Showing more agility than I would have credited him with, he hopped out, said, 'See you tomorrow', and was gone. I followed his instructions to drive on to Malahide. I parked and went into Gibney's Pub, a popular haunt with the Haugheys and their friends. I was joined a few minutes later by a group of breathless and somewhat irate photographers asking where 'he' was. I feigned total innocence. To this day some of the photographers refuse to believe me when I tell them exactly what happened, which was that Charlie sprinted across the road to O'Connor's gateway, hid behind a large tree until the photographers' cars had passed, and then walked up to the house and had his meal in peace while the rest of the country and the media continued to be convulsed by events.

Before I leave this issue, there was one other aspect to it that, while trivial in itself, exemplified the suspicion of everything Charlie and Fianna Fáil did at this time. The statement issued from Kinsaley after Connolly left was distributed by a Garda Superintendent, Billy Byrne of Coolock Station. This was a matter of convenience. Superintendent Byrne was on duty at the gates of Kinsaley, keeping an eye on some of the more enterprising photographers who would have liked to be nearer the house when Connolly arrived and departed. He also kept Charlie and me informed as to what was happening at the gates and who was there. The journalists were annoyed that there wasn't an opportunity to talk to the Taoiseach, and their annoyance increased when only a brief statement was issued. In these circumstances, the fact that a Government Information Service document was distributed by a senior garda caused something of a minor furore. Political and media critics accused the Taoiseach of attempting to politicize An Garda Síochána, and there were those who saw it as a small part of some putative jigsaw, one that indicated a rottenness at the heart of Charlie's management of affairs. The fact that Billy Byrne was an old school friend of Charlie, and had led the investigation of the case against his friend and election agent, Pat O'Connor, and his daughter, Niamh, when they were accused of double-voting in the previous general election (charges subsequently dismissed in court), was coincidental and had no bearing whatever on the central issue of the evening. But this was not how it was presented, and the Garda's willingness to help on the occasion was interpreted as something far more sinister.

From the moment Malcolm Macarthur was arrested there was an incessant demand for information. Many of these requests related to policing matters and were therefore referred directly to the Garda Press Office. But obviously there was an acute political interest as well and I felt that the only way of dealing with it was to hold a press conference. There ministers, or at least those who were willing to attend, could put matters in context and answer questions, particularly those relating to the Attorney General. Charlie knew that considerable damage had been done by virtue of the fact that a man accused of a brutal murder had been arrested in the home of an ex-officio member of the government, so he agreed to my proposal.

Usually at a time of crisis politicians gravitate towards the centre for fear they might miss something. In this instance, however, they did not want any proximity to the mess that had unfolded. Charlie was left to take the press conference alone in the Fianna Fáil party room on the fifth floor of Leinster House. I sat with him as a mostly hostile media quizzed him about every aspect of recent events. Having been asked to describe the entire scenario for the umpteenth time, Charlie used the fateful words 'grotesque, unbelievable, bizarre and unprecedented' to describe it. Then, in response to a question about whether he would like to congratulate the officers involved in the investigation, Charlie said that he certainly would in view of the fact that they had got 'the right man'. I knew immediately that he had made a faux pas. A man had been arrested and, while all the circumstantial evidence available pointed towards a particular conclusion, it would be disastrous if a subsequent prosecution was thrown out on the grounds that the case had been prejudiced by the Taoiseach. A couple of journalists present immediately picked up on the gaffe and began making faces at me. Charlie didn't like being interrupted while conducting press conferences – not, as was alleged, because he wanted to give the impression that he had all the answers; he just did not like to be distracted from the main thrust of what he wanted to say. If he made a mistake, which was quite rare, then it could be corrected later. So I didn't intervene, but as soon as the press conference was over I brought it to his attention. 'Oh, God, I didn't, did I?' he said. In briefings later that day I tried to make the point that it was a slip of the tongue and nothing of any consequence should be attached to the words used by the Taoiseach. But that didn't wash. In the highly charged atmosphere there were those who insisted on believing that it had been no slip of the tongue but a deliberate attempt to pervert the course of justice.

For ever afterwards the label GUBU was not only used by Charlie's long-time critics in the media and opposition, but also adopted as a convenient stick to beat the drum of anti-Haughey sentiment within Fianna Fáil. Those who had lined up against him in December 1979, together with those who had supported McCreevy in his critical comments about the direction of the party early in 1982, comments that led the way for the challenge to Charlie's leadership after the election, saw all these events as a glorious accumulation of negative perceptions of their *bête noire*. Those who made their views known publicly, however difficult they were to hear or accept, deserved credit for their principled stance. Those who moved in the shadows, egging on others while keeping their own identities secret, these were the ones for whom Charlie reserved the contempt that was their due. That when he came to chair a press conference on the Macarthur affair he was abandoned by some of his most senior ministers showed the depth of sentiment against him, and provided a disturbing insight into how even the most ardent of his supporters would wilt when the going got tough.

The loss of the Attorney General, even in such traumatic and unusual circumstances, was not going to put Charlie off his stride. John Murray was quickly appointed to the position. Connolly had been part of Charlie's defence team during the arms trial, but Murray was from a new generation of lawyers. He was the son-in-law of a member of the High Court, Judge Brian Walsh, who was somebody whom Charlie admired and looked up to. But nothing seemed to go right for the government, and particularly the Taoiseach, after the Macarthur affair, and it is fair to say that at this time my job was next to impossible. Unwittingly or otherwise, the media were drawn into the pervasive atmosphere of crisis and they, unwittingly or otherwise (otherwise I sometimes felt), played a part in perpetuating that atmosphere. On top of the unrelenting and legitimate coverage of the woeful state of the economy and the unemployment situation, influential media outlets also took a barely disguised view that under Charlie Ireland was doomed.

There seemed to be an endless stream of Doherty-related stories. The Dowra affair – in which an assault charge against Doherty's brother-in-law, Tom Nangle, a garda, was dismissed when a key prosecution witness, who lived in Fermanagh, was conveniently detained for questioning by the RUC on the day of the court hearing – hadn't the least impact on me, and I have no recollection of talking to reporters about it. But I do remember Seán Doherty saying to me that anything I might hear involving interference with the police in Northern Ireland was 'total bullshit'. That was in late September. Shortly afterwards I expended considerable time dealing with a story that a few weeks previously Doherty and a well-known country and western singer were allegedly found in a crashed car somewhere in Kerry after a game of poker with other senior ministers. Like all stories of this kind, there was a grain of truth in there somewhere. Yes, Doherty had had a late night out with friends after a day's racing in Listowel. Yes, there was a card game. Yes, there was another politician present, but it was a local TD, not a minister. Yes, a car did crash. However, it wasn't the minister's car, but one in which his security detail had travelled. There was no country and western singer. She was elsewhere in the country and had an alibi to prove it. When the crash happened there was no minister in the car. In fact the driver was alone. And so on and so on. It was impossible to get anyone to accept the facts of the story. From early on Saturday morning I spent hours taking journalists' calls, and eventually I contacted Doherty and had a lengthy and frank conversation with him about the details of the alleged incident. Seán could be totally disarming in one-to-one conversations. He would blithely tell you what the basic circumstances of a given situation were and didn't seem to worry too much about what might or might not be read into it. His attitude on this occasion was no different. He made no secret of the fact that there had been a late-night gathering and much drinking. It was he who told me of the exact circumstances of what happened regarding the car crash. Subsequently, though much later, these facts were confirmed. By then it was too late.

At the time, as in many Irish households, Saturday morning was reserved for shopping, and Sheila waited patiently for me while all this was going on. When I thought I had finally finished with the matter, the phone rang again. Despite her urging me to leave it, I answered with the words: 'This is the führer's bunker!' There was a long and ominous silence on the other end of the line and then a familiar voice said: 'This is the führer!' Charlie knew I was under pressure and he had been trying to get hold of me for an hour or so. 'How bad is it?' he asked. When I told him it was very bad, he ranted about Doherty's idiocy. This was a familiar pattern.

Recalling Charlie's occasional rants reminds me of an amusing exchange I had with Pádraig Ó hAnnracháin about this time that had shades of Nero fiddling while Rome burned. In frustration at the escalation of events that was threatening to submerge the government, I took to fits of using appalling bad language. God knows there was good reason for it. Charlie heard me in full flight on one occasion, and I think he may even have been the cause of the outburst. He said nothing and walked away. Later I was visited by a sheepish-looking Pádraig Ó hAnnracháin, who said that the Taoiseach would be obliged if I didn't lower the tone of his office by indulging in such profanities in his presence in the future. Ó hAnnracháin added, 'You wouldn't know when you would break out like that again. It could be in front of outsiders. It could embarrass the Taoiseach.' In fairness to Ó hAnnracháin there was a wry grin on his face and I knew that he was merely passing on a message, however ludicrous it was in the circumstances. The very fabric of political life in the country at the time was coming asunder, and the Taoiseach was worried about my language. This was pretty rich considering that Charlie had a good command of the vernacular himself. However, it had to be admitted that for a subordinate to 'eff and blind' in the presence of the Taoiseach, or about the Taoiseach, however much the Taoiseach himself might also eff and blind, was neither decorous nor respectful to the office. Ó hAnnracháin was sent away with a flea in his ear, but from then on I tried to curb my language, particularly when Charlie was in the vicinity.

Charlie's own use of language has become the stuff of legend, particularly after an infamous interview was published in *Hot Press* in the mid eighties with expletives undeleted. P. J. Mara, who had persuaded Charlie to give the interview to John Waters, believing it would provide a younger generation with a different perspective on the leader of Fianna Fáil, knew that there would be trouble when the magazine hit the stands. He recruited the services of his friend – everybody's friend – Brian Lenihan, who breezily entered Charlie's office on the day the interview was published and proclaimed it to be a brilliant coup. 'Inspired!' he said. Young people would love it: they wanted to see their politicians speaking and acting in a less stuffy way. Charlie was nobody's fool and instantly recognized that this was an attempt to convince him that black was white, and that the negative coverage of his interview in the mainstream media was far outweighed by his 'man of the people' presentation in *Hot Press*. 'Lenihan, get out of here and take that bastard Mara with you', was the response.

Having said all this, I have listened to many stories about how the air turned blue because of Charlie's Nixonian-style outbursts, and I have to say that I rarely heard him indulge in any incontinent use of expletives. He knew there was a time and a place for strong language and was perfectly capable of controlling his tongue. His generation were rather Victorian in that they were embarrassed by lapses into bad language, a characteristic perhaps reinforced by Catholic education; and when they did so they felt they had let the side down. They might become embroiled in all sorts of other questionable activities, for which they would see no need to apologize, but they apologized profusely when crude language slipped out. Charlie didn't need to use expletives to get his views across: force of personality alone ensured that people understood exactly what he meant. His occasional use of such language only gave added force to an already clearly stated opinion.

I'm glad to say that I cured myself of the habit, probably as a result of the strictures laid down by Charlie Haughey all those years ago.

14. Fianna Fáil falls apart

Though he presented a robust and resolute appearance in public, at times Charlie appeared to cave in, especially when there was blood in the water and the sharks were circling. The fact is that there was often blood in the water, and Ray MacSharry was the only one confident enough to take him aside, talk toughly to him and reinvigorate him in such a way that he came out fighting. MacSharry had been loyal from the beginning. Others were too, but they lacked the strength of character to go to him and deal with him on a man-to-man basis. These were the people who would make expansive and exaggerated statements of support in public, but who would also keep a wary eye out for any possibility of a wind change. They were typified by Pádraig Flynn: he prided himself on being some kind of political weathervane as far as Charlie's support in the parliamentary party and elsewhere was concerned. Ray Burke, the man who dubbed Albert Reynolds's supporters 'the country and western set', said Flynn was like the barber's cat, 'full of wind and piss'.

Haughey trusted MacSharry. In fact, MacSharry was probably one of the few politicians for whom Charlie had any real respect. Much has been made of Charlie's remark that Bertie Ahern was the most devious and the most cunning deputy in the party, but that was a statement of fact, not of respect. He respected MacSharry because, of all those around him, the Sligoman was fearless and told him the unpalatable facts of political life that others were either afraid to tell him or refrained from telling him because there was little advantage in being the bearer of bad news. He knew how far he could go with Haughey, and there were many occasions when, whatever the crisis, real or imagined – and there are lots of imaginary crises in politics – MacSharry was sent for to provide advice as to the course of action to be followed.

Those of us in the front line were always glad to see MacSharry arriving because we knew that some element of reason would prevail. 'Mac' (as he was called by those who knew him well) always gave the impression that he was above whatever crisis was obsessing us all. He struck me as a man who, early in life, had decided that he was not going to be put upon by anybody, let alone those who might have thought that they were his intellectual superiors. And even in his own party – O'Malley and O'Donoghue come to mind – there were some of those. He wasn't a natural plotter, but when the necessity arose he was as good as the best. He also brought a cool head to dealing with the media because, unusually for a politician, he didn't have an automatic paranoia about journalists.

Pádraig Ó hAnnracháin, who was keeping an uncharacteristically low profile, was in constant contact with his old friend John Healy of the *Irish Times*; but he was wasting his time because Healy had failed to recognize that a new era of political journalism had dawned. Even in my relatively short time on the scene – eight years by 1982 – the whole landscape had changed. Many reporters who matured, career-wise, at the beginning of the eighties had been inspired by *All the President's Men*, the book and the film about how the Watergate scandal was revealed. Now an army of ambitious young journalists wanted high-profile exclusives, not staid, ministerial kite-flying. Matters were examined far more forensically and little, if any, quarter was given. Whereas in the past only a handful of press people covered Leinster House, in the late seventies and early eighties the numbers increased phenomenally. This media army gravitated to the bars and restaurants in the Dáil and its environs, where, naturally, they heard all kinds of yarns, both true and apocryphal. In this changed environment political gossip was as likely to be considered newsworthy as a policy shift. A minor diary piece would be followed by denials or clarifications, and so the news cycle became self-generating. Since it is in the nature of the political animal to feed the media, some TDs got caught up in this new way of doing business, often in the vain expectation that the favour would be returned at some future date.

In the face of this onslaught, Charlie's instruction that my colleagues and I were to take a minimalist approach to assisting the
media was the worst possible strategy. In the absence of official
information from my office or from the GIS, people went rooting
around in the undergrowth and, given the fractious state of Fianna
Fáil and the calibre of some of those personalities Charlie had
promoted, inevitably they found truffles. Trying to guide reporters
in the circumstances was about as effective as trying to hold back
the tide. For this new style of reporting, nothing could be better
than turmoil in the country's largest political party; they relished
the sight of its leader in the cross-hairs of a sniper's rifle and the
prospect that someone was about to pull the trigger.

I am not suggesting that the new approach to reporting politics
was all bad. Far from it. It was less deferential – which was good.
The political system had, up to that point, survived on a curious
mixture of mystique and awe (some of it created by journalists like
John Healy, who liked to be seen to be on the inside track), and
was based on the misguided notion that Irish politics involved the
exercise of great power for the good of the people and that one
tampered with it or questioned it at one's peril. It was confron-
tational – which was also good, as long as the confrontation was
about searching for the truth, not following a campaigning agenda
that sometimes would not let the facts get in the way of a good
story. And it certainly got under the skin of politics, which was
fantastic for the journalists, the media proprietors and the public.

At this time you could discern fairly accurately people's attitude
to Charlie Haughey from the way they addressed him. Those
who were fervent supporters and admirers called Charlie 'Boss'.
Those who disliked him rarely ever addressed him as 'Taoiseach'
and when they did it was with an intonation that indicated how
repugnant it was to have to do so. Some journalists also adopted
this style. For instance, in any discussions with me, one senior
reporter never referred to him as anything other than 'Haughey'.
Many journalists could barely hide their hostility. When they were
in Charlie's immediate vicinity the air bristled. I could never work
out exactly what the hostility was based upon. Of course, they

rationalized it in a way that gave a certain credibility to their attitude: he was an arriviste; he made his money in questionable circumstances, though nobody could quite work out what the circumstances were; he displayed naked ambition; he aroused the basest of political feelings in a country that had striven long and hard to forget the savagery of a civil war; he was unsound on the Northern question and might not subscribe wholeheartedly to the 'unity by consent' line; he had questionable morals, and much more besides. It always fascinated me to watch these people present themselves as objective seekers of truth when every cell in their bodies screamed aversion to the Taoiseach of the day. Interestingly many of these reporters were women – subsequently dubbed 'the clitorati' by the inimitable P. J. Mara. He was also responsible for naming one of them 'Miss Botulism '82' after a particularly vicious piece on Charlie.

There were two media personalities whose relationships with Charlie were particularly intriguing to the media and political cognoscenti (in other words, the clientele of Doheny & Nesbitt's) including myself: Bruce Arnold, the influential political commentator who had a column in the *Irish Independent*, and Tony O'Reilly, the owner of Independent Newspapers. Notwithstanding Charlie's very good relations with the editors of some of O'Reilly's papers – particularly Vinnie Doyle of the *Evening Herald* and Michael Hand of the *Sunday Independent* – there was little love lost between the two principals. I don't recall a single occasion when the two men met after Charlie became Taoiseach, and the mention of O'Reilly's name in Charlie's presence usually resulted in a frosty stare. Yet they were of the same age and came from similar backgrounds. Both were from Dublin's northside, although O'Reilly attended the more upmarket Belvedere College whereas Charlie went to the Christian Brothers in Fairview. Charlie had been Minister for Agriculture and O'Reilly had been in charge of two important semi-state food companies, Bord Bainne and the Irish Sugar Company.

Rumour had it that Jack Lynch had offered O'Reilly the post of Minister for Agriculture in the late sixties. The story was repeated again and again by John Healy in his column. It is true that the two men knew and liked each other – both had been sporting heroes and Jack certainly admired O'Reilly's management skills – but to offer a high-profile cabinet job to somebody not even remotely involved in party politics would have been completely at odds with the political culture of the time and caused considerable ill-feeling amongst TDs, to say nothing of serving ministers. When I asked Jack Lynch about the story I got neither a denial nor a confirmation. O'Reilly had a holiday home in west Cork at which Jack was sometimes a dinner guest. I was left with the impression that at some stage when he was Taoiseach in the late sixties he had asked O'Reilly for advice about something or other and, having received some words of wisdom, said something to the effect that he wished he had him in his cabinet as Minister for Agriculture. I can imagine him making such a remark. I can also imagine him doing so in the hope that it might be interpreted in a certain way that would do his relationship with Tony O'Reilly no harm.

When Charlie became leader of Fianna Fáil and the *Irish Independent* (as distinct from the Independent Group) took a less than friendly attitude to both him and his government, the conspiracy theorists got to work. The explanation, the experts decided, was that Lynch had indeed offered O'Reilly a cabinet post back in the sixties but that his new Minister for Finance, Charlie Haughey, had vetoed it because he feared O'Reilly might outshine him and eventually pose a threat to his leadership ambitions. Whatever the truth of Jack's offer, there could be none in the story of Charlie's veto: Jack was too wily an operator ever to give one of his ministers a power of veto over anything. Finally, despite all the talk, and despite the *Irish Independent*'s critical stance, it could not be said that O'Reilly appeared to be interfering with his editors.

During my time as Fianna Fáil's Press Officer, and subsequently as Government Press Secretary, I had many dealings with Bruce Arnold. Apart from the usual healthy tensions that accompany any such relationship, I had no difficulty with his reporting of political events in the Dáil or generally. (And I assume that he didn't have any difficulty with me either: partly because I never sensed any hostility from him but also because, according to Gemma Hussey's diaries – when she became Minister for Education in December 1982 after the government changed and I had returned to that department as Press Officer – Bruce told her I was 'first class'.) When Charlie succeeded Jack, there seemed to be a distinct change of attitude and tone in Bruce's reporting. At one time they had been on good terms and Bruce had written speeches for Charlie, but for some reason the relationship between them broke down. Charlie would never speak to me about it, no matter how many times I tried to entice him to do so. (Even more intriguing was the information in the ether, though I never actually got to the bottom of it, that there was some family connection between Bruce's ancestors and the Kinsaley estate.)

By the time Charlie became Taoiseach there was open hostility between them. One Friday afternoon Charlie read me the riot act after he returned to his office and found Bruce sitting there, waiting for him, without an appointment, demanding an interview about some matter he deemed urgent. I was told that as the person in charge of media relations I should have known better than to allow Bruce Arnold 'of all people' near his private office. While Bruce and I laughed about it afterwards, the fact of the matter was that he was far pushier than anyone else in the political correspondents' room and epitomized the change in the media's approach to covering politics. He seemed to be more articulate, more sophisticated and more informed than any of his colleagues, and had a persuasiveness that allowed him to get away with far more than any other political reporter or commentator at the time. I have always put this down to an intimidating charm that was supplemented by a distinctive English accent.

Throughout the various upheavals in Fianna Fáil in the 1980s Bruce always seemed to be on the inside track and a few steps ahead of every other journalist. He knew who the dissidents were, where they were meeting and what their plans were. Before the abortive heave in February '82 he had published a list of those who would support Des O'Malley in a leadership vote. It was tantamount to ensuring that the heave would be aborted; many of those listed

were at pains to declare their devotion to Charlie. The men leading
the intended revolt were furious with him. His bad relationship
with Charlie went even further south after this episode, because
the tenor of his reporting suggested that he thought Ireland
would be better served if George Colley, or one of the other
anti-Haugheyites, was in charge. At least his views were clear.

But, for me, there was a far trickier aspect to Bruce's reporting
than how Charlie felt about it. I had to deal with the official
parliamentary lobby every day and its members were deeply suspicious of Bruce. The more he wrote – authoritatively or otherwise
– about internal Fianna Fáil affairs, the more they feared that they
would be adversely affected, and that my colleagues and I in the
information service would start to treat them as warily as they
assumed we must be treating him and the new wave of gung-ho
political commentators. They liked to be seen as standard bearers
for objectivity and, from some touchy remarks, it was clear that
they feared we would start to doubt this and to see them as trying
to influence events in the way we perceived Bruce's reporting did.
We, in turn, were at pains to signal to them that we held them and
their professionalism in the highest regard. It was all quite weari-
some and they were fooling themselves if they thought that I or
anyone else believed in their complete objectivity. Nobody
expected that, least of all Charlie Haughey. It didn't take an Einstein
to decipher where their true loyalties lay on any given occasion.
Just like now, journalists who presented themselves as unaligned
reporters often had stronger friendships with TDs in one party
than another. And, undoubtedly, close relationships had developed
between some of the political correspondents and members of Fine
Gael and Labour who had been senior ministers in the 1973–7
government. (That period was somehow regarded as the golden
age of relationships between a government and the political lobby,
so it was an interesting lesson for all involved to realize, after the
1977 election, that the politicians who were so kindly regarded
by the media establishment were not all that popular with the
electorate.)

When it emerged that Bruce's phone, along with Geraldine

Kennedy's, had been tapped on the instructions of Seán Doherty during the height of these upheavals in 1982, I was completely astounded. As part of my job I had conversations with many journalists, including Bruce Arnold and Geraldine Kennedy, that I certainly wouldn't have wanted overheard or recorded. Whatever was happening between Charlie and the media, there was no excuse for what Doherty did. And there is no excuse for Charlie either.

Doherty subsequently said that he showed the transcripts of the recordings to the Taoiseach; Charlie denied this. But whether he did or not, it is difficult for me to accept that one of Charlie's ministers could have taken all of the actions he did without some knowledge on the part of his boss, however peripheral. The rule that I've applied to Jack Lynch's conduct during the arms crisis also applies here: Charlie may not have troubled himself with the detail of what Doherty was up to, but he operated a very centralized system of government, so he cannot have been entirely in the dark.

In the autumn of 1982, the combination of those in Fianna Fáil who wanted to be rid of Charlie – never having accepted the legitimacy of his election to the leadership in the first instance – and reporters who believed that the Irish equivalent of Watergate was within their grasp, created an explosive atmosphere. This was something that very few people, if any, within the government itself or amongst those advising it could contend with successfully. The party disappointed its thousands of supporters throughout the country by discarding its legendary discipline and unity, and turning itself into a cauldron of dissent, disaffection and deceit.

On the day that Charlie was elected leader of Fianna Fáil, and I had found Dessie O'Malley, Jim Gibbons, Bobby Molloy and Des Hanafin in George Colley's office after the vote, I had happened on the nucleus of the permanent opposition to Haughey within his own party. These were the core dissidents. There were others, including Senator Eoin Ryan, but on every occasion on which there was a heave against Haughey, one or other or all of these would not be far from the front line. One or other or all would begin the process in a fashion that became familiar to those of us who knew what was happening. A quiet briefing of a few compliant journalists, resulting in a speculative preview of the likelihood of a leadership challenge, was the equivalent of putting the match to the tinder-wood. Then these men emerged from the shadows and into the glare of the TV cameras blinking in a dazed way as if the developing inferno was a shattering and unforeseen event. Carefully scripted language gave the appropriate signals to those in the parliamentary party anxious to be led into battle. In normal times, I had sometimes found these men reluctant to take part in media outings that would have been useful in explaining or defending government policy; in fact, they seemed to regard most of the media with deep suspicion. So it always struck me as odd that they managed to know the right journalist to call and the right buttons to press to achieve the most controversial coverage.

What made the circumstances surrounding the prospect of another heave against Charlie all the more unreal was the hesitancy of the challengers. Everybody knew there was discontent. Everybody knew the identity of those who professed to be discontented. What nobody knew, least of all those who claimed to be disaffected, was who would actually do the deed. Who would pull the trigger? The truth was that, like many other expressions of revolt, they couldn't agree amongst themselves as to who should be nominated as the alternative to Charlie; the reality was that there was nobody behind whom the rebels could unite. The core issue was to remove the incumbent. Other things would then follow.

George Colley was an unlikely leader. Dessie O'Malley, long believed to be Jack's own preference as his successor, carried too much baggage – he had been somewhat autocratic as Chief Whip and controversial when in Justice – to be acceptable to a majority of the parliamentary party. There were senior figures in the party who might have thought that they could provide an alternative: Gerry Collins, Ray MacSharry, John Wilson, Albert Reynolds, Brian Lenihan. But none of these could command the necessary support to win and, even if they did, it would be by such a thin margin that the same problems would arise in due course.

In retrospect, MacSharry is probably the best leader Fianna Fáil never had. His subsequent career both in Europe and in the private sector manifestly proved that he had the type of qualities necessary to deal with controversial political issues, and do so with a firm hand. Initially, the O'Malleys, the Gibbonses and the Molloys of the Fianna Fáil political world had looked on MacSharry with scepticism and didn't seem to give his views much weight. That he remained friendly with Charlie through his wilderness years was a black mark against him in the eyes of those who supported Jack Lynch. The general attitude of the party establishment was epitomized in the reaction of Jack Lynch when I went to him in 1977, at Mac's own request, to lobby for his appointment to a junior ministry. Jack was immediately on the defensive and wanted to know who had 'put me up' to the suggestion. When the lawyer Hugh O'Flaherty also lobbied on his behalf, Jack seemed to have second thoughts and appointed MacSharry to the Department of Finance to assist George Colley with some of the increased load arising out of membership of the European Community. He turned in an extremely creditable performance and developed a very good working relationship with Colley, despite the fact that both men knew, without ever discussing the matter, that MacSharry would support Charlie in a leadership contest. He was straight with the two candidates when that time came in December 1979, refusing to publicly endorse Charlie until he had had a chance to explain his position to Colley.

When leadership crises loomed, everybody, not only Haughey, turned to MacSharry. He became the commanding officer, the controller of tactics within Charlie's camp, and he was ruthless in his determination to defeat the rebels. To their cost, those challenging Haughey failed to recognize either the determination or the capability of the Sligoman. For him, it wasn't simply a matter of keeping Charlie at the helm at all costs, but a matter of greater significance. In his view the most irresponsible rebels were those people who had had charge of the party and, having lost it, wanted to wrest it back by any means they could. He was not fooled by the argument made by the dissidents – and strongly supported by a couple of tame economists with strong party links – that the national economic condition would be different or better under either

George Colley or Dessie O'Malley. Similarly, he didn't support the view that back benchers' unease about their future prospects would be allayed by putting a different leader's face on the election posters.

Until such time as somebody was prepared to put his head above the parapet and lead the revolt, the business of government was practically paralysed. While there was nothing officially in train, the prospect of another challenge to Charlie's leadership dominated political discourse. Newspapers, radio and television conducted their own research and opinion polls amongst the members of the parliamentary party, the Fianna Fáil national executive and the wider party throughout the country. There were reports of meetings in constituencies the length and breadth of the country at which motions in support of the Taoiseach were proposed: some passed by massive majorities, some passed by a frighteningly small margin and some were defeated. The net effect was that the leadership of Fianna Fáil, and therefore of the country, was the only political game in town. Fianna Fáil's TDs were too stressed or too distracted to give proper attention to matters of state or to routine constituency business. But those directly involved in the challenge knew this. And, ironically, the challengers also knew that this apparent lack of governance by the Haughey administration was part of their strength.

Charlie adopted varying responses to leadership challenges, ranging from a claim that they were merely concoctions of a hostile section of the media to full-scale battle stations. The single most difficult person he had to deal with was not, surprisingly, Dessie O'Malley, but Charlie McCreevy, who had once been a vociferous supporter. At this time McCreevy was something of a pimpernel. Nobody was sure if he was a lone voice or actually represented anything approaching a credible number of uneasy TDs. The older elements, or what might be loosely described as the 'establishment' of the party – Colley, O'Malley, Collins, Wilson and others – didn't know him. There was only one source on where he was coming from, whom he represented and what he wanted, and that was his constituency colleague Paddy Power, the senior TD for

Kildare. Since Power was dismissive, at first sight it looked as if McCreevy might be on something of a solo run and had little, if any, support amongst his parliamentary colleagues.

But Power hadn't got the right measure of McCreevy. He was determined to put the leadership of the party back on the agenda after O'Malley's abortive heave in February. Malone's Cake Shop in Naas, the venue for an alleged meeting of dissidents, attained the type of national recognition an ambitious marketing guru could only dream about. McCreevy was the only TD who consistently spoke out openly against Charlie Haughey and therefore provided something of a lightning conductor for others in the party to voice their own opposition. The media regarded the developments taking place within Fianna Fáil as a type of popular blood-sport. McCreevy played a clever game, providing them with colourful copy and spicy insights into what life was like under the leadership of Charlie Haughey. Although he was indirectly making my life more difficult, I never spoke to McCreevy about what he was doing. It was a party-political matter and none of my business. I met him frequently around Leinster House, and those were amicable encounters in which he was his usual amiable self and always referred to me as F.J. (for Francis Joseph).

Through September the air grew thick with accusations and recriminations. Friendships were sundered. Previously accepted personal associations became suspect and the camaraderie and *esprit de corps* that characterized most of the party – at least outwardly – vanished. The most disturbing part of it all was that there didn't seem to be any remedy for this state of affairs. Those few (Brian Lenihan comes to mind) who made any attempts to reconcile the warring factions got caught in the crossfire and retreated, bloodied and bowed. Rumour became the order of the day. People met in small groups, which quickly dispersed when an interloper, innocent or not, arrived. Nobody made declaratory statements; everything was tentative. Few disclosed their position on anything, but when someone did, their comments were so circumscribed as to be meaningless, though their words still became immediately suspect, and were parsed for hidden meanings and hidden loyalties.

It was completely and totally dispiriting. It is impossible to imagine how those who had dedicated themselves in a genuine way – or in as genuine a way as any politician can – to the furtherance of the best interests of the party managed to survive in such a poisonous atmosphere. It is pointless at this remove to apportion blame for this sorry state of affairs, though I would be dishonest if I said I was not interested in blame. Suffice to say there was blame on all sides. This wasn't a situation that happened overnight. It was a volcano that had been waiting to erupt ever since the day Seán Lemass retired. The very fact that there was a contest to choose his successor, a commonplace occurrence in modern politics, was new to Fianna Fáil. He himself had been assumed into office to succeed de Valera.

The upheaval was actually the culmination of persistent and careful suppression of tensions in the party since the latter years of de Valera's reign. Young ministers like Blaney, Haughey, Lynch, Colley and Donogh O'Malley felt that he had stayed too long at the helm and that Lemass, notwithstanding his good intentions, had come to the job too late in life to make any of the changes that would accord with the new mood abroad in the country. Lynch, of course, was to be the stopgap until the time was right for a real dynamo to fill the position. In de Valera's and even Lemass's time the spirit of deference to the leader was still alive and well. Whatever differences existed with regard to either policy or personality – and there were many instances of both – were subsumed into what was believed, with something approaching fundamentalist fervour, to be the greater good of the party as a whole, which in turn was viewed as being in the best interests of the country. The fact that a senior minister would challenge the leader's legitimacy was not completely new. The fact that it would be done in public was. As for a back bench TD conducting a one-man public campaign against the leader – unthinkable.

Ray MacSharry recognized that one of Charlie's big problems was that it was extremely difficult to undo the notion that his opponents had carefully fostered in the public mind: that the perilous state of the national finances and Charlie Haughey's leadership were inextricably linked. It was unbelievably hypocritical. Those rebels who had served under Jack Lynch knew that they had been wrong to allow Lynch to indulge in the profligacy, however populist, of the first six months of the new government in 1977. Back then, when Charlie Haughey spoke out against the lunacy of actually keeping the manifesto's promises, it was dismissed as sour grapes and attributed to a fear that Jack's popularity would inevitably mean that his favourite, George Colley, would succeed to the leadership. By the autumn of 1982, those who had basked in the sunshine of public popularity five years earlier now wanted to forget their connections with the manifesto and to put the blame for the undoubted ills of the country solely on the shoulders of Charlie Haughey. So it was implied, fairly strongly, that the economy had, in some indefinable way, become the personal fiefdom of the Taoiseach and that all of its ills could be laid at his doorstep. This was given added credibility as a result of a claim that Charlie was the real Minister for Finance and that there was a revolution in the making within some of the senior ranks of the Department of Finance arising from the level of his alleged interference with national economic policy.

The strategy worked, as these things always do, because there was a grain of truth in the rumours: there had been and still were tensions between Charlie and Finance. The truth is that the Department of Finance never likes politicians 'interfering' in what it considers to be its bailiwick. And when they do interfere, by coming up with ideas and plans of their own, they leave themselves wide open to the charge of using the management of the public finances for electoral gain. Until he appointed Ray MacSharry to the post in March 1982, Charlie hadn't had a finance minister he was happy with: his first minister, Michael O'Kennedy, had no background in financial matters and was far more suited to Foreign Affairs. O'Kennedy's successor, Gene Fitzgerald, hadn't even wanted the job and was fully aware of his limitations for it.

Charlie had been a strong Minister for Finance and he was not slow to put forward his own ideas. To him the oil crisis that had caused such havoc to the 1973–7 coalition government's best-laid plans had stultified thinking in Finance, and there was nobody of the calibre of a Ken Whitaker within its ranks to encourage officials to, as it were, think outside the box. He obviously believed that the economy could be managed in such a way as to alleviate some of its horrendous problems – not least of which were crippling interest rates and devastatingly high unemployment figures – without causing unnecessary structural damage. Because of the strength of his views, expressed forcibly but cogently, the impression was created that unless he got his own way nothing would happen.

Having been frustrated by what he saw as the conservatism of the Finance mandarins, he instructed Pádraig Ó hUiginn, of his own department, to prepare a national economic plan along the lines of Ken Whitaker's revolutionary *Programmes for Economic Expansion*, which had galvanized Seán Lemass's period in office. In private the Department of Finance went ballistic. In public it sniffed its nose and let it be known, via the usual reliable channels, political and journalistic, that it, and it alone, was the progenitor of economic policy and that anything else, regardless of its origin, should be looked at with serious suspicion. Ó hUiginn took time off from the office and produced a draft document that was presented to ministers for discussion.

When the penultimate draft of this programme was being considered at a Sunday morning meeting in the Department of the Taoiseach, the senior representative of the Department of Finance present – an Assistant Secretary – demurred when he saw some of the contents of the document. Challenged to substantiate his criticisms by a fellow civil servant, albeit one from the Department of the Taoiseach, he replied that he wasn't the only one who would not allow his name to be associated with it; he could not condone Finance's imprimatur being given to what he called a 'hookey document'. Immediate and terrible war ensued. There were sharp exchanges between Ó hUiginn and the official, culminating in the latter leaving and not participating further in the meeting. This was all between civil servants and Charlie Haughey was not involved, but to hear the stories of the incident later you could be forgiven for believing that the Taoiseach and a senior Finance official had actually exchanged blows over what could or could not be included in a policy document to be launched by the government. The atmosphere was such that the notion that Fianna Fáil was abusing the department gained some credibility, which wasn't diminished by those within its ranks who gave off-the-record briefings to both the media and opposition politicians.

When you threw in the reported actions of the Minister for Justice, particularly a number of highly questionable interventions in internal Garda affairs, it is no wonder that the credulous thought a *coup d'état* was imminent. And, strange as it may seem in retrospect, there were even sober-minded and intelligent people, motivated solely by what was in the best interests of the country, who bought into this presentation of the intentions and activities of the elected government of the day and contributed, unintentionally, as much, if not more, to undemocratic activity as those whom they accused. People's suspicions, so easily aroused where politics are concerned, were whipped into a frenzy of lurid speculation as to the real intentions of those in power. There is no doubt that very strange things did happen, and that power was abused, in 1982. While I accept that when extraordinary events occur they will automatically attract extraordinary levels of both scrutiny and criticism – that is the nature of democracy – none the less I maintain that the way in which matters were reported and commented upon not only contributed to an unnecessary mood of hysteria but also nurtured it.

Dessie O'Malley's and Martin O'Donoghue's resignations from the cabinet on 5 October brought things to a head. Charlie argued that loyalty to the Taoiseach was of paramount importance if there was to be any unity of purpose in the cabinet. O'Malley and O'Donoghue felt they could not express loyalty to Charlie, so they resigned from their ministries. Gerry Collins tried to dissuade O'Malley from going; it threw his own willingness to remain into stark relief. The resignations were a defining moment for Fianna Fáil: none of these two men's colleagues joined them. I imagine that O'Malley was astonished because I had a brief conversation with him in which he expressed surprise that I was remaining in my post as Government Press Secretary. The implication was that because he had decided to resign others would automatically do likewise. As with many other aspects of his political career, O'Malley got a rude awakening when he discovered that there is a distinct difference between a politician threatening to resign and actually doing so, and that expressions of support tend to melt away like early-morning frost as soon as the moment of truth arrives. The following day a motion of no confidence in Charlie put forward by McCreevy was defeated by fifty-eight votes to twenty-one. When Charlie returned to his office afterwards there were no signs of elation or relief. Once again it was simply a case of getting on with business.

In the wake of the controversy, Charlie attempted to shift the focus back to the running of the country. After much discussion amongst ministers, the new economic programme, entitled *The Way Forward*, was published on 21 October, a week before the Dáil was due to reassemble. In the upper echelons of Finance it immediately became known as *The Way Backwards*. Notwithstanding the fact that the row between the civil servants had taken place in the privacy of the Taoiseach's office, it was disconcerting to hear the Finance official's criticisms being repeated – almost verbatim from what I knew of what had occurred – in the Dáil shortly after the ill-fated document was publicly launched.

The political correspondents, who had seen it all before, were privately cynical in their approach to the brave new plan for fiscal austerity that was to be the panacea for all the ills that had beset the economy from 1978 onwards; some of them told me that they thought that *The Way Forward* was all smoke and mirrors. It was hard to blame them: the history of Fianna Fáil governments actually doing what they proposed in terms of hard decisions was not good, so this in itself made people suspicious about the real intent of the document. However, their reportage was even-handed and there was enough positive reaction to please Charlie. And that was it. *The Way Forward* was a one-day wonder. Apart from the odd occasion when it was referred to in derogatory terms during Dáil exchanges, the document that had caused so much sound and fury signified little and was largely forgotten.

Two weeks later, on 4 November, the Fianna Fáil government fell. One TD, Bill Loughnane from Clare, had died in early October. Another, Jim Gibbons, had had two heart attacks. The Workers Party held the balance of power and it was not impressed by the expenditure cuts proposed in *The Way Forward*. When Garret FitzGerald proposed a motion of no confidence in the Fianna Fáil administration, the three Workers Party deputies voted against the government and it lost the vote. During the election campaign, shrewd readers of the political leaves such as Ray Burke, Albert Reynolds and Ray MacSharry privately admitted to me that the chances of being re-elected were very slim. None of them wanted to be dependent on the support of smaller groups, and, while none of them would own up to this, I got the distinct impression that they would prefer a period in opposition that would enable them to regroup and take whatever measures were necessary to ensure that a reunited party was returned to government as quickly as possible. When Fianna Fáil won seventy-five seats, thus giving the combined Fine Gael and Labour parties a comfortable majority, it looked like they were going to get the opportunity to do just that. For my part I knew that I would be moved from my job in Government Buildings and that once again I would have to get used to a whole new set of political masters.

15. The end of an era

Though I hadn't realized it at the time, when Fianna Fáil left office in December 1982, it was the end of an era for me. I knew I would be leaving the Department of the Taoiseach, but I didn't know I would be leaving it for the last time. And though I would serve the Fine Gael–Labour coalition for over three years, and go through many ups and downs with two ministers, nothing would ever compare to the drama or the intensity of being at the heart of Fianna Fáil during some of the most tumultuous years of its history.

After the election was over, Charlie invited me to come back to work for Fianna Fáil as its Press Secretary. I gave his offer some thought, but the prospect of returning to the daily routine of infighting, bolstering and massaging egos, and vainly trying to provide cogent reasons why Fianna Fáil should be returned to government, didn't appeal. I preferred to stay in the civil service, not only because of the security of the job, but also because I had become tired of constantly having to navigate my way through stormy waters and longed for calm in my working life. Although it would have been convenient for him if I had said yes to the offer, and would have saved the party the trouble of having to search for someone suitable, Charlie gave no sign that he was disappointed when I declined. I sought, and got, a transfer back to Education, where I had been very happy under the previous coalition government.

I had remained in touch with John Boland during the ten months Fine Gael was in opposition. After the pasting he had got for his handling of the school entry age row, I doubted that he would be returning to Education, but I knew he was hoping for a good position in the cabinet. The previous May he had done his party a great service in running a successful by-election campaign in Dublin West. The vacancy for a TD had arisen when Charlie Haughey, hoping to strengthen his position in the Dáil, had hit on the bright idea of making the constituency's Fine Gael TD, Dick Burke, Ireland's European Commissioner. Boland told me later that he despised Burke for accepting the post and he was determined to ensure that his party would not be humiliated. By all accounts, including his own, he ran the campaign with military precision and brooked no opposition, not even from Garret. He was jubilant when a relatively unknown candidate, Liam Skelly, was elected against all the odds.

John thought that the world was his oyster as a result of his success, but he was to discover that in politics gratitude is short-lived. While Garret FitzGerald has recorded that he made John Boland Minister for the Public Service because he thought he was tough enough to take on the public service and its unions, there is no doubt that it was a demotion. John's enemies, people close to Garret, believed that, despite his undoubted tactical abilities, he could not be trusted with a high-profile ministry. Effectively the department was the personnel section of the entire public service and a division of the Department of Finance. However, whenever there was a need to buy off a politician with a cabinet post, it was suddenly detached from Finance and became a stand-alone ministry. Overseeing and running this department was dull and unexciting work for an ambitious politician.

When John called me to tell me what he had been offered, I knew that he was on the brink of refusing the job. He regarded Public Service as the political equivalent of Siberia. As usual he was more than blunt in his comments about Garret, about those around him and about the reasons why he was being sidelined, as he saw it. He knew that Fine Gael had attracted highly ambitious people who wanted to piggyback on Garret's undoubted popularity, and the only way their ambitions could be realized was by ditching the old guard. In this case there was the added factor that he was far too blunt either for his own good or for the comfort of any government in which he might serve. Boland went through the arguments why he should not accept the Taoiseach's offer, the main one being that he would not enjoy the work. I told him he

would be mad to refuse: he should swallow his pride and get his
feet under the cabinet table as fast as he possibly could. Otherwise
he would be left out in the cold, probably for ever. I spoke to him
for more than an hour, trying to persuade him that it would be far
better, in his own long-term political interests, to say yes. After
widespread consultations with colleagues he trusted and respected,
such as Paddy Cooney, he finally agreed to go to what he regarded
as a non-department, one without a remit, without power and
without any prospect of giving him a political profile. Sadly, John
remained bitter about the matter for the rest of his time in politics.
His anger eventually permeated everything he put his hand to in
the department and in the relationships he developed – or, more
accurately, didn't develop – with its officials.

When the cabinet was announced, he rang me again and
pleaded with me to leave Education and go to the Public Service
with him. But he didn't make the invitation very enticing: he
described the department as the equivalent of a mental institution
to which he had been involuntarily committed. I had already
decided to take my chances with the Department of Education,
where I had made some friends and for which I had developed a
particular liking. Also, I didn't want to become something of a
departmental nomad every time there was a ministerial reshuffle.
Boland was disappointed, but he didn't push the matter.

The new Minister for Education was Gemma Hussey. I did not
know her and had never even spoken to her. Boland kept his own
counsel when I told him of my decision. It was only later that I
discovered that he resented her because he believed that by expressing a preference for Education when she realized a cabinet post
was on offer, she had been partly responsible for his not being
reappointed as minister. John regarded Gemma Hussey with ill-
concealed contempt and believed that she was not a committed
Fine Gaeler, that she had come into the party via a combination of
coat-tailing on Garret's popularity and friendship with his wife,
Joan, and that she would stay the course only for the duration of
what he perceived to be her passing interest in parliamentary
politics. A number of times I heard him ask her, apparently inno-

cently, 'Tell me, how long have you been in Fine Gael now, Gemma?' Anyone who knew Boland knew what a loaded question that was. His judgements seemed harsh and I was not in a position to evaluate them. I had no knowledge of Gemma Hussey's reasons for joining Fine Gael, nor of her political ambitions. There is no doubt that John was a misogynist when it came to politics. While he agreed that the system needed women to take part, he believed that Garret was moving far too quickly in encouraging women to join Fine Gael and to become involved in its higher reaches. He knew this would inevitably lead to women participating in an almost dilettantish way, losing faith in the process when confronted with the predictable hurdles, and then departing just as quickly, leaving chaos and emotional trauma in their wake. Truth be told, most of his male colleagues agreed with him.

At first my relationship with Gemma Hussey was no different from that with any other minister I had ever worked with. As I mentioned earlier, she had been reassured by Bruce Arnold's view that I was sound, and seemed initially well disposed towards me. I had no view on her at all. From the outset her approach was typical of any new minister, in that she was determined to be portrayed in the best light possible in the media. None the less she was hesitant in her relations with them, mainly because she appeared unsure of her capacity to deal with the problems that Education throws up – in the main mundane issues but ones that have a nasty habit of spiralling out of control and causing apparently huge and intractable crises. Gemma veered towards what she clearly considered to be her natural habitat: the intelligentsia of the media, people such as Bruce Arnold and John Bowman of RTÉ. She thought that the education correspondents were far too intrusive, in both their attention to policy matters and in their daily quest for news stories. Somewhat alarmingly, as far as I was concerned at least, she thought she could manage matters in such a way as to minimize the negative aspects of the education portfolio. Given the nature of the demands on the education budget, and the experienced trade unionists with whom she had to deal, I felt that she was starting out on a very dangerous footing. I tried to explain the facts of political life in

Education, but after a while, when I could see I was getting nowhere, I gave up.

Straightaway Gemma was plunged into a typically sticky situation when she announced a plan to impose school transport charges. Like many another new Minister for Education, she had little hands-on experience of the practical workings of the school transport system; it was certainly not one of the loftier issues she was hoping to deal with as a minister. For years very little investment had been made in the service and it was a complete shambles. After she announced the charges, there was uproar. Gemma began to take the criticism personally. She was given the very same advice that was given to all other ministers in her position: stand firm, ride out the storm and matters will settle down again. It had worked like a treat on every occasion previously, except the odd time when it was discovered that a child somewhere, usually in a remote part of the country, was being refused a seat on the school bus because, as was the case in one instance, he lived five yards outside the specified limit. In these circumstances a statement was issued on behalf of the minister undertaking to have the matter examined immediately and expressing appropriate concern that such an incident could take place in modern Ireland.

As the days passed, in spite of the Secretary of the Department, other officials and myself explaining to her that the critical coverage she was receiving was perfectly normal and could be dealt with, Gemma insisted on calling in the new Government Press Secretary, Peter Prendergast, to advise on how matters should be handled and resolved. In political terms Peter Prendergast was something of a trusted family relative and I suspect that he was partly responsible for her entry into Fine Gael; she had been an independent senator and joined the party only after Garret became its leader. As he admitted to me and other department officials when he arrived in Marlborough Street, Peter knew less about school transport than she did. He took a phlegmatic approach and told her that the coverage was par for the course.

By the time we had got through the initial media storm, the relationship between myself and Gemma was irreparably strained.

Her published diaries record that I was out sick for the crucial period when the controversy was raging, but I am adamant that I hardly missed a day through illness in all the time I worked in the civil service. I can only imagine that, because she was unhappy with my approach to managing the media, and because she sought other counsel, I disappeared off her radar for a while. I felt that Gemma's unease with her media relations – apart from a fear of disappointing her political patron, Garret FitzGerald – arose out of the fact that her Press Officer – me – had been closely associated with her Fine Gael predecessor, a colleague who was hardly a soulmate, as well as having been Government Press Secretary to the man right-thinking Fine Gaelers regarded as the Darth Vadar of Irish politics, Charlie Haughey. Gemma was not good at hiding her feelings, and I knew from relatively early on that a clash between us was only a matter of time. This didn't particularly bother me. I had had rows with ministers and politicians since I first went into politics in 1974. Quite a few of these had been with politicians whom I regarded as having far greater experience, and indeed capacity, than Gemma Hussey, and I had survived. But what you cannot survive when you are the Press Officer in a department is being cut out of the loop. If the minister doesn't speak to you, vital decisions about handling information are ignored, avoided, left too late or ultimately botched. And the minister gets frustrated and angry because, it seems, the media are out to get him or her and the public doesn't understand what wonderful work is being done on its behalf. By definition, then, through very little fault of your own, you are not doing your job. Being cut out of the loop is as good as being given your marching orders.

Instinctively I knew that the type of trusting relationship that I needed with Gemma was never going to develop and I waited for the inevitable divorce. It occurred on a Friday afternoon over a cup of tea in her office. Liam Ó Laidhin, the Secretary of the department, tipped me off at lunchtime not to be surprised if I got a call from the minister's office with a view to having a word; I knew by his demeanour that it wasn't going to be a nice chat about the weather. The call duly came, the silver teapot was produced, and Gemma was at her most hesitantly charming, displaying all the characteristics of someone who has been confronted with a dilemma she isn't quite sure how to deal with. Liam was present to smooth over any unpleasantness that might arise – afterwards he told me that he thought the minister was afraid that I would react badly to what she had to say – and when he saw that she was making a bad fist of things he intervened to say that the minister wanted me to take on new duties and become responsible for departmental liaison with UNESCO (the United Nations Educational, Scientific and Cultural Organization).

Gemma got her second wind at this stage and said that, much as she would have liked it to be otherwise, the relationship between us hadn't worked and wasn't going to work. She knew that I had got on very well with John Boland, 'but I am a very different person to John'.

The message couldn't be clearer: I was Boland's man. Worse still, although it was not said, she regarded me as a Haughey man. I felt like laughing at the utter predictability of the situation, but I confined myself to politely saying that I fully understood that it was the minister's privilege to choose whomsoever she wished to work with and that I would respect her decision. I did put something of a sting in the tail to the effect that I was a civil servant and, regardless of how much she might like to get rid of me permanently, she couldn't. She bridled at the suggestion that she might be trying to sack me, but then she gave the game away by saying that she did not agree with the system of making appointments to the civil service 'in the public interest'. In other words, she would not have had the problem of dealing with me if Jack Lynch had not made me a senior civil servant in 1977. We parted politely with my agreeing to whatever arrangements were necessary to give effect to her decision.

Unfortunately, Gemma overegged the pudding by turning her own hand to news management. While I was contemplating what I would actually do – under no circumstances was I going to confine myself to dealing with UNESCO matters – she rang Christina Murphy of the *Irish Times*. Her line was that I wanted to work with

John Boland. Christina rang me the following Monday morning and I knew immediately that this could turn into a row about a minister removing a civil servant ostensibly because she did not trust his political background. I had a very good relationship with Christina and I pleaded with her not to write about it, at least until matters settled down, and she agreed. Gemma also rang John Boland's house that Friday afternoon to tell him what she had done. That she thought it necessary to do so seemed to suggest defensiveness on her part – or else she was hoping that Boland would insist on taking me off her hands altogether. When she failed to contact Boland, she told his wife, Kay, what had happened.

John Boland rang me at 2 a.m. on the Saturday. He told me that I had made a mistake in not accepting his offer of a post in the Department of the Public Service – while on the other hand telling me that 'When the clowns start kissing you, Frank, it's time to leave the circus.' Apparently Fine Gael HQ had a group of people that kept an eye on the government's media profile; and when it was reviewing the Department of Education, the comment was made that it was somewhat impossible to expect good publicity for it or its minister when a former Fianna Fáil Government Press Secretary was in charge of press relations. I was outraged by the idea that I was considered some kind of Fianna Fáil Trojan horse, particularly considering my hard work for a previous Fine Gael minister.

Boland invited me to join the Department of the Public Service immediately. When I arrived there on the Monday morning, I found him like a caged lion. The single most important issue that the Minister of the Public Service had to deal with every year was the long, drawn-out process of negotiating with the public service trade unions about national pay agreements. Given the size of the public service payroll, and the fact that at this time, in some economists' opinions, it was increasing uncontrollably, these talks were very important for the management of the economy. The normal routine was that the senior civil servant in the department led the discussions on behalf of the government and the minister became involved only when a final imprimatur was required from the Department of Finance. But Boland got stuck into the discussions of the nitty-gritty of pay scales and terms and conditions.

I was in Public Service for just under three years, until February 1986, when I moved with Boland to Environment. Because I, unlike many of his officials, got on well with the minister, from time to time I found myself acting as a type of independent arbitrator within the department. It wasn't my job, but it was something to do. In general, life was quite boring in Public Service and it lacked the vibrancy of either the Department of the Taoiseach or the Department of Education. Boland managed to launch two initiatives while he was in 'the mad-house': the establishment of the Top Level Appointments Commission, which, for the first time in the history of the state, allowed for competition for senior posts in the civil service; and the setting up of the Office of the Ombudsman and the appointment of its first occupant, Michael Mills.

Boland had a love–hate relationship with the service. Both his parents had worked there. His father had died relatively young, leaving his mother to rear a family in difficult circumstances. Because of the marriage ban, which required female civil servants to resign when they married, the establishment in the service had made it difficult for his widowed mother to return to work and earn a living, though she eventually succeeded in doing so. There is no doubt that his mother's experience coloured some of his attitudes to the more stereotypical civil servant who preferred to do everything by the book, without room for compassion or compromise. He was determined to make changes to the system of appointing senior civil servants. High-level vacancies were filled on the basis of seniority only. Boland described the approach as being one of 'Buggins' Turn' – a term to which the civil servants took grave exception – which he believed was deliberately manipulated to allow as many senior civil servants as possible to reach the top of the pay scale at Permanent Secretary and Assistant Secretary levels, regardless of suitability or ability, and to retire on generous pensions. Boland, together with those who had had experience of the workings and management of the service, believed that it was time to introduce a system of meritocracy. He had no reason to feel undue deference towards these men (as most senior civil servants still were), and every reason to feel that they should have to prove themselves rather than get an easy passage to their well-paid positions and secure and comfortable retirements.

Boland knew that this was something that he had only one shot at. If there were any delays in getting the reform through, his proposals for changing the way senior civil servants were appointed would wither on the vine and stand no chance of ever being revived. He knew that if he circulated the customary memorandum to colleagues in advance of the cabinet meeting, his proposal would be 'strangled at birth' by senior officials in every department who wouldn't want any change to the status quo. The only way to succeed was to propose it unannounced and have it agreed quickly. A 'twelve o'clock' item was the accepted method for a minister to introduce an urgent matter without having to circulate documentation in advance. However, using the procedure for a non-urgent proposal such as this was frowned on and his colleagues' receptiveness to it would depend on the force of the arguments he made at the meeting. He swore Kevin Murphy, the Secretary-General of the department, to secrecy, and between them they produced a set of proposals that would result in a complete sea-change in the way senior civil servants were appointed.

I hadn't a clue what he was up to. All he told me was that he was involved in the preparation of something that might cause controversy but that he would prefer, for my own good, not to tell me more until it had progressed. He did say that it related to the management of the civil service, and from that I knew that feathers would be ruffled. He didn't take me into his confidence until the very last minute before departing to the cabinet meeting at which he was going to present his ideas. Garret was surprised at the speed with which he wanted to proceed, but when Boland received wide support at cabinet, the new method of selecting senior civil servants was agreed almost immediately. He was ecstatic and could hardly contain himself with excitement and glee. Not so the civil service, where he now became reviled. However, the new system ultimately raised morale and performance by providing unforeseen

opportunities for a younger cadre who had resigned themselves to
the vicissitudes of the old system.

A few months later, Boland told me he was thinking of appointing Michael Mills as the country's first Ombudsman. I was pleasantly
surprised because, although Michael was known to like and admire
Garret FitzGerald, he had no ties with Fine Gael, and I found it
astonishing that a politician would be prepared to appoint somebody to an important office who didn't have some connection with
his party, however tenuous. I can't remember ever hearing how
Michael was chosen for the post, but, whatever its origins, it was
an imaginative and popular decision, and Michael served two terms
in the role.

After I went to work for the Fine Gael–Labour government, I had
little public contact with Fianna Fáil. I was a fully fledged civil
servant, and the party and I observed the accepted convention that,
unless official duties required it, there was no interaction with the
opposition. At first I found this very difficult. But when I moved
to Public Service, because of the nature of the issues that arose with
my work there, I spent quite a bit of time in Leinster House, and
inevitably during these visits I would meet old friends from Fianna
Fáil who had got over their initial suspicion of my serving the
coalition. There had been a certain amount of sniggering in the
party as a result of the breakdown in my relationship with Gemma
Hussey, but ultimately the fact that I had not survived the course
with her worked in my favour. Amusingly, people in Fianna Fáil
preferred to believe that I had refused to serve under her rather
than that she had found it difficult to work with me.

After I had turned down the chance to become Fianna Fáil Press
Secretary in December 1982, the party took some time to get a
media person in place. Various people, including Seán Duignan of
RTÉ, were canvassed with a view to taking the job. Everyone
refused. P. J. Mara was very much in evidence in Fianna Fáil circles,
and seemed to be at a crossroads career-wise, but Charlie didn't
appoint him to the position immediately. This was the way Charlie
sometimes dealt with his most loyal and ardent supporters: P.J.

would go out of his way for Charlie, and had done so over the years, but it took a while for Charlie to be convinced that P.J., who after all had little enough experience of the media other than getting to know them socially, was the man for the job. It was Brian Lenihan, Ray Burke and, to a certain extent, Pádraig Ó hAnnracháin who persuaded Haughey that, despite his misgivings, P.J. should be given a chance, and eventually he operated under the title of 'Acting' Press Officer. P.J. certainly fulfilled their expectations and performed brilliantly in the most difficult of circumstances. After Ray MacSharry, he was probably the only man to be able to confront Charlie with unpleasant realities; and, while Charlie would give every impression of viewing his opinions with a nonchalance approaching disdain, none the less he listened to him.

Restoring Charlie and Fianna Fáil's tattered reputation was going to be an uphill struggle. In early 1983 it was well known in political circles that the journalists Joe Joyce and Peter Murtagh were trying to produce an exhaustive and definitive work on Charlie Haughey. The book was to include events that had occurred since Fianna Fáil had left government, including the leadership heave against Charlie after Michael Noonan, the new Minister for Justice, revealed that Bruce Arnold's and Geraldine Kennedy's phones has been tapped the previous year, and that Ray MacSharry had used Garda facilities to secretly record a conversation with Martin O'Donoghue. (Such was the atmosphere of suspicion in Fianna Fáil the previous October that when MacSharry heard that there was talk of paying him to stop supporting Charlie Haughey, talk that he felt could be damaging to him, he had decided that he needed to record a meeting sought by Martin O'Donoghue to discuss the party leadership; Seán Doherty arranged to provide him with a Garda tape-recorder and to have the tape transcribed by gardaí afterwards.) I had not been around Fianna Fáil for that heave, but I got a small insight into how things had deteriorated, if further deterioration was possible, when Ray Burke and Ber Cowen, the Laois–Offaly TD, called into my house on their way home from the funeral of Donegal TD Clem Coughlin in early February. That day Charlie took everybody by surprise by issuing a public statement that seemed to question the parliamentary party's right to decide on his continued leadership: he appealed for support from the wider party membership throughout the country. The two men were eating toasted cheese and ham sandwiches in front of the television when Charlie appeared on the news. Ray became so agitated that he nearly put his foot through the TV screen. Charlie survived the leadership vote on 7 February.

To protect their sources Joyce and Murtagh hired a room in Clare Street, near Leinster House, where all the off-the-record briefings took place. I didn't have any difficulty in meeting them; I was as interested in some of the things that they had to tell me as they were in anything that I might tell them. My eyes were opened by the level of detail they had on some events; it was obvious that they had spoken to senior members of Fianna Fáil, including former ministers. The trouble was that some of those who met with them were playing on both sides and reporting back what they had learnt. Despite the fact that Joyce and Murtagh were desperately anxious to preserve the anonymity of their sources, there were those who were keeping a wary eye on them and the men whom they met; there were many anxious moments for some of those who talked to them. The book they produced, *The Boss*, was a riveting read and it remains a political classic of its type.

As Fianna Fáil settled into opposition, there was a general recognition that unless something was done to bind up the wounds there would be an irretrievable breakdown of relations within the party and nobody could foresee consequences other than a reduction in its electoral prospects. Brian Lenihan and Ray MacSharry were amongst those who recognized the futility of the perennial squabbling and tried to create bridges between the pro- and anti-Haughey factions. The very idea that the malcontents would regroup and eventually announce the formation of a new political party would have been greeted with derision and was the furthest thing from anybody's thoughts, including those of the politicians who eventually made the jump.

However, the party establishment hadn't counted on the ambition and drive of the young deputy Mary Harney, which would give O'Malley the push he needed. When Charlie McCreevy had started on his anti-Haughey campaign Harney was close behind him. McCreevy was by far the more politically astute and clinical of the two, but she learnt quickly. She had gone to Trinity and had mixed in a set that eventually threw up a number of noted lawyers and business people. She had high expectations for herself, and it showed, but under Charlie Haughey she did not prosper. Jack Lynch had appointed her to the senate in 1977, but Lynch was yesterday's man, and most of her colleagues thought that she needed to serve her apprenticeship. Her lack of popularity was not helped by her association with McCreevy.

In February 1985 O'Malley refused to vote with Fianna Fáil against Barry Desmond's family-planning bill. He made a speech in which, with much ceremony, he declared that he would 'stand by the Republic' – as if everybody else was intent on doing the opposite. Great copy. Memorable phrase. Little else besides. But it was rousing stuff, and the chattering classes loved it. He was expelled from Fianna Fáil for what it quaintly terms 'conduct unbecoming'. In November Mary Harney refused to vote with Fianna Fáil against the Anglo-Irish Agreement and she too was expelled. Now Harney and her legal chums brought all their considerable influence to bear on O'Malley to urge him to form a new party. Any doubts that he might have had were dispelled by Michael McDowell, who had been closely associated with Garret FitzGerald in his Dublin South-East constituency but who had become disillusioned with Fine Gael and saw a new party under O'Malley as a fresh and potentially fertile political pasture. The Progressive Democrats were launched on 21 December 1985.

While Fianna Fáil's more cerebral members were dismayed by what the move signified, and believed that nothing would ever be the same in 'the Republican Party', the wider attitude appeared to be one of 'good riddance'. There was as much, if not more, discussion within Fine Gael about the new party's prospects, and the potentially negative impact it might have on its vote, as there was within Fianna Fáil. People like John Boland saw that the party might divert valuable middle-class support from its traditional haven, Fine Gael, and were worried. But even they could not have foreseen the ultimate irony: Fianna Fáil and the PDs' mutual dependency over the next two decades.

By the time John Boland moved to the Department of the Environment in the government reshuffle of February 1986, I had already been approached by various public relations companies, not least Wilson Hartnell in the form of the redoubtable Mary Finan, about the possibility of going to work for them. I was reluctant to resign from the civil service; whatever criticisms I might have of it and its modus operandi, it did provide a valuable safety net, so at first I gave these little consideration. As it happened, while I had been in Public Service, Boland had extended to three years the time that a serving civil servant could take a career break. After I had been approached a number of times by one company, Murray Consultants, I decided to find out if I was eligible for such a career break. I was, so I applied for it and handed in my notice. Boland was furious: my departure would create a vacancy that he would have to trouble himself to fill. He came up with the idea that the journalist Olivia O'Leary would be a good choice, and as far as I know he made approaches to her, but was rebuffed.

There is no doubt that Boland had been very kind to me, and that we had worked very well as a team. We would remain friendly long after I had left the public service and he was no longer a minister. But his initial reaction was telling. Politicians are always 'disappointed' when people they depend on decide on alternative career options for themselves. In their view, serving a minister is the equivalent of national, patriotic service. Because they are so often cast out of jobs before they consider themselves ready to move on, a staff member exercising choice over his or her own destiny seems like the height of self-indulgence and not something to be applauded. On top of that, they don't understand a fundamental truth: they are a breed apart. For the rest of us it is possible to have a surfeit of politics.

16. Watching from the margins

It is difficult now to explain the traumatic impact of no longer being around Leinster House. It takes quite a long time for the sense of being at the heart of things, the belief that you are actually achieving something, to wear off. There is the constant pull back, so I found it almost impossible to walk down Kildare Street without calling in for a chat. The ushers knew me, and they would nod me through without the usual necessity of being signed in by a TD or senator. I normally headed for the Dáil bar and if I didn't spot a familiar face there I would make my way up to the government or Fianna Fáil offices. Because I was involved in the lobbying business, and frequently met ministers and politicians of all parties on behalf of clients, for years to come it wasn't so unusual to see me wandering about the corridors. In any case, the fact that I had joined the private sector, and ultimately remained in it, didn't mean I had to be entirely cut off from politicians and the civil service. I continued to be involved with Fianna Fáil, and for a long time it felt as if the party's HQ had a direct line into my life; it was almost taken for granted that whatever crisis was raging, I would become involved.

What fascinated me most as the years passed was the relationship between Charlie Haughey and Dessie O'Malley. Such was their accommodation to each other after everything that had happened over the previous twenty years, that in the summer of 1989 they were able to enter government together. Notwithstanding the almost visceral animosity that existed between them, none the less there were no displays of histrionics, either in public or in private. Neither man frequented the gossip haunts in Leinster House – in truth there was only one, the bar – or outside, places such as Doheny & Nesbitt's and the Unicorn Restaurant on Merrion Row, or the Shelbourne Hotel, where those who considered themselves to be at the epicentre of power, or involuntarily on the margins, strutted their stuff. Charlie or Dessie didn't need to be seen in such places to prove to themselves or others that they were influential and important. In the latter years Dessie was inveigled into popular watering holes by some of the younger elements in his new party, but traditionally he stayed close to home, domestically and politically. The same was true for Haughey. He stayed northside, and, while he had complete contempt for those who spent their time pursuing impossible political dreams and sharing a racy mixture of gossip about himself and his cohorts, he wasn't above listening to the odd titbit that he stored away and used judiciously when the occasion demanded. Neither man lowered himself in the other's esteem, or in that of others, by providing the equivalent of political blood sports. There was no name-calling. There were no allusions to cancerous growths on the body politic. There seemed to be a cautious mutual regard that transcended the palpable animus, a situation that even their closest observers found difficult to understand or reconcile.

Why, after all that had happened around and between them, was Haughey always so conciliatory to O'Malley, even though O'Malley was not slow to put the boot in politically or to have others do it on his behalf? And why, when it came to the formation of a government in 1989, did O'Malley provide a lifeline to Haughey? If he had made PD support for Fianna Fáil conditional on Charlie not becoming Taoiseach and, by implication, his removal as leader of the party, he would probably have got it. The Fianna Fáil backwoodsmen might have despised him for making such a demand, but nobody is going to tell me that they would not have sacrificed Charlie in such circumstances. What did either man, or both, know that allowed them to work together in government and to operate as virtual equals in the running of a coalition government? My theory – and it's just a theory, but posited on the basis of having been around and closely involved with Fianna Fáil for many years, and years not long after the arms crisis – is that O'Malley realized, when it was too late, that his idol, Jack Lynch, was implicated in the arms imbroglio, not by direct action but by the lack of it. I think he came to see that he could not discount

Haughey's argument that the government as a whole had deliberately closed its eyes to the plan to import arms and I suspect that is what they spoke about at their private meeting in September 1970 before the arms trial.

When they worked together in government after the 1989 election there seemed to be a mellowed appreciation of their mutual roles. I was in and out of Leinster House quite a lot at that time, and I knew that the younger elements in the cabinet were mystified at each man's ability to provide space for the other and to ensure that their respective points of view were aired and taken into consideration. When there were differences it was Charlie who invariably conceded, to the suppressed rage of those who believed that they were his loyal supporters and wanted to get stuck into Dessie.

On one occasion I was involved peripherally in such a conflict at cabinet. The agenda contained an item tabled by the Minister for the Environment, Pádraig Flynn, whose brain would have fitted neatly into the tip of Dessie's little finger. Environment had sought tenders for the building of an incinerator, and I was lobbying Flynn on behalf of a French consortium (for my sins, this included organizing a visit by him to a plant outside Paris, followed by a memorable trip to the Crazy Horse cabaret in the Moulin Rouge). Flynn had rung me on the morning of the cabinet meeting to tell me that the matter would be dealt with that day. He said he was recommending my client's proposal for acceptance and would ring me as soon as the meeting was over. By three o'clock I hadn't heard anything so I called his Private Secretary to find out what had happened. Flynn himself came on the line and told me to get down to his office in the Customs House. Instinctively I knew that something had gone wrong, but I couldn't fathom what, given the eighteen months of effort that had gone into the proposal and how microscopically it had been examined, not only by the civil servants in Flynn's own department but by independent auditors.

When I arrived Flynn put in an Oscar-winning performance of incandescent rage: 'That little fucker, O'Malley, blame him. Why Charlie has to listen to the bollocks, I don't know, but I'm now left with this mess.' Eventually I found out that Dessie had questioned the very notion of allowing the project to go ahead at all and said that it was his understanding that a similar move was under consideration by the British government for the North; in those circumstances the cabinet should delay any decision, because if the matter were progressed in the North, the Republic could come to an arrangement to avail of that installation. Flynn had made the normal protests, explaining the lengthy process that had been gone through, but Dessie persisted and Charlie asked Flynn to have another look at the matter.

After talking to Flynn, I rang Dessie to try to brief him about the project. Initially he refused to accept my call, but, when he eventually did, he was glacial. At the next cabinet meeting he complained that an outsider had knowledge of what had been discussed at the previous week's meeting and that this was unacceptable. The Taoiseach evinced concern that cabinet confidentiality might have been breached. In truth, every Taoiseach knows that members of the cabinet talk to outsiders; it is merely a question of who they actually talk to, and why. With disarming disingenuousness Flynn admitted that since I was the lobbyist for the consortium that had been selected, he had been talking to me. Charlie made a show of exasperation and admonished Flynn with the words: 'Don't you know that Dunlop is a Machiavellian fucker? Stay away from him!'

The beginning of the end for Charlie was when he had to sack Brian Lenihan as Tánaiste and Minister for Defence during the presidential election in 1990. The election is the stuff of recent history and needs little to be added to it now, except to note that, even though I was disappointed by the damage Pádraig Flynn's crass comment about Mary Robinson's 'new-found' interest in her family did to Brian's faltering campaign, on which I was working, I was also quietly satisfied that Flynn had so publicly exposed the misogyny and bombast that lay beneath his folksy image. (In fairness to Flynn, Mary Robinson would probably have won the election anyway. Brian's usual sure touch deserted him when he tried to address the revelation that after the coalition government fell in January 1982 he had tried to contact President Hillery to encourage him to invite Charlie Haughey to form a government without the need for an election. Though he put in a creditable electoral performance, it wasn't enough to counteract the combined effects of the support Mary Robinson had built up throughout her extended election campaign and the transfers she got when Fine Gael's candidate, Austin Currie, was eliminated.)

The débâcle of the presidential election added to the perception that Charlie no longer possessed the capacity for survival that had marked his career up to then and gave further comfort to a new breed of dissidents. The final reckoning came in January 1992, when Seán Doherty revealed that Charlie had not only approved the tapping of journalists' phones ten years earlier, but had seen the transcripts of the calls. The PDs put it to Fianna Fáil to choose between Charlie or them. Naturally Fianna Fáil chose power. In passing, it is interesting to note that rumours abounded at the time of Seán Doherty's public statement. Why did he speak out, years after the event? What was patently clear is that a carefully calculated plan was hatched amongst Charlie's enemies – 'the country and western set' – as to how best to undermine O'Malley's support for Haughey, and it worked.

Only nine months after Albert Reynolds became Taoiseach, I found myself in the heart of another Fianna Fáil crisis. The coalition with the PDs had fallen apart after Reynolds and O'Malley clashed bitterly in their evidence to the tribunal that was looking into the operations of the beef industry, and a general election had been called. I really didn't want to have any involvement in the campaign. While it was known that I had a long history with the party, there was a new generation of activists, both at HQ itself and in the party generally, and there is nothing more unwelcome than a previous apparatchik reappearing and playing the role of the wise old owl. Having seen it all before, I was happy to leave matters to the younger, more starry-eyed volunteers; it was somebody else's turn to work the enthusiasm out of their system. But it became very clear, very early on after the campaign had started, that the party was seriously out of synch with the public mood and that the public blamed it for the break-up of the government. Ten days into the

campaign, even the densest Fianna Fáil politician could see that the
train had left the tracks, and the possibility of getting it back on again
was pretty remote. With Tom Savage, Reynolds's communications
adviser, ill and in hospital, I was asked by Reynolds to take over at
Fianna Fáil HQ and to try to bring some cohesion to the shambolic
campaign. When asked by the Taoiseach, I had no option but to
take on the job: Albert had always operated an open-door policy
to me, as he did with most people, and it would have been churlish
to refuse. There was a fractious mood in the party, the main
characteristic of which was that a very serious and questioning look
was being taken at the man who had ousted Charlie Haughey from
power.

   Albert had a very good reputation for getting things done. At a
time when it appeared that nothing could go right with the economy, he had taken the courageous decision, as Minister for Posts
and Telegraphs, to invest millions in modernizing the state's telecommunications infrastructure. He brought a different type of
perspective to the running of his departments: as a businessman, he
had an instinct for a good deal, but also knew that to accumulate
you had to take risks and to speculate. After Charlie, he drove the
next-largest car in the Dáil car park, a Mercedes 500. Fellow back
benchers cast envious eyes on Albert's wealth without realizing the
hard graft that had gone into making it. That wealth sat easily on
his shoulders, and he had none of the false sophistication that often
accompanies the nouveau riche; he spoke in the same accent, used
the same language and kept the same friends. He didn't drink, and
he liked nothing more than to sit up half the night discussing politics
and business over innumerable pots of tea. People admired him for
his casual approachability – something that stood him in great stead
as a minister and subsequently as Taoiseach. He was generous to a
fault with his time and his insights into the workings of the system,
and there were many back benchers who were grateful for his help
at times when things might not have been going according to plan.
He had both liked and admired Charlie before he won his seat in
Longford–Westmeath and remained loyal to him right through the
crises of the early eighties. His views about Jack Lynch or Martin

O'Donoghue or George Colley he kept to himself. This was another characteristic of Albert's: he knew when to remain quiet.

Around about 1990–91 Albert's lifelong friend, Mick Quinn, asked me to meet with Albert in his apartment in Ballsbridge on a number of occasions. These meetings, at which a few others were present, were a type of unofficial think-tank. The conversations were fairly wide ranging and specifically about things he would like to see done for the country. Mick told me that solving the Northern problem was Albert's only remaining political ambition, though Albert himself never mentioned this. There was no specific talk about the leadership of the party but, from time to time, when the matter inevitably came up, I was left in no doubt that Albert intended to be Charlie's successor.

Liam Lawlor was the only politician present at these meetings, but this was mainly because he was very friendly with Mick Quinn. They had gone to school together and maintained a friendship down through the years. Lawlor hoped to be given a junior ministerial post if Albert succeeded in becoming leader. I didn't like to tell him that his hopes would be seriously dashed. From being around politicians for nearly twenty years, I knew instinctively that Albert, like Charlie Haughey before him, didn't regard Lawlor as ministerial material. (On one occasion, after Lawlor had got himself into some political scrap, Charlie described him as 'an Exocet missile without a guidance system'.) After Albert was elected party leader, I spoke to Mick Quinn, at Lawlor's request, about the possibility of a post and Mick was adamant this would not happen. Lawlor, however, continued to lobby for a job.

Lawlor wasn't the only back bencher who was disappointed by Albert's appointments. In coming to power he had brought with him politicians who had taken a strong stance against Haughey – people like Charlie McCreevy, Brian Cowen and Noel Dempsey – and who would go on to form the new generation of senior politicians for the nineties. The result of his decimation of the Haughey cabinet was that there were quite a few very senior members of the party watching this impending electoral débâcle with salivating anticipation. They were waiting for the kill, even if this meant Fianna Fáil being ousted from power. Albert's weakness was that he had a stubborn streak and once he got an idea into his head it was very difficult to shift him. He was not very good in a crisis – and Fianna Fáil was in a deep electoral crisis in November 1992. In such circumstances he tended to get strident, his style became domineering, and he alienated experienced figures in the party who, although they might not have been supporters of his, could have helped him with the difficulties in which the party found itself.

When I arrived at Fianna Fáil's Upper Mount Street head-quarters, I discovered that the building looked like a sub-office of the Law Liberty, with cigar-smoking junior and senior counsel proffering, mostly uninvited, opinions on matters about which they hadn't the faintest knowledge and junior HQ staff being unable, or unwilling, to contradict them. But this was not unusual. Every time there is a general election the political parties are inundated with offers of assistance from a particular type of lawyer who depends on political patronage for either briefs or advancement and their enthusiasm is nauseatingly transparent. In the event of victory they rush to the front line in order to ensure that whatever paltry efforts they have made, usually on the back of others' hard work, are given due recognition; and in the case of defeat they slink away and in stentorian tones deny, like Peter himself, that they were ever involved. When an election campaign is in full throttle and a considerable amount of mundane work has to be done, these people are nothing but a nuisance. During the various campaigns held under Haughey's leadership they were not tolerated. If advice was required, it was asked for; otherwise the legal eagles were confined to their eyries. Pat Farrell, the party's General Secretary, agreed wholeheartedly that they should be removed from the engine-room – they were virtually occupying his office – though he cautioned me that some of them were close friends of Albert and that there might be repercussions if they were evicted too peremptorily.

With the hangers-on out of the way, it was time to get down to business: analysing the canvassers' reports. In terms of how a party is doing on the doorsteps, the first week of a campaign is the most deceptive. First, it takes time to organize the necessary canvassers and to allocate areas to specific teams. Second, and perhaps more importantly, people are not willing to give their opinions too freely to canvassers at the very outset of a campaign. Unless they have deep-seated political views, they prefer to wait and see how matters develop. The most dangerous response that a canvasser can encounter is polite silence. Such an attitude speaks volumes and normally does not bode well for the political party on the receiving end. When the first reports began to come in to us that November, they were neutral at best. There were no issues to speak of. People listened at the doors, took the relevant literature and either stayed silent or indicated that they were thinking of changing their vote. It was obvious that people were waiting their chance. There was no vindictiveness; just a quiet satisfaction that the time for retribution had come.

The national opinion polls were giving a gloomy picture, one that mirrored what Fianna Fáil itself was experiencing. The party's opinion polls were also very bad. I realized that we were experiencing what I call 'mood' politics. In essence we were operating in the slipstream of Mary Robinson's presidential election campaign, and the Labour Party knew that it didn't need to do very much, if anything at all, other than to stoke the fires of middle-class resentment against Fianna Fáil. Fianna Fáil couldn't admit it, but it knew that unless something drastic was done the outcome would be catastrophic. It would spell the end of Reynolds's leadership and would open up old wounds that most people – apart from those who were gleefully watching as Albert twisted in the wind – were desperately trying to heal.

Borrowing from American jargon, we decided to invent what we called 'tracking' polls. When we were confronted by media queries about our response to the less than encouraging message coming from the national opinion polls, we merely said that this did not accord with what we were finding in our tracking polls. It was an outrageous subterfuge on our part, but one that was both condoned by the party hierarchy and considered necessary to prevent Fianna Fáil supporters sliding into a resigned acceptance of the inevitable and doing nothing to counteract the perception that all was lost. There were many calls for the party to make these tracking polls available for public scrutiny, both during the election itself and subsequently. Since these polls had never been conducted, that was an impossibility.

The campaign was a torrid affair, marked by more than the usual internal bickering: this, apart from being the norm in Fianna Fáil, was an indication of the back benchers' simmering dissatisfaction with some of the government's decisions. Charlie McCreevy had been an unlikely Minister for Social Affairs and had brought an accountant's perspective to a post that demanded a modicum of compassion. McCreevy had introduced twelve new regulations for complying with eligibility for certain social welfare payments. These became known as the 'dirty dozen'. With the same granite-jawed determination that he was to show subsequently as Minister for Finance, McCreevy stood firm in the face of the wrath of his own back benchers, the opposition, particularly the Labour Party, and a welter of welfare groups, both statutory and voluntary. The canvass feedback was that the public didn't like McCreevy's approach. I was with Albert on his way to an RTÉ interview with Pat Kenny when he had a telephone conversation with McCreevy about the measures. Seán Duignan and I flinched when he said, 'Just fucking withdraw them,' and slammed down the car phone so violently we both thought he had broken it. It wasn't the best disposition in which to approach an interview. As it transpired, Albert performed well, and once again I was astonished at the ability of senior politicians to swing from one mood to another without any apparent effort and without the slightest indication that this is in any way unusual. It reminded me again that they are, to a large extent, actors who follow the script of the moment and move from one role to the next with consummate ease.

As the results of the election began to come in, it was clear that the Labour Party was on something of a roll and was set fair for a phenomenal result. It looked odds-on that there would be a coalition involving Fine Gael, Labour's thirty-three seats and a few other parties. Nobody, least of all Albert himself, imagined that the

Labour Party would seriously entertain overtures from Fianna Fáil, but the motions had to be gone through. Martin Mansergh dissected the Labour manifesto and prepared a discussion document. Fianna Fáil couldn't believe its luck when Labour responded as quickly as it did to the possibility of talks. Despite its dismal election, courtesy of Dick Spring, Fianna Fáil got back into office.

After Albert became Taoiseach I had less and less contact with Fianna Fáil per se. This had nothing to do with Albert and everything to do with life's natural progression. I had no intention of being like one of the old-timers who had lingered like a bad smell and made things difficult for Séamus Brennan and myself back in 1974. However, because of the nature of my business as a public affairs consultant, I had continuing contact with the government, including with Albert himself, and subsequently with Bertie Ahern when he became Taoiseach. These contacts were all on behalf of corporate clients and fell into the broad category of lobbying, which I conducted either on my own or with senior executives of the companies in question.

There was a funny postscript to my involvement with Fianna Fáil. Around the beginning of 1996 I was approached by a party official who wanted to know if I would be willing to give Joe Duffy a job if he was selected as a candidate for Fianna Fáil in the following general election. The hope was that Duffy, who was from Ballyfermot and had developed a high profile as a broadcaster on Gay Byrne's radio show, would allow himself to be selected for the constituency of Dublin West; and, because he would be obliged to resign from RTÉ, he would need work in the period between selection and the actual election, which presumably I could find for him. I don't know how far the notion went or whether Duffy was even approached about it. Whatever happened, I heard no more about it and I assumed that Duffy had either refused the invitation or that the powers that be in Fianna Fáil changed their minds. I briefly thought it a sign of the times – the obsession with celebrity, the focus on getting a big 'name' on the ticket instead of working on sound policies – but then I reminded myself that it was ever thus: the man I had first come into politics to work for, Jack Lynch, had become a Fianna Fáil TD simply because of his fame as a sportsman. It was one of my last encounters with the 'political world' before life and events took a decidedly different course. But that is all for another day.

Epilogue

Back in 1974, I had an academic interest in politics, but I knew nothing of the mechanics of government or of the operations of political parties. When I first felt the adrenalin rush that accompanies electoral success, it amazed me. I thought I understood it. I empathized with the winners and shared their sense of purpose. I was excited. Things were going to change. It was the dawn of a new age and a brave new world lay over the horizon. Even people who have no more involvement in politics than marking the ballot paper every few years experience the same euphoria, albeit with much less intensity, if their favoured candidates get elected. No matter how long I stayed in politics and no matter how much I learnt about its true nature, that moment of elation on election day always seized me.

However, politics is an area where you have to learn fast or be destroyed, and I learnt that politics is the art of illusion and the art of persuasion. Decades of brainwashing have led us to believe that politicians are motivated by a desire to protect and enhance the common good. In reality, the force that drives politicians is more primal than principled. It is about getting into office, staying in office and hanging on to power, or what the political world regards as power. And the curious thing is that even the electorate understands this, although that doesn't stop it getting its hopes up and letting past disappointments fade in the collective memory – until a particular event either arouses its anger or feeds the disillusionment that is its default position. That old cliché – the triumph of hope over experience – is what keeps our democracy going. You might call it a confederacy of reluctant cynics.

Politicians are like psychologists, though not very good ones. They like to think that they know what people are really thinking, but their ability to read the electorate's mind is woefully bad. It takes the political brain far longer to come to terms with a change in the public mood than it takes any other single interest group in society. It is fascinating to watch how they contend with such a shift and how they wriggle and writhe until they tune in to its rhythm. Time and time again I saw at first-hand how modern democracy works: the politicians follow the voters and public opinion, they don't lead them. When in electoral trouble, politicians have a happy knack of being able to convince themselves – or at least appearing to be convinced – that the inevitable will not happen. I suspect that this comes from a desire to show to those around them, mainly their own supporters at constituency level, a sense of invincibility.

In the main, civil servants own and run politicians. Given our multi-seat, proportional representation system of democracy, it cannot be otherwise. However, the notion that the government of the day is hidebound by official advice rankles with politicians. On assuming office, some politicians assume a hauteur that is embarrassing in its presumption of omnipotence and, in some really delusional instances, in its accompanying presumption of omniscience. Their great mantra is that they have 'a mandate from the people' – regardless of the fact that sometimes less than two thirds of those entitled to vote have actually done so, and a minister might have won his or her seat only on a final count, without reaching the quota – and that this mandate entitles them to propose and introduce measures that may run counter to precedent or to official advice. In any case, despite the bluster, very few of them ever do anything of the sort.

After over twenty-odd years of being in or around the political arena, it was clear to me that ministers who were portrayed as being the most difficult to work with – Dessie O'Malley, Charlie Haughey, John Boland and, to a lesser extent, people like Frank Cluskey, Bobby Molloy and Pat Rabbitte – were those who showed any independence of thought. If you heard a civil servant calling a minister 'a treat to work with', you knew instinctively that that minister was less effective than if he or she had been described as a difficult taskmaster.

The civil service has years of practice in dealing with politicians, both ministers and back benchers, and it does so very well. It is always one step ahead of politicians and knows how to manage them. I remember being bewildered by the disappearance of the generous print-run of the Fianna Fáil manifesto in 1977 and then being amused to discover, on entering the Department of the Taoiseach, that every civil servant from the rank of Assistant Principal up had an original copy. Civil servants are nothing if not polite. They provide politicians with all the apparent trappings of power – large, comfortable, well-appointed offices with conference facilities, staff at their beck and call, powerful chauffeur-driven cars and the latest gadgets. Most important of all, they give politicians advice. Civil service officials don't mind if a politician plagiarizes their thoughts and intentions. They are only too pleased when they find they have a compliant, obedient frontman or woman to make their case to the media and the public.

The truth is that politicians have little or no power worth speaking of. Few politicians have either the strength of character or the intellectual capacity to confront the machinery of state, which, regardless of the political persuasion of an elected government, proceeds unhindered with the day-to-day business of running and administering what is equivalent in scale to a huge multinational corporation. Politicians are akin to non-executive directors of companies; they provide colour but rarely much substance.

Over the years in Leinster House, talking to members of various governments, I became quick to discern which ministers were comfortable with their departments. Quite often I listened sceptically as a minister described how he had managed to challenge a particularly entrenched view or deal firmly with a strong-minded civil servant in his department. New ministers, inspired by such stories from their more experienced colleagues, went back to their departments fired up with the notion that they really were in charge, only to find some new obstacle to their plans. Those politicians who had lengthy and successful ministerial careers, and who actually achieved something substantive, learnt how to read the landscape when they arrived in a department and figured out who was worth listening to, what was worth taking a stand on, and when they should bow to the civil servants' counsel. While some of them may have had reservations about the capacity of their officials to provide the best possible advice in every situation, none had any doubts about their commitment.

It was perfectly normal to find that politicians with no previous experience of ministerial office – particularly those with little experience of being a TD – panicked when confronted with the array of responsibilities and decisions that was now their lot. But after a short time at the heart of government, when I understood the formidable capacity of the civil service, I also understood that such panic was unnecessary. The duration of the crisis depended on the person involved. Usually it was short-lived, although in one or two cases, despite massive confidence-boosting efforts by senior civil servants, there was no recovery. These ministers couldn't get over the shocking contrast between their new positions and the relative comfort of either opposition or the government back benches. The myriad duties and responsibilities, combined with the almost Byzantine procedures involved in arriving at even the simplest of decisions, didn't engender confidence. On such occasions the civil service comes into its own. Like a wise and comforting parent, it embraces the timid politician and provides protection and the requisite amount of reassurance that what he or she considers to be their best interests are being looked after.

Politicians who become ministers are rightly proud of their achievement in doing so. It is the acme of political ambition. There is little point in being in Dáil Éireann unless you become a minister. On appointment, new ministers evince, in public at least, a determination to provide better management of their particular department and, as a member of the collective government, to do the best for the country as a whole. And they mean it. But ministers, like their back bench colleagues, represent constituencies in which they have to compete with both members of their own party and those of the opposition; and they know that, however exhalted their own status, the electorate can be unforgiving and unless a particular type of service is provided their parliamentary careers may be short-lived.

The 1977 general election was instructive for those who doubted that all politics is local. On that occasion, a number of ministers with high national profiles – men such as Justin Keating and Conor Cruise O'Brien – lost their seats because, some senior colleagues believed, they paid too much attention to their media profiles and not enough to their constituencies. The lesson was not lost on succeeding generations of politicians and ministers. Regardless of what may or may not be of significance on the national stage, a minister must keep a weather eye on constituency matters. Of all the advisers and handlers that are now available to senior politicians, the single most important is the person who runs the constituency office. He or she is the politician's lifeline when it comes to local matters. This too is where the civil service scores heavily. While the minister is detained by the sometimes grubby necessities of local politics, the machinery of the department runs smoothly and churns out the required paperwork that perpetuates the belief that the politicians are in charge.

The single most important member of the hierarchy in a government department, after the Secretary-General, is the minister's Private Secretary. The Private Secretary is the link between the department and the political world. Because of their role as the effective controllers of ministerial lives, they gain a penetrating insight into the nuances of interpersonal relationships between ministers and politicians of the same party. They become experts at reading the tea leaves as far as ministerial, and government, policy preferences are concerned, and not only do they pass on this intelligence to the senior managers in their departments but bring this accumulated knowledge and skill with them when, as they invariably do, they move upwards in the service.

Contrary to appearances, and to claims of objective neutrality, civil servants can be and are very political in their approach. The most senior officials know what is and what is not acceptable in policy terms with each of the political parties in the state. There have been occasions when newly appointed ministers, in their first flush of enthusiasm – particularly in circumstances where their opponents had been in office for lengthy periods beforehand –

believed that it would not be possible for them to deal with the same civil servants who had served their predecessors. In one instance, for precisely this reason, a new minister from the Labour Party refused even to meet with the Secretary of the department to which he had been appointed; for over four years communication between the two men was conducted through the minister's Private Secretary. Obviously, long after the minister was gone from the department, the Secretary was serving his successor in the normal way.

Usually the problem between politicians and civil servants is not so much one of too much but not enough friction. I have seen the wiliest of politicians, some of whom have started out with incredibly acute extrasensory perception when it came to anything that might have an impact on their careers at constituency level, being slowly, subtly and inescapably trapped in the comfortable embrace of the civil service. The longer a politician is in office, the greater the danger – the virtual inevitability – that he or she will become unconsciously dependent on the reliability of the service provided by a department, and will become a mere cipher of that department, gradually weaned away from the realities of life. This shows itself starkly sometimes when, at a time of retrenchment, ministers, against all their ingrained political instincts, allow themselves to be inveigled into publicly defending economies in areas that they know full well will adversely affect the more vulnerable elements in society. They do so also in the full knowledge that not only are they alienating some of their own support base, but may well be driving undecided voters into the arms of competitors. This type of action (and it usually happens in one of three areas, or all three, if things are going particularly badly – health, education and social welfare) is given a patina of political respectability by the claim that somebody has to act responsibly in the interests of the national finances.

You can count on the fingers of one hand the number of politicians who, as ministers, either write any material for themselves or, more significantly, generate any original ideas for new policies. Every word uttered officially by most ministers – in public, in the Dáil, and at private meetings – is scripted by the civil servants in his or her department and each such utterance, written or spoken, is vetted by the Secretary-General of the minister's department. Writing speeches, or preparing material for use in speeches by politicians, is the bane of any civil servant's life. It is a vocation rather than a profession, and unfortunately it is not a calling that many civil servants have heeded. The furthest that most will usually go in writing a speech is to prepare a set of facts for the politician to weave into a deliverable script. Most politicians are easily satisfied in that they are grateful for anything that is put before them and that allows them to stand up and speak with the authority which they foolishly assume accompanies a written script. It is difficult to prepare something for another person to deliver, and there is always the danger that there will be a dissonance between what is required for a given occasion and what is actually delivered. That is why most of the material used in debates in the Dáil is so mundane, soulless and clinical. Of course the art of parliamentary oratory is long since dead. There might be some hope for political debate if providing a script for the media wasn't a precondition of speaking in the first instance. Be that as it may, the fact is that very few politicians feel comfortable speaking off the cuff any more. They are terrified of making a gaffe that might inhibit their career prospects or, alternatively, if their careers have already taken off, bring them to a premature conclusion.

There is great unwillingness on the part of politicians – certainly on the part of those who hold office, and those who may have only recently left office, voluntarily or otherwise – to admit to or to criticize errors or failings on the part of civil servants in any kind of public forum. Politicians operate on the age-old principle that you do not bite the hand that feeds you and you may not know when you will need that hand to feed you again. And while they show no such inhibition in private, their criticisms are mostly trivial in nature. Rarely did I hear ministers with whom I worked, or with whom I had professional dealings as a public affairs consultant, admit to shortcomings in the quality of advice provided to them. While some ministers occasionally bewailed the lack of political awareness on the part of those who devised policies, none the less they tended to accept what was put before them and endorse it.

As for the politicians with whom I worked, it will be no surprise if I say now that, for all his faults, the best of these was Charlie Haughey. The years since he left public life have been unkind to him. The revelations that have appeared and the microscopic examination of his private affairs have convinced those few who needed to be convinced that he should never have been Taoiseach, and these include people in his own party. They have created the required amount of fog and smoke to make any objective assessment impossible. For those who were used to proving their intellectual and moral superiority – particularly around the dinner tables of Dublin's southside – by frequent abuse of his lifestyle and political career, his retirement robbed them of a convenient whipping-boy, so his return to the public eye and his apparent disgrace gave them an extra rush of adrenalin.

If you took your lead from the newspapers of the time and if you read the books published about him or about Fianna Fáil's recent history, you might think that the period in which Charlie was in charge was some sort of interminable B-movie brawl. Yes, there was daily intrigue, infighting and back-stabbing, and all of the less attractive attributes of full-blooded politics. But to suggest that this was all that happened, and that nothing of substance was achieved, is simply wrong. A huge part of the problem with Charlie's image was in the presentation. He was secretive and, given his propensity not to trust too many people, very few, in fact, it was inevitable that his habit of keeping matters *in pectore* would result in a skewed picture emerging. In the absence of knowledge, conspiracy flourishes. In one instance, and one only, was his habitual secrecy justified – the matter of the difficult and sensitive overtures to parties in the North with a view to an ultimate settlement. With the exception of Martin Mansergh and Fr Alex Reid, who were acting as intermediaries with the Republicans, I don't believe he talked to anybody about it, and Albert Reynolds, who was fully briefed by Charlie after he took over as Taoiseach, was surprised at the nature and depth of the progress that had been made. Albert was to build on this groundwork and lay claim, justifiably, to be the politician who finally made the breakthrough that was required to end the deadlock.

I regard Charlie as a modern-day Talleyrand. Like Talleyrand he survived in circumstances where most other, if not all, politicians would have caved in. There was the whiff of cordite about him. There were the rumours. There was the grandeur with which he cushioned himself against life's vicissitudes. There was the private life. There was the money (in Talleyrand's case there were suspicions that he had allowed himself to become involved in what would nowadays be described as insider dealing on the French Bourse, something that Charlie hasn't yet been accused of). There was the fine line between great intelligence and the inability to distinguish between sycophancy and what was in his best interests. But, just as Talleyrand never seemed to display any emotion in the face of the most unpropitious circumstances, so Charlie portrayed a degree of sang-froid that left his opponents seething and allowed accusations of arrogant disregard for the feelings and opinions of others to flourish.

Above all there was the determination never to give in regardless of the circumstances. Where others would see only insurmountable difficulties, Charlie, like Talleyrand, would see only opportunities. I recall one occasion when we were flying to a function in Cavan. It was early in the morning and we ran into thick fog a short time after we took off. The helicopter pilot became edgy, and his nervousness made me nervous too. But not Charlie. He became the co-pilot and ordered the pilot and myself to search the skies for any blue patch we might see, however small, so that we might escape through it. Eventually, and to the great relief of the pilot and myself, Charlie pointed at our exit and we arrived safely. The pilot was unforgiving. 'I'm never flying with that man again', was his parting shot.

It will be interesting to see how the contributions made to the state by the last five taoisigh – Cosgrave, Lynch, Haughey, FitzGerald and Reynolds – are ultimately judged. I believe Haughey will stand head and shoulders over the others in the public memory and perhaps, in time, in public affection. We know of his own estimation of his career – 'I have done the state some service' – but what does he think it is? We can only hope that he is somewhere making a record of his time in public life.

It seems that in recent years we have fixed on what is known as consensus politics as the way we manage our lives. This allows the politicians to claim credit for mediocre leadership and to avoid the necessity of being decisive. It is a system whereby everybody is partially satisfied and nobody is completely dissatisfied.

One of the curiosities of politics generally is the apparent ability of people of diametrically opposing political philosophies and distinctly different backgrounds – educational, social and cultural – to work together. From time to time they have the strangest of bedfellows. You only have to think of Lynch and Haughey, the Corkonian and the Dubliner, the reluctant leader and the ambitious wannabe. Or, Haughey and O'Malley, one apparently the personification of Fianna Fáil's 'slightly constitutional' character, the other a scion of upper-middle-class Limerick. Think of, in latter years, Reynolds and Spring, or Bruton and de Rossa. The extraordinary thing is that, in general, these apparent misalliances worked, and worked well in terms of providing stable government. Whether they resulted in actual, tangible improvements as far as the electorate was concerned is a moot point.

But the one alliance that appears to be able to transcend policy differences and general elections is that between Fianna Fáil and the Progressive Democrats. There are still some who believe that this is because the Progressive Democrats are just disaffected Fianna Fáilers who, having set their face against their real *bête noire*, Charlie Haughey, would look pretty silly if they now turned around and rejoined the party they left at a more turbulent time. It would also mean that they would lose the dubious, but electorally attractive, cachet of being Fianna Fáil's moral guardians.

★

It took me a long time to come off the addiction of politics, to realize that politics is not everything, and that there are other ways, probably far better ways, of doing things, and that the vast majority of people, despite the unending attention devoted to the subject by the media and a passing interest in current affairs, don't pay a great deal of attention to politics per se – if they do, they have a predictably under-impressed view of the system and the people engaged in it.

There is no doubt that I thoroughly enjoyed my time working in the political arena, liked most of the people I met and admired quite a few of them. But, for all its allure, politics is also a vicious business and not for the faint-hearted. For those who are directly involved, it is both all-consuming and obsessive. To succeed in a political career demands certain basic characteristics, chief amongst these being a hard neck, the capacity to take abuse and an ability to suppress individual instincts in the interests of a collective wisdom that, in the main, has been devised purely for political advantage. Nice guys rarely survive, and if they do they tend to be so unusual that they become convenient icons for the political system as a whole, which is eager to demonstrate that not all politicians are self-interested cynics.

Purporting to be operating in the interests of the public weal, politicians' real focus is the pursuit of power. Politics is at one and the same time honourable but hypocritical, honest but full of dissemblers, disinterested but riven by self-interest, forward-looking but caught in a time warp. In short, it is a mirror of society as a whole, and the truth is that, as the disaffected and the disillusioned would have it, we get the politicians we deserve.

Acknowledgements

I would like to thank my wife, Sheila, and my daughter, Sinéad, for their patience and forbearance while I was writing this book. I would also like to thank Michael McLoughlin and Patricia Deevy of Penguin Ireland, particularly the latter, who invited me to embark on the project and helped bring it to fruition.

Index